Down in New Orleans

Down in New Orleans

Reflections from a Drowned City

Billy Sothern

Photographs by Nikki Page

UNIVERSITY OF CALIFORNIA PRESS

Berkeley   Los Angeles   London

The publisher gratefully acknowledges the generous contri-
bution to this book provided by the African American Studies
Endowment Fund of the University of California Press
Foundation, which is supported by a major gift from the
George Gund Foundation.

University of California Press, one of the most distinguished
university presses in the United States, enriches lives around
the world by advancing scholarship in the humanities, social
sciences, and natural sciences. Its activities are supported by
the UC Press Foundation and by philanthropic contribu-
tions from individuals and institutions. For more information, visit www.ucpress.edu.

University of California Press
Berkeley and Los Angeles, California

University of California Press, Ltd.
London, England

Library of Congress Cataloging-in-Publication Data

Sothern, Billy, 1977–
    Down in New Orleans : reflections from a drowned city /
Billy Sothern ; with photographs by Nikki Page.
        p.   cm.
    Includes bibliographical references and index.
    ISBN: 978-0-520-25149-6 (cloth : alk. paper)
    1. Hurricane Katrina, 2005.   2. Hurricanes—Louisiana—
New Orleans.   3. Disaster victims—Louisiana—New Or-
leans.   4. Emergency management—Government policy—
United States.   I. Title.

HV636 2005. L8 s68   2007
976.3'35064—dc22   2007000213

Manufactured in the United States of America

16   15   14   13   12   11   10   09   08   07
10   9   8   7   6   5   4   3   2   1

This book is printed on Natures Book, which contains 50%
post-consumer waste and meets the minimum requirements
of ANSI/NISO z39.48–1992 (R 1997) (*Permanence of Paper*).

For Helen Hill and Paul Gailiunas,
two of the finest New Orleanians,
and our struggling but beautiful city,
inestimably poorer in their absence

Times are not good here. The city is crumbling into ashes. It has been buried under a lava flood of taxes and frauds and mal-administrations so that it has become only a study for archaeologists. Its condition is so bad that when I write about it, as I intend to do soon, nobody will believe I am telling the truth. But it is better to live here in sackcloth and ashes than to own the whole state of Ohio.

Lafcadio Hearn, letter to a friend in Cincinnati in 1879,
after living in New Orleans for two years through the
height of a yellow fever epidemic

To love. To be loved. To never forget your own insignificance. To never get used to the unspeakable violence and the vulgar disparity of life around you. To seek joy in the saddest places. To pursue beauty to its lair. To never simplify what is complicated or complicate what is simple. To respect strength, never power. Above all, to watch. To try and understand. To never look away. And never, never, to forget.

Arundhati Roy, *The End of Imagination*

CONTENTS

ACKNOWLEDGMENTS

Numerous people helped to make this book possible.

At the Capital Appeals Project, Jelpi Picou, my erudite and tolerant boss, has been uniformly generous, encouraging, and patient during this project, while Eleni Antonopoulos, Richard Bourke, Aneel Chablani, Ben Cohen, and Liz Cumming have ensured that our clients were well taken care of in my absence.

Chris Eades, Sarah Kaufman, and Shauneen Lambe convinced me to come to New Orleans in the first place, and I followed their examples in dedicating myself to working for others here. Surely this book would never have happened without their influence.

In thinking through these ideas and stories, I spoke to scores of people, many of whom appear in the book. These people include Luke Allen, Dan Bright, Brandon Darby, Daryn Deluco, Meg Garvey, Rachel Jones, Professor Peirce Lewis, Alex McMurray, Alfredo Moran, Lefty Parker, Kathryn Richmond-Zeitoun, Jeff Rouse, Michelle Shin and Albert Bass at Common Ground, Rebecca Snedeker, Eve Troeh, Kim Watts, Brice White, and Abdulrahman Zeitoun. They were all generous with their time, suggestions, and stories. The people at the Louisiana Room of the New Orleans Public Library were very patient and helpful in identifying resources and materials on anything and everything relating to New Orleans history.

Several people provided encouragement without which I would not have endeavored to begin writing this book; they include JoAnn Wypijewski, the other folks at the Kopkind (a wonderful "summer thinking retreat for political journalists and activists"), and Elisabeth Sifton. Will Gorham was generous to read nearly every part of the book as soon as I finished it and has been an amazing editor and friend through all of this.

I am embarrassed by the number of people who supported me and listened to my endless rants about New Orleans since my adoptive hometown began crumbling into the rising water, especially Siobhan Boyer, Marcia Beard, Jesse Furgesson, Sarah and Emily Kunstler, Mike Lenore, Wallace Lester, Jill McDonough, Ian Robertson, Scheherazade Salimi, John Sifton, and my dad, Bill Sothern. And a special thanks to Will and Siobhan, John and Scheherazade, and Susan Strane and Bill Starr for opening their homes and providing me shelter after the storm.

Many of these folks, and others including Barry Gerharz, John Howell, Bruce Jackson, Cynthia Joyce, David Koen, Maryann Miller, David and Sara Olivier, Katy Reckdahl, Sara Roahen, Rob Walker, Prisca Weems, Lola Vollen and everyone at McSweeney's Voice of Witness series, Kerry Lauerman at *Salon*, and Roane Carey at *The Nation*, read early versions of the book or its chapters or helped me think through the central ideas. The book is better for their assistance.

I owe Naomi Schneider at the University of California Press

an enormous debt of gratitude for conceiving of this project and making it possible. She is the kind of person who usually appears only in the dreams of young writers. Kate Warne at the Press has also been very helpful in seeing that these pages found their way into the printed book in which they now appear. Madeleine Adams and Jan Nichols have been wonderful copy editors, identifying not only many issues of language and style but providing terrific insights on the difficult issues that the book attempts to address.

New York University School of Law's Office of Student Financial Services has made all of my quixotic endeavors possible, both with this book and in my legal career, through the generous support of its loan repayment assistance program, which services my staggering educational debt.

Last, boundless thanks to Nikki Page, my co-conspirator, who has been my partner in this project and all other things worth remembering.

EARLIER VERSIONS OF some of the chapters have appeared elsewhere: "Left to Die" and "Gideon's Blues" appeared in "Left to Die," *The Nation*, January 2, 2006; the interview from which "Left to Die" was written appeared, in part, in "Dan Bright: The Prisoner," *Paris Review*, Spring 2006, and in *After the Flood* (San Francisco: McSweeney's, 2006); the interview from which "Bring the War Home" was written also appeared in *After the Flood*; "Going Home" appeared in "Carondelet Street or Bust," *Salon*, September 19, 2005; "Second Line" appeared in "Second-Line Revival," *The Nation Online*, January 26, 2006; "Live from the Circle Bar" appeared in "Live from the Circle Bar," *Punk Planet*, January/February 2006, and "Letter from the Circle Bar," *Counterpunch*,

October 22, 2005; "In the Parish" appeared in "A Question of Blood," *The Nation Online*, March 27, 2007; "Not Resigned" appeared in "Taken by the Tide," *New York Times*, January 10, 2007. Elements of other chapters appeared in "Dreams Unrealized," *Salon*, September 4, 2005, and "How the Other Half Lived: The Need for a Progressive Vision in the Face of Horror," *Counterpunch*, September 13, 2005.

"Azalea" words and music by Duke Ellington, copyright (c) 1942 (renewed 1969) by Famous Music LLC in the U.S.A. Rights for the world outside the U.S.A. controlled by EMI Robbins Catalog, Inc. (Publishing) and Warner Bros. Publications U.S., Inc. (Print). International copyright secured. All rights reserved.

Happy Talk Band/Luke Spurr Allen, "Ash Wednesday," *Total Death Benefit*, Chicken Little Music, 2004.

Q. Electronics, "Drum Buddy Introduction," Drum Buddy Demonstration Vol. 1, Rhinestone Records.

Excerpt from *Don Quixote* by Miguel de Cervantes Saavedra, translated by Samuel Putnam, copyright 1949 by The Viking Press, Inc. Used by permission of Viking Penguin, a division of Penguin Group (USA) Inc.

PROLOGUE

Our talk drained rather quickly off into silence and we lay thinking, analyzing, remembering, in the human and artist's sense
praying, chiefly over matters of the present and of that immediate
past which was part of the present; and each of these matters had
in that time the extreme clearness, and edge, and honor, which I
shall now try to give you; until at length we too fell asleep.

James Agee, *Let Us Now Praise Famous Men*

I began writing the pieces that comprise this book out of a sense
of urgency, compelled by seeing my adopted home crumbling
into the rising water that followed Hurricane Katrina while the
rest of the country looked on dumbfounded, believing that the
horrifying things appearing on their televisions were aberrations,
uncharacteristic of either our country or New Orleans. Each time
I heard someone exclaim in shock at the city's resemblance to a
"third-world country," I needed to respond that the city had long
displayed such signs to anyone who cared to look at them. Indeed,
those things that appeared aberrational in the days after Hurri-

cane Katrina not only were obvious on the surface of life in New Orleans before the storm, but remain obvious in cities, towns, and rural outposts throughout the country where people live in poverty. Nonetheless, the faces of those people are nearly invisible in our political and cultural landscape.

This book presents the stories of my friends, colleagues, neighbors, and fellow New Orleanians. Their individual stories are sad, maddening, and ennobling in turn, representing the dignity of human beings even under the most adverse circumstances. These stories also reflect bigger truths about the pressing issues of our day. The issues that will define us to future generations—the consequences of conservative governance, our continuing national struggle to confront issues of race and poverty, environmental disregard, mass incarceration, immigration, and the "war on terror"—appeared in New Orleans as magnifications of the thousands of instances in which these matters arise in daily American life. In this regard, the story of New Orleans following Hurricane Katrina is, even though it may be hard to accept, the story of America at the beginning of a new millennium. Though we see ourselves as leaders in the world and attempt to spread abroad our ethics of democracy and equality, though we celebrate the supposed "victory" of the civil rights struggle with various holidays each year, we face many of the same grave obstacles to human and civil rights that we condemn in other countries and regret in our own past. These shortcomings were made plain by Hurricane Katrina's landfall and its consequences in New Orleans.

The book also presents my own story: evacuating my home; anxiously awaiting news while living off the charity of friends and family; returning home to New Orleans, a city I love, to rebuild my home and continue my work as a lawyer, representing men on

Louisiana's death row. Although I was reluctant to write about myself, to make the story of the country's biggest natural disaster all about me, I began to see the bigger history of Hurricane Katrina reflected in my own story, and I began to see the human impact of the storm in the lives of my friends and neighbors. For those of us who lived in New Orleans in the year following the storm, it came as no surprise to read headlines like "A Legacy of the Storm: Depression and Suicide" or "Post-Katrina Depression Triples Suicide Rate in New Orleans."[1] Post-Katrina New Orleans hasn't been an easy place to live, it hasn't been an easy place to be in love, it hasn't been an easy place to take care of yourself or see the bright side of things. For that reason, let me offer this disclaimer: I am neither a journalist nor a historian and I haven't endeavored to tell this story in a manner that attempts impersonal detachment. No more or less than anyone else who lived here, I am part of the story of New Orleans.

Over the five years that I have lived here, my friends and family have continually asked me when I was moving back home to New York, where I am originally from and where most of them live. Though it was meant lovingly, I hated the question. Why would they assume that everyone needs to return to New York eventually? Why didn't they understand that I live here and that *this* is my home? Perhaps I was angry at their presumption because I was never too sure that I actually did live here, that I could become a New Orleanian, and their doubts merely confirmed my own uncertainty. Now that I have moved back to this city on the brink of ruin and doubled down with my home and life here, however, there can no longer be any room for doubt. As much as I can be, I am now from here. No one asks me anymore when I am coming home to New York. New Orleans is my home, and it matters to me enormously that I get our story right.

PART I

Heading Straight for Us

The Days Before and After
Hurricane Katrina

CHAPTER I

A Man Leaves Home

Boarded Up for the Storm, Carondelet Street

WE DROVE NORTH INTO Mississippi as the late-summer Sabbath sun rose over New Orleans. I was passed out in the backseat of our old gray Volvo, competing for space with Max and Mabel, our two dogs. I was dirty and sticky after a night on top of a twenty-eight-foot ladder boarding up the windows of my home and was made all the more uncomfortable by the heat—we were unable to use the air conditioning for fear that the car might stall, as it often did with the toxic combination of staggering heat, traffic, and air conditioning. Through my half-sleep, I could tell from the quiet conversation between my wife, Nikki Page, and my old friend from New York, Mike Lenore, that we had not made it far in our hours on the road in the bumper-to-bumper traffic fleeing the city. The sound of increasing panic was evident in the voices of public officials and announcers on AM radio. It was the end of a very long day and the beginning of a long and life-altering year for the residents of New Orleans and for our country.

My first hint of the coming storm that was to shape my life, take the lives of neighbors, and alter the face of my city, had come in an e-mail the previous Friday afternoon from one of my colleagues, Joe, who announced with significant incredulity that another colleague was evacuating to a little house in Lake Charles, Louisiana, that the office owned: "Steve Singer is evacuating—yes evacuating—because the hurricane is apparently coming our way." I remember thinking, "Ah Steve, prone to panic," and completely dismissing the coming storm from my thoughts.

Thoughts of the coming storm became harder to avoid the following day, as people began calling us from around the country. My dad told me that CNN was reporting that Mayor Ray Nagin had ordered thirty thousand body bags. I studiously avoided having evacuation conversations with my wife, who I knew was eager to leave. She would ask what I thought about leaving, and I would delay answering, knowing that postponing the decision was itself a decision, a decision to stay in the 1850s home that we had restored from the ground up, the only home that either of us had ever really known. She made me make tentative plans to stay with college friends, Will Gorham and Siobhan Boyer, who lived in Oxford, Mississippi.

Mike, Nikki, and I had moved from New York about four years earlier to live in New Orleans and do social justice work in the cracks of the edifice erected in the wake of the civil rights movement. Mike and I came to New Orleans to represent poor people on death row, he as an investigator, I as an attorney. Nikki, an artist and teacher by disposition, came to teach art to children in the city's crumbling public school system. None of us, however, were martyred saints of New Orleans, a city that does not tolerate too much false asceticism.

I first came to New Orleans in 1999, while I was in law school at New York University, to work for a nonprofit agency specializing in death penalty defense run by a charismatic British lawyer and self-perceived radical, Clive Stafford Smith, and staffed by young lawyers and activists from around the world. They had come from faraway countries, some of them among the richest countries in the world, to work on behalf of men facing the death penalty in Louisiana, Mississippi, Alabama, and other states in what they called the "death belt." Many of them had never been to New York or San Francisco, or any place north of the Mason-Dixon Line, for that matter, and they were shocked by the racism and poverty they saw on a daily basis. Many of them had traveled to other parts of the world on human rights missions and had come to the American South because they regarded the human rights crisis at Angola State Penitentiary, which houses Louisiana's death row, as at least as significant as the human rights crisis in Louanda, the capital city of Angola.

And what they see here is shocking. They visit homes in rural communities where cracks in the floors make visible the stinking raw sewage that drips from homemade plumbing. They see our clients' families, all of whom have a son facing the death penalty and are unable to feed their other children or provide them with medical care. They see school systems failing to identify or treat mentally ill children. They see prisons where mentally retarded inmates are expected to represent themselves in their complex court appeals because there are no public defenders. They see prison inmates suffer and die at the hands of the state for unimaginably horrifying acts committed against innocents. It is the soup-to-nuts tour of human misery and, for our visitors from overseas, it is distinctly American.

I tried to explain to these colleagues that Louisiana was not America, that although things were not perfect up north, there was at least a show of tolerance and social justice. But they had driven as much as fifteen hours north, twelve hours east, and twenty hours west while working on various cases and they had never seen anything contrary to what they witnessed in and around New Orleans. If an expanse of territory in which you could fit nearly all of Europe did not represent America, then what country was it? They were right, and the answer was obvious. What they had seen was at least as American as the multi-ethnic high school in New York City where I once stared out the window at the Statue of Liberty.

Although, for me, this part of the country had been consigned to history lessons about the civil rights era, and for my parents' generation it was the location of a triumph-through-struggle story, the clearer perspective of these guests in our country allowed me to see my own homeland with fresh eyes. Just as it had taken reading Alexis de Tocqueville's words for nineteenth-century Americans to be able to see their young country without their built-in biases, I had to travel to the South and spend time with young Europeans and Australians to see my country as a whole and realize that the way we do things is not the only way that they can (or should) be done.

Inspired by their examples, I came back to New Orleans following my graduation from law school with the promise of meaningful work, though not much in the way of compensation. The money did not matter, in large measure because the cost of living in New Orleans was so much lower than in New York, and because I had never perceived my law degree as a tool for acquiring wealth.

The apartment I left in Brooklyn, a charmless basement unit beneath an ugly brick house built in the 1960s, was forty minutes by train from Manhattan, and we paid twelve hundred dollars a month for it. My wife, who had preceded me to New Orleans to find a place for us to live, had rented a house, which she assured me I would love, for hundreds of dollars a month less. When I arrived in my U-Haul truck, after a twenty-two-hour drive from

New York, I could not believe that I could possibly live in that house. It was an elegant old center-hall Creole cottage with a large gaslit yoke hanging in front of a transom above an eight-foot cypress front door. The house was about a fifteen-minute walk from my office downtown. When I walked through the front door into the center hallway, it was clear that our entire New York apartment could easily have fit within the hall, which itself was used merely as a pass-through to the rest of the house. Then I was shown the courtyard, in the center of which a purple angel's trumpet tree grew and where satsuma and fig trees bore fruit. Someone pointed out the "slave quarters," a narrow frame building extending from the main house, in which there were two other apartments. I asked whether the house predated the Emancipation Proclamation and was told that it did so by several years. As if to comfort me, it was then explained that the house had been built by free men of color rather than whites, and it was they who owned the slaves here. I chewed on this puzzling fact about our country's racial history and did not feel at all easier about living in a house where people had been compelled against their will to work and live. Attempting to understand this tangible evidence of New Orleans's troubled past, I began my life in New Orleans.

We lived in that house for two years and were married there, in an event that I believe may have exorcized at least some of the place's demons. I had an office in the back corner of one of the rooms and would sit working on my death penalty cases with my back to a fifty-foot expanse in which grand parties must have been attended by slave owners, to whom slaves served the city's classic Creole cuisine. I occupied a speck of space and time in a home and a city where the difficult aspects of American history spread out in every direction.

With several thousand dollars that we had saved from our wedding, we eventually bought our own home in the Central City neighborhood, a part of town that many New Orleanians were afraid of, and into which they ventured only for the divine pleasures of the neighborhood's many churches or for the food at Uglesich's Restaurant, a classic Croatian seafood restaurant opened in 1920.

Central City was one of the neighborhoods in which jazz was born, and it was where Buddy Bolden, a pioneering trumpet player who was never recorded, grew up. It had been a center of Jewish life in the city until New Orleans fell apart in the 1960s. By the time we moved there, all but one of the synagogues either were boarded up or had been reinvented as full gospel ministries, but our old pine door frames still bore the marks of mezuzahs from residents in generations past. Those holes, in fact, were some of the very few historic relics of the 1850s townhouse that remained. All of the interior walls had collapsed. The moldings had been stripped. The interior cypress doors were long gone, likely sold to "historic salvage" stores for food or drugs. When my friend Alfredo first entered the house before we bought it, he said that there were pots full of raw sewage on the floor; apparently, the plumbing had stopped working long before. The house was listing heavily to one side. Someone had to buy it and fix it up or it would fall over.

We resurrected the house between long days spent working at our regular jobs. Eventually, except for a bit of missing paint here and there, it became a proper home. My wife, who had never lived anywhere she could be proud of, and I, who had never lived anywhere with a sense of permanence, finally had a home of our own—a beautiful place that we had made ourselves in a city we loved, all the while struggling to make the city better for the people who had not had a choice about living here. Maybe this is why I was so reluctant to leave when I heard of coming storms. Though I had prevailed on Nikki in summers past to stay for hurricanes in spite of pleas from our local apocalyptic meteorologists, she had definite plans to leave by the time I woke up on Saturday morning. I made no effort to prevent her from leaving, but explained that I wanted to stay, that I did not think the storm would be a big deal. Conveniently, we had an appointment with our couples counselor that afternoon, a pony-tailed man in his fifties whom we had been seeing in an effort to disentangle some nascent marital strife. As the storm barreled toward our city, a storm that ultimately killed more than a thousand people, my wife and I had a mediated conversation about my sense of manhood in light of my powerlessness against a giant storm and Nikki's desire to be safe in a world that often spun out of control. I cannot remember whether it was Nikki or I, but one of us invoked Job as a metaphor for our feelings. By the end of the appointment, I resolved that evacuating was something that I needed to do for Nikki, that a few days off up in Oxford would be a nice vacation, and that the very slight possibility that the worst could happen— that the city would flood, leaving me and Nikki in our attic in rising water with our dogs and cat—could not be risked in light of how punishing each "I told you we should leave" would be. Each time I have thought of that appointment subsequently, I have cringed with embarrassment at our privilege and the absurdity that our decision to leave was not only facilitated by the fact that we had two running cars, plenty of credit to buy gas, and a place to stay in Oxford, Mississippi, but also by our access to a person whom we pay to tell us, two adults, how to make the right decisions in life. Hurricane Katrina left plenty of Jobs in its wake, but we are not among them. At least this time, neither of us had to have it out, face-to-face, with the whirlwind.

Still uneasy with the decision to leave, I set out with extra vigor to convince others that they should leave as well—if I wasn't going to brave the storm, no one should. I took this message to the Circle Bar, my local, where Mike was working, and asked him what his plans were. He had none, but people coming into the bar—both those who were planning to stay in town and those who were planning to leave—were increasingly anxious, and he was beginning to get scared. As I was telling him that he could come with us, we were interrupted by Lefty Parker, the bar's manager, who derided us for our concerns and declared, with postpunk nonchalance, that nothing could get him to leave. As I was particularly vulnerable to his pose, and almost certainly would have shared it if not for my wife's resistance, I barked back with special vehemence, "I hope you think of this moment as your smug mouth slips beneath the poopy water."

We all paused, and then laughed uncomfortably, as that was a genuine fear. To avoid that imagined fate, people were abandoning their city and homes.

Mike told me that he would be getting off work at midnight and would make his decision by then. I told him that we were planning to leave around that time to avoid the ridiculous daylight traffic out of the city. It was heartening that Mike, a cool character not prone to panic, without pressure from a partner, appeared likely to make the same decision I had.

I returned home to the arduous task of boarding up the windows, with generous help from my neighbor Nick Suhor, who rented the other side of our double. Although neither of us is an incompetent bumbler, neither are we particularly adroit at 10:30 at night on a twenty-eight-foot ladder with a drill strapped on, while struggling with heavy, awkward pieces of plywood. During the hours it took us to board up the windows, it occurred to me numerous times that the chances of wind damage to the house were far outweighed by the very real likelihood of our sustaining serious injury while boarding it up. With my sense of self more tattered than usual and with the help of someone whose financial stake in the home was far less than my own, I persisted until every board was hung and Nick and I were shaking with exhaustion. It was 1:30 in the morning. The air was humid and still.

Mike arrived while we were finishing up. He had decided to come along. He thanked us again and again for taking him with us, noting that otherwise, he wouldn't be able to leave at all and wouldn't know where to go. Without a car or friends in the surrounding area, Mike did indeed have few options, but far more than many of the people he had left behind at the bar or back in his Ninth Ward neighborhood did.

Exhausted by stress and hard work, I took a brief nap on the couch. I was awakened by Nikki, in a panic that I could not comprehend about her cat, Bitch, a little tortoise-shell that she had named with characteristic third-wave feminist flair. It was not until I was upstairs that I could see Bitch's predicament. She had squeezed her little body halfway through a small plastic window in her cat carrier and was wedged so that she could go neither out nor in, compressing her torso so that she had difficulty breathing. Nikki was panicking as all of her anxiety about the coming storm and our precarious lives became focused on the cat. With a bracing order, "Calm down," I told her to get her super-sharp sewing scissors so we could cut through the plastic. Once we got down to business, it became clear that cutting the cat free would be more difficult than I'd anticipated because the plastic ring that bound her was so tight against her flesh and buried so deeply in her fur that I worried I would cut her if I tried to cut the ring. Nikki comforted the cat while pressing her side away from the ring as I cut, and suddenly she was free. Nikki and I hugged as though we had beaten death, even though this was merely one of its little sideshows.

I told Nikki that I thought that we should leave the cat behind rather than force her to spend hours back in the little plastic cage; she would be happier romping around the dog-free house for a few days. But Nikki insisted that we take the cat with us to Oxford. I had already convinced her that it was unnecessary for her to take her computer and her art supplies for our three-day trip, and I lost the will to argue about the cat.

It was nearly four in the morning by the time the car was packed and we were ready to go. Our neighbors, Nick and his girlfriend Tiffany Cotlar, were on a similar schedule and had just finished packing their little Mini Cooper with a hamper containing a big, white Moluccan cockatoo and were locking the door to the other side of our house. We had all been listening to the news that the hurricane was coming right at us, so saying goodbye in front of the house seemed awfully permanent after the countless greetings we had exchanged in passing over the previous year.

Nikki and I drove our Volvo and our Jeep in caravan over to a high-rise parking lot downtown, where the Jeep wouldn't be vulnerable to flooding. I left it on the fourth floor, wondering about a world where that might not be high enough. I took the elevator down, got into the backseat of the Volvo with Max and Mabel, and fell asleep before we hit the interstate.

CHAPTER 2

A Stranger Comes to Town

Taylor Grocery, Outside of Oxford, Mississippi

WE PULLED UP TO Will and Siobhan's simple house on the outskirts of Oxford early Sunday evening and parked beneath a cluster of three tall pines. We dragged ourselves out of the car, not bothering to remove the bags of fast-food trash, and walked up to their door.

I knew Will from college and had seen him only a handful of times in the intervening years. He and his wife were both graduate students at Ole Miss, Will in creative writing, Siobhan in biology, studying wetlands. The last time I saw Will had been about three years earlier, the only time I had been in Oxford. I stayed at his house while conducting interviews of jurors who had sentenced a man to death for a murder committed in a neighboring county. In the evening after the first day of interviews, Will expressed an interest in doing the additional interviews with me the following day. I thought that would be interesting for him and would show him a corner of my life representing people on death row, which I was always eager for friends to see and understand. Later, we had a long night of Jim Beam on the rocks, and I remember Will playing Phil Ochs's "Love Me, I'm a Liberal" on a record player over and over, to the glee of my English friend and colleague, Chris Eades, who had been conducting the interviews with me. Chris, a Londoner who had been working on death penalty cases in the Deep South for the five years since he left law school in England, always took delight in the hypocrisy of American liberals. He had met very few of this sort in the Deep South, where he saw such great need, but on visits to New York City he had met liberals in droves among his American girlfriend's Wesleyan classmates who were pursuing careers in the arts or academia. Such reflections surely animated his almost perverse joy at hearing Phil sing of American liberalism.

As we emerged from hangovers the following morning, it became clear that Will was no longer keen on exploring the back roads of Oxford in search of hanging jurors, so Chris, incredibly flatulent as a result of the previous night's drinking, reluctantly agreed to join me. It was a long day in the rented economy car. We narrowly escaped a run-in with local sheriff's deputies on the doorstep of a juror's home, an ugly scene in which we were accused of attempting to break in. The day required considerable stoicism on my part. Up until the moment I saw Will's face greeting Nikki, Mike, and me warmly at the door, I was not sure whether I had forgiven him for that episode three years earlier.

We were exhausted and not at all the kind of guests we would normally aspire to be. As we learned on the radio on the way up, however, we were not guests but rather "refugees" from the coming storm. At that point, the label seemed little more than an ironic tag; after all, we had left voluntarily and we would be home again soon.

Nikki and I settled into the peaceful front room and slept long and hard on the big bed, willfully oblivious to everything that was happening around us. I awoke early Monday morning confused as to where I was and, upon remembering all that hung in the balance, desperate for news.

Siobhan gave me directions to a coffee shop with wireless Internet access on the old historic square in Oxford, and I drove into town on streets congested with expensive SUVs driven by handsome young men and women returning to college. This was the first of many times I saw the emblematic "Save Colonel Reb" bumper sticker, a reference to the troubling pattern of historic discrimination against the college's football mascot, a character rather closely resembling KFC's Colonel Sanders. The image of Colonel Reb made it unmistakable that the team were the Rebels in a very specific and narrow sense.

When I got to the coffee shop, people with laptops filled the tables. After getting an iced coffee, I surveyed the scene more closely and realized that I recognized people from New Orleans, not people I knew but people I had seen regularly at coffee shops, bars, and restaurants back home. Some huddled in small groups with families and friends, reviewing the morning's news about the hurricane. And the news looked relatively good, as I discovered when I logged on to the *Times-Picayune* and the *New York Times* Web sites. In Crawford, Texas, President Bush reportedly believed that New Orleans had dodged a bullet (a belief echoed in the media), and therefore his perennial vacation continued unabated.[1] Although even then the reports were ambiguous and hinted at the potential for dramatic problems, I found myself believing that the worst had been avoided, as it had been for so many years.

I bought a cigar in the shop next door, lit it, and walked around the square trying to justify having spent the money to come to Oxford unnecessarily and therefore redoubling my effort to treat the trip as a vacation. I peeked into Square Books, an elegant bookstore housed in a pretty, old building that is owned by the town's mayor. As I leafed through books from shelf after shelf of volumes by William Faulkner and other titans of literature from this part of the country, I made plans to visit Rowan Oak, Faulkner's home, where he tended roses and mapped out the plot of one of his books in longhand on the plaster walls.

I reconnected with Nikki and Mike and we resolved to meet up with other folks we knew in town and go grab some catfish at Taylor Grocery, an amazing old country store that had been converted to a catfish restaurant in Taylor, a one-street town eight miles south of Oxford. Nikki invited her friend Miranda Lake, a New Orleans artist who had also come to Oxford, but she was not interested in lunch and also declined our invitation to a dinner we had planned with Will and Siobhan for that night. Her prerogative, I figured.

We ate an amazing lunch of catfish, hush puppies, chocolate cake, and sweet tea and soaked up the atmosphere of the Grocery, a place that managed to be an idealized picture of the charm of the Deep South without being a caricature. During lunch we talked nervously about returning home in the next day or two and how nice it was to be out in the country, away from the oppressive heat and smells of late-summer New Orleans.

Back in the car, the local Mississippi Public Radio station began to offer detailed descriptions of the utter devastation of towns along the Mississippi coast and forecast that the storm would pass over Oxford that night with far diminished strength.

We bought some beer and wine and returned to the house, where we prepared a big dinner. We opened a couple of nice bottles of wine and talked, relaxed, ate, and drank. Nikki clicked photos of the revelry. We played Boggle; as usual, Nikki dominated. The wind began to howl outside and the rain poured down hard. The power flickered and then went out altogether. Siobhan got out some candles and we settled in for more conversation. In the iridescent candlelight, everything seemed in order in the world and I was happy to have an opportunity, however forced, to reconnect with an old friend. But I could not forget New Orleans and, in particular, Miranda's unwillingness to join us in these festivities.

Nikki had told me earlier that Miranda, whose early life had at times presented itself as a series of unforeseeable tragedies, had none of the optimism in which the rest of us were indulging. While we were off at Taylor Grocery eating catfish and imagining everything was okay, Miranda remained cloistered in her motel room with her dogs and her boyfriend, seemingly already grieving the loss of her city. As this was my city, too, and I was trying to believe that there was nothing to grieve, I felt impatient with her negativity. I suppose that, like Cassandra in Troy, there have always been people too sensitive to the realities of what is unfolding to allow themselves to take comfort in what so easily placates the rest of us.

Sadly, there were so many others, back home in New Orleans, who did not have the luxury of ignorance or comfort.

CHAPTER 3

"This Blues Is Just Too Big"

Red Raider's, Lamar Boulevard, Memphis

THE NEWS ON WEDNESDAY morning was sobering. Mayor Nagin was on television estimating the death toll in New Orleans, "Minimum, hundreds. Most likely, thousands."[1] Hope for a quick return home had dissipated with his further appraisal, "The city will not be functional for two or three months."[2] Even President Bush had caught wind of the disaster, explaining what he had seen of New Orleans during his Air Force One flyover: "It's totally wiped out. . . . It's devastating; it's got to be doubly devastating on the ground."[3] The White House went on to announce what we had begun to suspect, "This could well be the worst natural disaster in our nation's history."[4]

All we had left to do was despair.

There had been some clear indications that things were looking bad on Tuesday, as we nursed minor hangovers from our dinner party Monday night. Mike, who had been teetering on the edge of leaving New Orleans for years, spent Tuesday hemming and hawing until he finally resolved to fly to New York and look for work.

Mike had been living the New Orleans life for years since leaving his job as an investigator in death penalty appeals, the job that had first brought him to New Orleans. He lived alone in a cheap and crumbling, but elegant, old New Orleans apartment. He worked a few nights a week at two New Orleans rock 'n' roll bars, the Saint and the Circle Bar, and drank at them for free on the other side of the bar on the nights he wasn't working. He played upright bass in the Happy Talk Band, a roots rock band with a passionate local following. Most days, he awoke late in the afternoon to complete the *New York Times* crossword puzzle in less than ten minutes (at least early in the week) and then spend a few hours in local coffee shops drinking tea before heading to work. Whenever I spent time with Mike, regardless of where we were in the city, people who knew him would come up and say hello with the expectation of some intelligent and witty banter. Mike, an inveterate New York Jew who grew up in a middle-income housing project in the shadow of the Brooklyn Bridge, had made himself very much at home in New Orleans.

Mike and I met as teenagers at a bike shop on Lafayette Street, the easternmost border of SoHo in Manhattan. He had worked at the shop since he was thirteen and projected the wonkish competence and self-assurance found among young men who work at places like bike shops and vintage record stores. These characteristics were perhaps exaggerated at our first meeting because Mia, the girl with whom I had gone to the shop and with whom I had a precollege romance, had been the apple of Mike's eye for years. Though Mike said he was too busy to talk, Mia prevailed on him to meet us at a little park around the corner. Mia and I settled on a bench in the park with some sandwiches that we had purchased at a nearby deli and Mike soon joined us. Mia explained that she had wanted Mike and me to meet because she thought we would like each other. Mike asked a couple of cursory questions about where I had bought my sandwich and then addressed Mia exclusively before walking away, with barely a nod to me.

About six years later, Mike and I became reacquainted, again through a mutual friend, Sarah, with whom Mike had gone to Wesleyan and with whom I worked as a summer volunteer at a New Orleans anti–death penalty law office during law school. Like Mia, Sarah was sure that Mike and I would become fast friends. This time, without the impediment of a mutual love interest, the friendship came to fruition.

In the fall of 2000, Mike resolved to leave his job as a police misconduct investigator and to move to New Orleans. I was in my third year of law school and, though still uncertain, expected that I would take a job as a public defender in New York City upon graduating. Having just made a new (and simultaneously old) friend, I was sad to see Mike go and resolved to convince him of the merits of remaining in New York. When, with this purpose in mind, I invited him out for a drink, he responded, "Why don't we meet at a bar in the East Village and we can talk all about it?"— which implicitly settled the matter: the East Village and the rest of New York City had become an expensive place to live, full of hipster bars overcrowded with young professionals, wealthier facsimiles of us who, unlike us, were not looking for a place to talk about leaving the city where they had grown up, but were, through disposable income and aesthetics, permanently changing the character of the city for the worse.

I understood Mike's motives completely, as I had my own ambivalence about the city. I had seen it change from an economically and socially diverse web of neighborhoods and communities, like my family's neighborhood on Roosevelt Island, which was diverse by design, to an increasingly disturbing mirror of the economic and social divides in the rest of the country.

Mike left New York to move to New Orleans, and this appeared to me to be an original act, defying the preset path of those in New York City's orbit. It seemed to me that Mike, though his self-effacement and sarcasm would not allow him to admit it, was following in the slightly overgrown path of people who had, a generation earlier, gone down South to do good work for a cause bigger than themselves.

For a number of reasons, including the inspiration and positive reports we got from Mike, Nikki and I moved to New Orleans the following summer, just before September 11. I had an amazing job that no one else wanted, representing people facing the death penalty, a job that (contrary to representations over the phone) came with no compensation. My wife had a big studio for her art in our beautiful, crumbling house. And, perhaps most important, I had an old friend in Mike, whom I hadn't known for long but who had somehow graduated to the status of someone I had known from the "old country." Unlike in New York, where I saw my good friends occasionally, the intimacy of New Orleans led to me to see Mike all the time. And though I had other close friends through work, the stress and frustration of representing people condemned to die mean that people in my field tend not to stay around for long. So Mike became my constant, a connection to my own history.

In the gathering despair of that Tuesday, with little money and no foreseeable hope for a job back in flood-devastated New Orleans, Mike booked a one-way plane ticket to New York.

Nikki and I agreed to drive Mike to the airport in Memphis, where we planned to pick up some art supplies for Nikki, now that it was clear that she would not be home in her studio anytime soon. Cynthia Joyce, an acquaintance from New Orleans who had become a fast friend when I ran into her in the coffee shop in Oxford the previous day, decided to join our Wednesday road trip, which promised, if nothing else, a compulsory break from the steady stream of CNN and Internet news.

We drove the back way to Memphis, a shortcut off the interstate, and came into town on Lamar Boulevard, the old Highway 78, under the white, hot, late-morning sun. We passed abandoned strip malls, run-down motels with abandoned cars parked in front of vacant rooms, porn bookstores, men milling around in parking lots, and old ladies shuffling into thrift stores. Although it was a charmless and miserable sprawl, it was more like New Orleans than any place I had seen since leaving there the previous weekend. I imagined a disaster in this struggling community, with the poorest people being left to fend for themselves, and I realized that it would be just like the disaster that had struck New Orleans.

We made it to the older, historic part of town and found the art supplies store that Nikki had heard about. Unsure whether we would ever go home, or even if we still had a home, Nikki set about replacing everything she might have lost. I tried to counsel moderation, offering empty assurances that we would be home soon, that our home was still standing. Uninterested in witnessing our marital/disaster strife, Mike and Cynthia walked across the street to a record store. Nikki wandered the art supplies store throwing things into her basket, mostly ignoring me and happy to be back in her element. With some satisfaction, she brought her supplies to the check-out counter.

Cynthia and Mike returned. Cynthia was eager to report that Shannon McNally, a New Orleans singer, was playing in the record store. She explained that, as she hummed along to the lyrics, "And you'll make it through the first part of a broken heart.

Yes you'll make it through the worst part of a broken heart," the guy behind the counter had explained, "She's from New Orleans."

After a barbeque lunch, we made our way to the airport. On the way, we talked about all the unknowns that Mike's departure made us conscious of—when he would return to New Orleans, whether his house and all of his belongings had survived, how long he would be in New York, and what he would do for work once he got there. I mentioned to Mike that the combination of his departure, my sadness about New Orleans, and the barbeque in my stomach had made me nauseous. "Nauseated," he corrected me.[5]

When we arrived at the departure drop-off, Mike, uncharacteristically, hugged each of us. When there was nothing left to do or say, he walked into the airport. My heart sank as I got back into the car.

"I only met him yesterday and I am *really* sad to see him go," Cynthia said. I couldn't respond and continue to suppress the tears I felt welling up, so I sat silently and turned on the radio as we came off the ramp onto the highway.

The local NPR station was reporting the afternoon's news of the New Orleans disaster. I was glad not to talk, not to hear anyone else talk, just to listen to reporting about issues bigger than my sadness about my friend and my anxieties about my own life. The newscaster introduced a well-known New Orleans writer, Andrei Codrescu, who in the past had affected me deeply with his probing essays. In his familiar thick Romanian accent, marked with his own clear grief, he explained what we felt:

> So here we are sinking into the water around us, drowning in our own waste, poverty, incompetence, and the greed of

those who came before us. This is the time for straight reporting, of heartbreaking stories, of heroic rescues and super-
human efforts by good-hearted individuals and the weary but
always ready charities. It's not a time for anger. But I can't
help wondering, what is going to survive of our culture? We
already know who's going to pay for all this. The poor. They
always do. The whole country's garbage flows down the Mississippi to them. Until now, they turned all that waste into
song. They took the sins of America onto themselves, but
this blues now is just too big.[6]

I kept my eyes on the road and bit my lip, hearing Nikki and
Cynthia sobbing, and worried that if I started to cry, I might
never stop. My blues was too big.

PART II

This Could Be Anywhere

*Katrina's Immediate Aftermath,
Late Summer 2006*

CHAPTER 4

A Dollar Short

Remains of the St. Thomas Projects

WHEN THE LEVEES THAT HELD Lake Pontchartrain and the Mississippi River out of New Orleans broke at critical points along canals, on the Monday following the storm, the vast majority of the city, along with one hundred thousand of its residents who had not evacuated, took on water at an alarming rate. Many of those who remained suffered the dual indignity of the threat of death and the knowledge that their younger, richer, whiter counterparts had been able to flee. Although the causes and the consequences of the breaches may be hard to grasp and explain, the reality of thousands of mostly poor and black people wading through fetid rising water, or breaking through their roofs with axes lest they drown, is biblical in its simplicity. Those who stayed included many of the city's poorest residents, in a city where more than a quarter of all people live below the poverty line.[1]

The millions of vacationers who came here every year before Katrina were mostly unaware of this poverty. French Quarter tourists were rarely exposed to the reality beneath the Disneyland Gomorrah that is projected as "N'Awlins," a phrasing I have never heard a local use and a place, as far as I can tell, that I have never encountered despite my years in the city. The seemingly average, white, middle-class Americans whooped it up on Bourbon Street without any thought of the third-world lives of so many of the city's citizens that existed under their noses. The husband and wife, clad in khaki shorts, feather boa, and Mardi Gras beads well out of season, beheld a child tap-dancing on the street for money and clapped along to his beat without considering the obvious fact that this was an early school-day afternoon and that the child should be learning to read, not dancing for money. Somehow they did not see their own child beneath the dancer's black visage. Nor, perhaps, did they see the crumbling buildings where the city's poor live as they traveled by cab from the French Quarter to Commander's Palace. They were on vacation and this was not their problem.

Tourists look past these sights in the same manner travelers in the developing world do, with a passing thought that "the poor will always be among us," or some other comforting platitude. It is the hard-hearted view that we all must adopt when confronted with the manifold misery that exists in the world, and that the world, apparently, can't exist without. Perhaps the tourists believe that such misery can be similarly viewed in the South, rationalizing that, in the wake of the civil rights movement, America has washed its hands of the stains of slavery, Jim Crow, and racism.

For those of us who live here, even the wealthy and the privileged, it is impossible to ignore race and poverty; regardless of one's politics or beliefs about the causes of poverty and its link to race, these factors are central in our civic discourse and define daily life in the city. It is hard to ignore the consequences of poverty when you can't send your children to public schools because the schools are almost universally failing; when you can't walk the streets at night out of fear for your safety because of a murder rate more than six times the per capita murder rate of New York City; when, even in the richest neighborhoods, craters seemingly large enough to swallow cars go untended in the city's streets because our public coffers are empty. Although poverty certainly exists in other American cities and towns—in unexpected places such as Miami, where an even greater segment of the population lives below the poverty line than in New Orleans, and in more predictable places such as East St. Louis, Detroit, and Newark—I have never been to a city in the United States whose life and character were so defined by the struggles of its poorest citizens.

My own work here highlighted these issues because my clients' families, the witnesses in my clients' cases, the vast majority of the victims' families—indeed, the entire universe surrounding nearly everything related to the brutal murders that my clients are accused of committing—all live in poor communities of color.

When I first arrived in 1999, I met Bart Stappard, a Dutch human rights lawyer who had represented people on death row and, in the course of that work, began a neighborhood legal clinic in a small shotgun house in the shadow of the St. Thomas Housing Project. The little office was right next door to the Hope House, the place where a young nun, Sister Helen Prejean, began her work. In the opening of her book *Dead Man Walking*, she described the St. Thomas: "Not death row exactly, but close. Death is rampant here—from guns, disease, addiction. Medical care scarcely exists."[2]

When I first saw St. Thomas, a series of sturdy two- and three-story solid masonry brick buildings, each divided into numerous apartments, that feeling of death was palpable. Although the entryways still boasted filigreed ironwork, half of the windows were boarded up and many doors hung from single hinges. Windowless frames exposed abandoned interiors covered with graffiti. Children played in the trash-strewn courtyards and life moved on for people whose only possible home was this. A group of kids played a game they called "crazy can." They set up two empty soup tins about ten yards apart and a pitcher, standing at one end, tried to knock down the opposite tin with a ball. If he missed the tin, or if a kid standing in front of the tin hit the ball with a stick, the pitcher would run back and forth between the cans until the ball was retrieved. From a birthday party for my English boss, I recognized the game as a variety of cricket and wondered how it had found its way into this forgotten alley.

St. Thomas's buildings were constructed with great idealism and optimism, as the first housing project in the United States built pursuant to a piece of New Deal legislation passed in 1937.[3] The loan used to construct them had been signed by President Roosevelt himself. They were to provide clean, safe, affordable housing for white families made homeless by the Great Depression. They lived up to this ideal, more or less, until the mid-1960s, when the Civil Rights Act compelled racial integration of the projects and the bottom fell out of the social services offered to residents. White flight and a lack of jobs pushed the area into steady decay over the next four decades, leaving rampant poverty, failed schools, and a horrifying level of violent crime in its wake.[4]

I walked around the projects that day with a woman who attended law school with me in New York and who was also in New Orleans that summer working on poverty law issues. She was an Indian-American who had traveled back and forth to India her entire life. I asked her how the poverty and desperation she saw in the courtyards between these buildings compared to what she saw in India, a country of staggering poverty. She responded simply, "In India people are poorer, they have so little, but they have dignity. This looks so hopeless, not like India at all."

In 2001, these projects were razed with public funding under the U.S. Department of Housing and Urban Development's "Hope Six" program, and a private company built "mixed-income" housing in its place, to the delight of many business owners and residents who had moved into the old, historic neighborhood in recent years.[5] Almost none of the original residents were allowed to return. Some of the displaced families were given rent vouchers for private, low-rent apartments in the city's decrepit housing market. Others ended up in other housing projects in areas where gentrification had not yet spurred on the razing of public housing. (The transfer of families to other projects was fatal for some young men, as the mixing of groups from rival projects and neighborhoods led to increased violence in these already war-torn communities.)[6]

Many of the people who had lived in these projects were the city's persistent "working poor," people who toil in the city's minimum-wage jobs in the tourist industry or service market, or in other low-wage positions in the city's meager economy. Prior to Katrina, these positions offered low wages, no benefits, little job protection, and minimal possibility of advancement. In part, this was attributable to Louisiana's status as a Right to Work state, where the protections and collective bargaining advantages that come from union membership are rare. Unable to harness the power of organized labor to improve the working conditions of low-wage workers, and finding deaf ears in the state house in Baton Rouge, the people of New Orleans began a campaign in the late 1990s in support of a citywide referendum to increase the city's minimum wage to $6.15 an hour, a dollar more than was required by federal law. The proponents of the measure, which was spearheaded by the grassroots group ACORN (Association of Community Organizations for Reform Now), argued forcefully that an increased minimum wage would assist in lowering poverty rates in the city, which could, in turn, begin to address the pervasive crime, neighborhood blight, illiteracy, hunger, and other social ills that were epidemic in the city's poorest neighborhoods. Wade Rathke, one of the organizers of the New Orleans campaign and ACORN's founder, explained just how narrow the range of options is for the city's residents: "The city's poor public education system has produced a class of adults who have little choice but to join the legions of low-wage workers serving the hospitality industry."[7]

Living wage campaigns were being initiated across the country at this time by groups and individuals who were seeing full-time workers, despite their diligence, on soup kitchen lines with their families. As a local minister, Rev. Kenneth Thibadoux of the Asia Baptist Church, told the city council at the time, "This is about survival, keeping our heads above water, doing everything we can while we can."[8]

The Chamber of Commerce, the business lobby, and the state Republican Party worked fiercely against the living wage campaign. On its face, their argument was essentially that an increase in the minimum wage in New Orleans would make the city an even more inhospitable place to do business and thus would drive yet more businesses out of the city, leading to even fewer jobs. This is a core "free market" argument: what's good for business is good for workers. It belies the fact that many of the states with the freest markets, the fewest regulations, and the most probusiness agendas are Louisiana's neighbors to the north and east, states that, like ours, tolerate the rape of our land and the exploitation of our people without any tangible benefit to our public fisc or infrastructure. We get the cancer of industry and this does not even afford us functioning schools.

For years, the business community prevented the living wage measure from being put to the voters, but finally in 2001 the people had a chance to decide for themselves. Given their familiarity with the realities of trickle-down economics, New Orleans voters came out overwhelmingly in favor of the referendum, by a margin of 63 to 37 percent. Rathke, the organizer, said at the time, "We strongly believe that the people's voice is finally getting to be heard, and they're answering with a roar."[9]

A study conducted for ACORN at the time that the measure passed estimated that almost fifty thousand people would receive immediate raises as a consequence of the measure and that an additional twenty-seven thousand would receive significant increases in salary as part of the ripple effect among low-wage workers.[10] Thus, more than seventy-five thousand citizens of New Orleans, or about a third of its working population, would have received meaningful raises as a consequence of the measure, raises that could have provided food, transportation, housing, and dignity.[11]

It should be no surprise that the same forces that attempted to prevent this vote in the first place had no qualms about undermining democratic self-rule, even once it was evident what the people wanted for themselves, their families, and their communities. Immediately, and with absolutely no concerns about the "judicial activism" that they revile in other public policy matters, these groups took their case to the courts. The opposition came complete with posters hung around town threatening violence against individuals who had worked to make the living wage increase a reality.

The living wage prevailed in the first round of litigation before an elected civil district court judge, Judge Rosemary Ledet, in New Orleans. She rejected the business group's argument that "localized minimum wage ordinances would have a negative impact on business development" and drew back the veil on their argument, stating that it "is based on economic theory premised on [their] belief that there should be no mandatory minimum wage, whether prescribed by federal state or local law."[12] In other words, business's argument was that any minimum wage, including the living wage mandated in the measure passed by New Orleans voters, hindered the free flow of business and the right to contract. This was the same thinking that I heard over and over in law school from the future big business lawyers of America, the Federalist Society, and the "law and economic" types who were heading down here to clerk for the federal Fifth Circuit Court of Appeals and further eviscerate our rights. They argued that individuals should be permitted to sell their organs on the free market to the highest bidder and that, regardless of the factor of poverty, they were making a rational, market-based determination that reflected their freedom and humanity. As they saw it, preventing businesses from paying whatever wage, however low the market would bear, criminalizing the sale of one's own organs, and disallowing consumer loans that would allow poor people to buy refrigerators at 30 percent interest were all part of a liberal paternalism that disrespects individual freedom and self-determination.

Sadly, the Louisiana Supreme Court, a court before which I argue death penalty cases, and which has been infected, like many other state supreme courts, with the antitort, probusiness Chamber of Commerce lobby, was perfectly willing to engage in this monstrous discourse. The Court found the minimum-wage increase unconstitutional because it conflicted with an early act by the state legislature prohibiting such actions on the grounds that they "would lead to economic instability and decline and to a decrease in the standard of living for Louisiana's citizens."[13]

The biggest insult of this entire episode was that the opponents of a living wage felt the need to put the whole discussion in terms of raising the standard of living of New Orleanians. How impossibly transparent is it when the city's powerful hotel industry, restaurant lobby, and other major employers claim to be advocating on behalf of the interests of poor people while they attempt to thwart a democratically passed initiative that would compel them to pay people at the lowest rungs of society seven or eight dollars a day more for their hard work?

Advocates of free markets would be more tolerable if they simply laid bare their real passion—their belief that "market efficiency" is paramount and, further, that they should be able to do whatever the hell they want because they are the big and powerful market and have earned that right. Honest tyrants of the past have been bold enough to say with clarity that "might makes right." This view has a long pedigree, expressed by Machiavelli and Sun Tzu in volumes digested for businessmen and sitting with uncracked spines in bookcases in the corner offices of finance big shots in Wall Street towers.[14]

Instead, we are left with the ugliness of business claiming that measures that would help business make more money and force people deeper into poverty are, in fact, good for those people and for business. This argument, made in all corners these days, has always reminded me of a drunk uncle who, during my teens, chastised me for not drinking. Through an alcoholic slur, which he tried to even out because my sobriety made him self-conscious, he explained, "A couple of glasses of wine a day are good for your heart. One should drink." Indeed, how much comfort would we all take if our darkest vices proved beneficial to ourselves and others.

Sadly, at least in New Orleans, that appears not to have been the case. Here, in spite of the "humanitarian" work done by the business lobby in voiding the minimum-wage increase that foolish people wanted for themselves, poverty has persisted and deepened. During the dark days after the storm, when so many of my fellow New Orleanians were trapped here because they had no transportation or means to live, my friend David Koen, an activist New Orleans lawyer who helps people escape predatory loans and usurious mortgages, wondered aloud about how much difference it might have made for families unable to evacuate if the family breadwinner had made a dollar more an hour.

Imagine a mother working at one of our grand hotels making a dollar more an hour for her thirty-five hours a week spent cleaning strangers' toilets and changing their bedsheets. That's $140 more income every month. For a two-income family, that's $280 every month. Though this modest raise is not likely to afford anyone the new S-Class Mercedes that the Hilton shareholders drive, it is certainly adequate for a used Kia and some gas money.

Neither an increase in the minimum wage nor the profits of corporations that do business in New Orleans managed to trickle down to poor New Orleanians before Hurricane Katrina. The question remains whether the people living in housing projects and poor neighborhoods across New Orleans who sat anxiously on their roofs amidst the flood or in horror at the Superdome would have benefited more quickly from the dollar provided in the referendum or the invisible hand of unregulated capitalism. All we know is what they chose for themselves and what was chosen for them.

CHAPTER 5

Poor, Nasty, Brutish, and Short

The Business District and Superdome from Broad Avenue

"WE HAD BABIES IN THERE. Little babies being raped!" exclaimed the New Orleans police chief, Eddie Compass, in tears. He was on *Oprah* recounting the atrocities that occurred in the Superdome while thousands remained stranded there in the aftermath of Hurricane Katrina.[1] It was a gruesome picture that seemed consistent with the images of total collapse and mayhem that streamed over the airwaves in the days following the storm.

Mayor Ray Nagin made comments that corroborated the police chief's account: "About three days we were basically rationing, fighting, people were—that's why the people, in my opinion, they got to this almost animalistic state because they didn't have the resources. . . . We have people standing out there, that have been in that frickin' Superdome for five days watching dead bodies, watching hooligans killing people, raping people."[2]

These tales of child rape—probably the most horrifying and needless crime that most people can imagine—corresponded comfortably with the images of looting that were ubiquitous in the early days after the storm. The needless and perverse self-gratification embodied in the act of rape informed the world's views on the looting of stores by the predominantly black residents who had been left behind. The looting, like the rapes in the Superdome, appeared to be prompted by vice rather than need.

It seemed that for these people, the rapists and looters, the storm was not a nightmare in which they were trapped but instead an opportunity for expression of their true natures, which before the storm had been only barely curbed by the constraints of society. Furthermore, little distinction was made between sociopaths and those who were merely stuck, as though poor New Orleanians had been complicit in hiding a sleeper cell of criminals in their communities and were now getting their due.

Although one might be tempted to argue that poor communities are not, in fact, complicit in their own troubles, but instead victims of them, in this case the much more sensible argument is that the very elements of the narrative—rape, murder, and, in many cases, looting—were fictions or distortions.

THE SUPERDOME HAS long been considered the de facto hurricane shelter in New Orleans. As is now emblazoned in the consciousness of many Americans, it is a massive dome sitting on a huge cylinder. It is simultaneously otherworldly in appearance, as if a spaceship had landed in a busy downtown, and solid and confidence-inspiring, as old banks and government buildings used to be. In storms past, the radio announcers would invariably announce that the Superdome was or wasn't yet accepting evacuees, but there was a general sense throughout the city that the Superdome was the place to go in case of disaster. My home is about ten blocks from the dome, and in years past, when I failed to heed hurricane evacuation warnings, I have taken comfort in the notion that I could easily make it on foot to the Superdome, where, no doubt, there would be people on hand to help me. Apparently, I was not the only one in New Orleans under this cruel illusion, and the government officials, who had failed to disabuse us of this idea, had not done anything to prepare the dome for more than a really exciting Sugar Bowl or Saints game.

People began arriving en masse at the dome on Monday when the levees were breached and water rose in large parts of the city. They arrived on foot, as those who had cars, as well as those with an inclination to commandeer transportation, had already left or were leaving town. Many of the poorest and hardest-hit parts of the city, such as the Lower Ninth Ward, are miles from the Superdome. Imagine the Herculean effort required, in waist- and chest-deep water, to evacuate your family from your home and then make your way for miles through an abandoned and lawless city to get to the Superdome. Thousands of people, clearly, imagined that there would be some relief at the end of this effort but, like a mirage in a desert, it was an illusion. The reality at the Superdome was worse for many than what they had left behind, and the belief that there *must* be someone at the end of their travails who would provide help or assistance must have stung immeasurably as it evaporated.

By Tuesday, there were more than ten thousand people at the Superdome; by Wednesday, twenty-five thousand people; by Thursday, thirty thousand people.[3] Children and elderly, the sick and the disabled. The poor. The dispossessed. The very people most in need of help were there, stuck in a situation that was entirely foreseeable but somehow either unanticipated or ignored by the people who could have made a difference, not just in those days before and after the storm but in the preceding decades in which all of this could easily have been anticipated.

The images of rape and murder ran in perfect tandem with other media depictions in the days following the storm. The most horrifying portrayals concerned attacks by city residents on people attempting to assist in the rescue effort. I remember hearing on National Public Radio and CNN in the days following the storm that the airlift effort was being hampered by roving gangs trying to shoot down rescue helicopters and that Charity Hospital, Louisiana's first public hospital, created by the populist governor Huey Long, was under sniper attack while rescuers tried to evacuate the hospital.[4] Michael Brown, the errant director of the Federal Emergency Management Agency (FEMA), went so far as to tell reporters that his agency was attempting to work "under conditions of urban warfare," as if New Orleans had become Mogadishu or Sarajevo in the 1990s.[5]

For me, the most frightening of these depictions concerned the New Orleans Children's Hospital. The *Times-Picayune* reported, "Gov. Blanco spokeswoman Denise Bottcher described a disturbing scene unfolding in uptown New Orleans, where looters were trying to break into Children's Hospital. Bottcher said the director of the hospital fears for the safety of the staff and the 100 kids inside the hospital. The director said the hospital is locked, but that the looters were trying to break in and had gathered outside the facility. The director has sought help from the police, but, due to rising flood waters, police have not been able to respond."[6]

Looters, like the hoodlums who had already raped children and women in shelters, were now trying, en masse, to break into a hospital for children and help was nowhere to be found. Could it be made any more clear that the barbarians were at the gate?

Other looting, by far less vicious characters, occurred throughout the city. People unable to get provisions through any other means were compelled to take what they needed from stores and businesses. A friend of mine who stayed behind and rode his bike over to the Wal-Mart that had been built on the site of the former St. Thomas Housing Project, described the wide array of people he saw there, "There were old black church ladies with Jesus bumper stickers, there were young kids, there were firefighters getting water and canned food."

And surely there were many who, in the total lawlessness, took things they didn't need, like jeans, CDs, and televisions. One young man carrying several pairs of jeans out of a store was asked by a reporter whether it was his store. He replied, "No. That's everybody's store."[7] Although this may be an overly expansive view of property rights, it is certainly understandable in an environment where it appears that the world has come to end, among people for whom being left behind in the storm was only the most recent of a series of insults.

On the other hand, taking canned food, water, medicine, and other necessary provisions from deserted stores in a seemingly forsaken city seems to be a very understandable and human act, not a crime. Regardless of one's opinion of Emma Goldman or her position that it is the "sacred right" of hungry men to steal bread, only the most pious would rather watch their family or loved ones starve or suffer from thirst than take what they needed without harming others. At that point, who cares if it is "wrong" or a "crime"?

This human understanding of the suffering of desperate people seemed to inhere in a photograph and caption put on the Web by one of the newswire services in the worst days following the storm. The image depicted two young white people, a man and a woman, wading through chest-deep water with soda and white bread in tow. The caption from AFP/Getty read, "Two residents wade through chest-deep water after finding bread and soda from a local grocery store in New Orleans."[8]

The photo and its caption would be entirely unexceptional except for its contrast with numerous other captions to photos of black residents that appeared on the wire. For instance, an image of two black women holding grocery bags and a bottle of bleach walking through calf-deep water, was captioned, "Looters carry bags of groceries through floodwaters after taking the merchandise away from a wind damaged convenience store in New Orleans."[9]

Another wire service photo showed a black teenager with short dreadlocks and yellow collared shirt, chest-deep in flood water, clinging to a cardboard twelve-pack of drinks and pulling a large floating garbage bag. The caption to that photo read, "A young man walks through chest deep flood water after looting a grocery store in New Orleans."[10]

The sad correlation of the terms *looter* and *looting* with blacks and *resident* and *finding* with whites epitomizes the subjective lens through which America sees, and is frightened by, its black minority while maintaining an open mind toward otherwise identical images of whites.[11] The captions certainly suggest that the entire media depiction of the chaos in New Orleans following Hurricane Katrina would have been very different if there had been more white faces in the turmoil, or if all of this had occurred in Westport, Connecticut.

SINCE THE STORM, I have heard many lamentable things about the situation in the Superdome. On a rainy afternoon in an Oxford, Mississippi, motel in those first days after the storm, a man approached my friend and, upon learning that they were both from the same white-flight neighborhood of Jefferson Parish, announced with a half-smile, "All those blacks in one place. Can you imagine the smell?"

Then, of course, there were the widespread Internet jokes about the storm and the lawlessness in New Orleans. One, originating from former state senator David Duke's Web site, mocks a Heineken advertisement. A balding black man is shown wading through thigh-high water with a plastic bin of beers. The words beneath the image read, "In a grab and run test, Heineken was the number one beer of choice for looters in the New Orleans metropolitan area. When asked, most agreed that Colt 45 or Red Dog was their main beer of purchase, but when money doesn't matter, they grab for the finest beer around, Heineken."[12]

Another joke passed along by the Fox News set, and sung to the tune of "The Battle of New Orleans," synthesized some of the above views with its own narrow view of the role that government ought to serve in the lives of its most desperate citizens.

The New Battle of New Orleans rhymed Superdome and "make themselves right at home," while depicting theft, looting, and rape. The song mocks people for "not getting their sorry asses out" of New Orleans, for receiving FEMA checks, and for wanting to return home to New Orleans. And the song didn't fail to make clear that the "them" was black people in a couplet where the songwriter supports the army's need to shoot "back," and then ridicules people who complain that such action was motivated by the fact that the victims where "black." The sarcastic final line, mocking people who feel that the government is at fault for what happened in New Orleans, is just more of the same ugliness and cynicism at the needless suffering of our fellow citizens.[13]

To me, blaming people and mocking them for their own vulnerability is vastly more discouraging than naked and, sadly, expected racism in light of the suffering of these people. Many in America likely agree with the man in the Oxford motel and with David Duke, and the song appears to reflect a dominant voice in the American political mainstream.[14] In the song, the echoes of the mythic "welfare queen," threatening black superpredators, the mantra of "personal responsibility," and the other quivers of right-wing race-baiting are evident. The core of the song, and of these principles, is that people should take care of themselves or live with the consequences. In this instance, the song seems to assume that people *could* have left and *chose* not to because they were waiting for someone else to "get their sorry asses out." In the logic of the song, "they" made bad choices, committed horrible acts, and now whine because they expect the government to bail them out for their mistakes.

Certainly, there were some who made the wrong choice and took a chance that the storm would turn, a chance that everyone who lives here has taken at one time or another. But what about the majority, those who didn't choose but instead couldn't leave because they were poor or old? Didn't they have the right to believe that they wouldn't simply be left behind to fend for themselves? The elderly, the veterans, the children, even the misguided, uninformed, or stupid—isn't there something on the other end of the social contract for these people in their time of greatest need? Isn't this the role of government?

Somehow, however, in the days immediately following the

storm, this was not the story; the dominant narrative focused on the lawlessness of the victims. The police, the military, the whole apparatus of the American government that has felled entire nations in an afternoon, were no match for this disaster because these people were destroying themselves by shooting at helicopters, raping babies and old women, and killing one another.

Hurricane Katrina and interpretation of the blurry and indistinct events that occurred in New Orleans served as a compulsory Rorschach test for a country that has long been troubled by the dynamics of inequality. Staring at the inkblot, the press and people across this country saw their worst suspicions about America's poor and minorities confirmed. They saw rape and looting by blacks untethered by the constraints of law and order. They saw their own nightmare about driving through a frightening neighborhood late at night. They saw the empty results of a civil rights movement that we seem to celebrate all year long these days but fail to really honor. They saw a failed system of government "entitlements."

Unlike a Rorschach, however, much of what Americans saw was not a matter of subjective interpretation in the cool light of day. They were simply wrong about what they thought they saw. There was not a single reported rape or murder in the Superdome or Convention Center. No one looted the Children's Hospital. Not one shot was fired at helicopters or Charity Hospital.[15] And where looting did occur, it was mostly of businesses, and, in retrospect, we can see that instances of looting were interpreted through the lens of race.

It seems that all of us, with the provocation of the media and its distortions, were somehow willing to believe things had sunk to the "law of the jungle" among those who had been left behind. It is reminiscent of the Bertrand Russell quotation, "Men tend to have the beliefs that suit their passions." In other words, what we thought we saw says more about us than about what we were seeing.

CHAPTER 6

Not in My Backyard

Crescent City Connection from behind Wal-Mart

ONCE IT BECAME CLEAR that help was not on the way and that people needed to fend for themselves, groups began attempting to evacuate the city on their own two feet. From the business district, where both the Superdome and Convention Center are located, the most natural point of egress from the city is the Crescent City Connection, a twin-span bridge that arches over the Mississippi River and connects the east bank of New Orleans with the west bank neighborhood of Algiers, part of the city of New Orleans, as well as Jefferson Parish's west bank.

Not only was the bridge a natural point of egress, it was also the escape route prescribed to desperate groups of tourists by police after they were forced to leave their hotels in the French Quarter. Larry Bradshaw, a paramedic from San Francisco who was visiting the city for a convention, told CBS News, "A gentleman came out [of the police command post] and identified himself as one of the commanders. And he said, 'I have a solution. I have buses waiting for you across the bridge.' "[1] Because Bradshaw's group had received previous empty solutions, they pressed the commander, who turned to the gathered crowd and stated emphatically, "I swear to you that buses are there."[2]

With that, Bradshaw and a group of other tourists began the mile-and-a-half walk from Canal Street to the bridge. Along the way, they ran into hundreds of people, mostly black, and told them the good news—that buses were a half hour's walk away.

Hundreds joined the group, including "families," "babies in strollers," "people using crutches," and "elderly clasping walkers and people in wheelchairs," hopeful that they had found a way out.[3] By the time they reached the ramp to the bridge, Bradshaw estimated that the group was 95 percent black. Rain began pouring down but, given its proximity to escape, the large group moved forward undeterred—that is, until they saw a line of police barring the road ahead once they reached the top of the steep ramp. As the group approached the line, the police, all of whom were white, according to witnesses, began firing shotguns over their heads. People scattered, but a few, including Bradshaw, attempted to address the police. He told them that they had been sent there by a New Orleans Police Department commander and that there were buses waiting for them. The police responded that the group would not be permitted to cross, because "This is not New Orleans," and "We're not going to have any Superdomes over here."[4]

Bradshaw read between the lines. "To me, that was code language or code words for, 'We're not having black people coming into our neighborhood.'"[5]

The story of what happened on the bridge was, briefly, a point of interest in the national press and in the conversation across the country about race, poverty, and Hurricane Katrina. The actions of the police were quickly addressed, however, and the story was largely put to bed by public officials adept at deflecting claims of racial discrimination and a national press corps ill-suited to pursuing hard questions about race in American life.

The initial iteration of this story in the press seemed sympathetic to the injustice suffered by those refused on the bridge. In succeeding days, however, both the Jefferson Parish sheriff,

Harry Lee, and the Gretna police chief, Arthur Lawson, provided their own explanations for their motivations in repelling and shooting at frightened people.

Lawson explained, "We had no preparations. You know, we're a small city on the west bank of the river. We had people being told to come over here, that we were going to have buses, we were going to have food, we were going to have water, and we were going to have shelter. And we had none. . . . Our people had left. Our city was locked down and secured, for the sake of the citizens that left their valuables here to be protected by us."[6]

After that explanation gained traction, Lawson took a more aggressive stance in rebutting critics who regarded his actions as "racist and callous." "I'm very pissed off. . . . I am because I have been painted as a racist and this good community's good reputation has been blemished because of something we did because the City of New Orleans was ill prepared to handle the situation that they had and expected us to evacuate their city without preparation, without any notice, without any contact."[7]

Sheriff Harry Lee, the longtime Asian American head of the Jefferson Parish Sheriff's Office, made similar remarks: "FEMA didn't have any food for those people in Gretna. They didn't give me any food. I didn't have any water. My obligation was to the citizens of Jefferson Parish."[8]

These explanations might be easier for me to accept if I had not come across the ugly specter of racism in Jefferson Parish so many times in my work in the courts there and in researching racial justice issues in the parish. I have worked on cases in which an assistant district attorney, a person charged with enforcing the laws of the state, wore a necktie with a hand-painted noose on it during the death penalty prosecution of a young black man.

Then, as now, Jefferson Parish officials defended their actions, asserting that race had nothing to do with the tie. Paul Connick, the Jefferson Parish district attorney, explained, "The impression you get at first blush is that these guys are wearing these ties into the courtroom and creating prejudicial issues, racial issues. That has not happened. More importantly to me, personally and professionally, that is not what my office is about."[9] (The district attorney's office ultimately agreed that the tie would not be worn again after I filed a motion attempting to address the symbolic significance of the noose, in which I quoted the full text of the poem, then song, "Strange Fruit.")

The Jefferson Parish District Attorney's Office's use of race in the courtroom is not limited to mere symbolism. A comprehensive report on the use of discretionary challenges to minority jurors in criminal trials there found that black citizens were more than three times more likely than whites to be excluded by Jefferson Parish district attorneys. The study, which looked at 10,900 potential jurors in 390 jury selections, concluded that the district attorneys' actions resulted in minority voices being excluded from 80 percent of trials, in spite of the fact that the parish is nearly 23 percent black.[10] The report concluded that the statistical likelihood that the finding wasn't contingent on race was significantly less than the chance of getting struck by lightning.[11] When the press confronted Jefferson Parish district attorney Paul Connick with these statistics, he vehemently denied that race played any role in jury selection and explained, "They're just throwing the numbers out and making the inference that it's all racially motivated."[12]

A brief window into the rationale behind these policies was revealed in *State v. Edward Harris*, a case that the Louisiana

Supreme Court overturned after finding that an assistant district attorney had discriminated in her exclusion of a black juror. When the trial court questioned her about her challenge of the juror, she didn't even offer a pretext for his exclusion, explaining, "He's a single black male on the [jury] panel . . . He was black . . . and I don't want him identifying with the defendant." When the judge asked her to explain her rationale in light of the U.S. Supreme Court precedents prohibiting the use of race in jury selection, she replied that this civil rights protection was "old law." Apparently the elected Jefferson Parish judge agreed with her because he overruled the defense's objections to the challenge.[13]

Since the Louisiana Supreme Court's decision in the Harris case, the U.S. Supreme Court has decided a sequence of cases in which, thankfully, it has affirmed that the line of cases protecting minority participation on juries is very much a live and binding area of law, in spite of any claims to the contrary.[14]

Another more symbolic issue arose recently, concerning a target that Sheriff Harry Lee's deputies were using for shooting practice. While Sarah and Emily Kunstler were filming *The Road to Justice*, a documentary about my client Ryan Matthews, who had been exonerated from death row, they came across a handmade wooden target behind the Jefferson Parish Correctional Center in Gretna. It was cut in the shape of an overweight man, with extra-large white googly eyes, large red lips, and an orange jumpsuit painted on. From the photo they took, it was clear that the target was a caricature of a black man done in the old-fashioned, racist Sambo style. This is what Jefferson Parish sheriff's deputies, who were among the forces that barred the bridge, were using for target practice.

When Sheriff Lee was questioned about the target, he made

several remarkable statements. He commented, "A critic could say that the painting is not representative of a Caucasian eye or a Caucasian mouth, but it doesn't look much like an African mouth either." He suggested that it could even be "a Chinaman," but "the eyes aren't slanted enough to be a Chinaman."[15] Ultimately he defended the target, explaining, "I'm looking at this thing that people say is offensive. I've looked at it, I don't find it offensive, and I have no interest in correcting it."[16]

From Harry Lee, who has been popularly elected sheriff by overwhelming margins of Jefferson Parish voters for almost three decades, no one would have reasonably expected a different response. In his time in elected office, Lee has made a policy of speaking his mind and expressing his views without any regard for the fact that his comments or policies might offend minorities, who make up almost 30 percent of Jefferson Parish's citizens.

Comments made by Lee at a news conference following a rash of robberies in Jefferson Parish in the 1980s typify his approach to racial profiling: "If there are some young blacks driving a car late at night in a predominantly white area, they will be stopped. . . . If you live in a predominantly white neighborhood and two blacks are in a car behind you, there's a pretty good chance they're up to no good. . . . It's obvious two young blacks driving a rinky-dink car in a predominately white neighborhood—I'm not talking about on the main thoroughfare, but if they're on one of the side streets and they're cruising around—they'll be stopped."[17] When these comments provoked outrage, Lee asserted that the comments were practical, not racist.

He displayed similar self-styled pragmatism when he pulled a street crimes unit from a predominantly black neighborhood in 1994, in response to community members' protesting the deaths while in the custody of sheriff's deputies of two men from their neighborhood. In a statement to the press, Lee explained his motivation: "To hell with them. I don't need that. I haven't heard one word of support from one black person. There are plenty of other neighborhoods that would want the Street Crimes Unit."[18]

Although Lee's overtly bigoted and confrontational attitudes on race may not play well in the rest of the country, there are a lot of reasons to believe that his approach to race has bolstered his political career in Jefferson Parish. Indeed, former state representative David Duke, the most racially divisive politician in recent memory to have gained national attention, ascended to national politics from origins in Jefferson Parish.

David Duke, a former imperial wizard of the Ku Klux Klan and founder of the National Association for the Advancement of White People, was elected to the Louisiana State House of Representatives in 1989 as the representative of the Metairie district, a middle-class suburb in Jefferson Parish. Encouraged by his success, Duke ran for governor in 1991. He defeated his Republican opponent, the incumbent governor Buddy Roemer, in the primary, and was pitted against Democratic candidate Edwin Edwards in the general election. Although Edwards went on to win the governorship with 60 percent of the vote—due in part to local organizing against Duke because of his past leadership of the Klan—Duke did surprisingly well. After the election, he bragged, "I won my constituency. I won 55 percent of the white vote."[19] Duke could also brag that he won a majority in many districts of his home parish.[20] Like Lee, Duke maintained throughout his campaign that he was no racist but, instead, merely represented the interests of the "great American middle class."[21]

Also foreshadowing the Gretna bridge incident was a series of instances in which Jefferson Parish lawmakers attempted to erect barricades to keep poor black residents from traveling into neighboring white neighborhoods within Jefferson Parish, as well as a high-profile incident in 1987 in which Jefferson Parish officials erected a barricade along the parish line to prevent residents from largely black Orleans Parish from entering Jefferson Parish. The wood and concrete walls along the parish line, which were dubbed "the Berlin Wall" by black residents on the New Orleans side of the wall, were erected by order of the Jefferson Parish Council only three months after Sheriff Lee mandated pulling over black drivers in white neighborhoods.[22] Building of the walls was ostensibly motivated by citizens' complaints that the flow of traffic from the city let criminals enter the parish. The then mayor of New Orleans, Sidney Barthelemy, cried foul and had the barricades bulldozed, insisting that Jefferson Parish "can't lock my people in," thereby blocking the New Orleans neighborhood's access to highways and hospitals.[23]

The Jefferson Parish Council, led by Chairman Bob Evans, responded by challenging the mayor's legal ability to demolish the barriers and by urging that they be rebuilt within days. After being informed by the State Transportation Authority that the barricades were illegal, however, the Council relented. Regardless, Evans insisted that the barriers were erected to prevent crime and "nothing racial was intended."[24]

Again in 2005, we were told that race played no role in the barricade that prevented hundreds of black people, desperate for their lives, from escaping over the Crescent City Connection from the flood in New Orleans. As with other embattled "straight-shooting" Jefferson Parish officials, Chief Lawson, who ordered the barricade, experienced his own post-Katrina popularity bounce. The Gretna City Council unanimously voted to support the police chief's actions. Signs could be found throughout the town reading, "God bless Chief Lawson," and "Balls is spelled Arthur Lawson." When interviewed by reporters, most local residents were supportive. One explained, "We were ecstatic. They were looting and they were shooting, and we didn't want that over here."[25] "If you are in your house and they're rioting all around to get in, are you going to let them in? We saved our city and protected our people. Our plan worked, and we're going to stick with our plan," Lawson said in a September interview. "Next hurricane, we're going to secure our city the same way."[26]

Although context makes it impossible to believe the universal denials of racism on the part of Jefferson Parish officials, we can be sure that on the last score—that he would do it all again—Lawson is not lying. We can also be sure that such pragmatism will spread—north, south, east, and west—if it remains unpoliced and unexamined by either the press or the government.

CHAPTER 7

Left to Die

Temporary Prison Tent for Orleans Parish Inmates

At a press conference on the morning of August 28, Mayor Nagin was asked about his decision not to evacuate OPP [Orleans Parish Prison]. He referred the question to Sheriff Gusman, who said: "[W]e have backup generators to accommodate any power loss. . . . We're fully staffed. We're under our emergency operations plan. . . . [W]e've been working with the police department—*so we're going to keep our prisoners where they belong.*"

"Treated Like Trash," report of the
Juvenile Justice Project of Louisiana

IF, AS DOSTOYEVSKY CLAIMED, a society's degree of civilization can be measured by its treatment of prisoners, we are in even deeper trouble in New Orleans than many realize. In this city, Hurricane Katrina spurred on the biggest prison crisis since Attica. Unlike Attica, which brought about a period of thoughtful examination of American prison policies, the crisis in New Orleans has failed to create a meaningful conversation about the treatment of American prisoners. The lack of concern highlights the extent to which prisons have become invisible in the United States over the past thirty years while marking the lives of more than two million Americans on any given day, five times the per capita incarceration rate at the time the Attica riots occurred.[1]

The New Orleans jail sits behind the old gothic Orleans Parish Criminal Court and backs up on Interstate 10 in a rundown area of the city. On the days following Hurricane Katrina, the entire complex sat beneath feet of water. At that time, the jail housed more than seven thousand prisoners, the majority of whom were pretrial detainees—people entitled to the fundamental presumption of innocence, but without the funds for bail or a lawyer to get them out of jail before trial. There was a larger than usual population of pretrial inmates in the jail when the storm came, a result of police sweeps in which people were arrested for petty crimes such as loitering or trespass, exacerbated by other parish jails' evacuating their prisoners to New Orleans in anticipation of the hurricane.

Despite the universal awareness of the risk of flooding in the city, the low-lying jail failed to execute any real evacuation plan. Instead, even faster than some New Orleans police abandoned the citizens of New Orleans, many of the sheriff's deputies who guard the city's prisoners abandoned their charges, leaving men, women, and children wondering whether they were going to die as water rose in their locked cells. As one prisoner, Dan Bright, remarked, "They left us to die there."[2]

In many respects, Dan's experience in the days and weeks following Hurricane Katrina exemplifies the experience of his fellow prisoners who survived the storm in the Orleans Parish Prison. The Saturday before the storm, he had been driving around the city in his car, a 1997 Jaguar XJ6 that had been given to him by his aunt. He was pulled over by the police, who approached the car and asked for his license and insurance information, never explaining the reason why he had been pulled over. Dan told me that he had his own suspicions: "I knew why they pulled me over—they thought that the car was stolen or that I was a drug dealer. Especially in New Orleans, if a guy is driving a nice car, he better have an Armani suit on."

Dan was arrested on the basis of a misdemeanor charge from several months earlier, a domestic dispute with a former girlfriend. When he was brought to OPP, he heard from guards and other inmates that police were arresting everyone they found on the streets that night, on any basis, in order to "clear the street" in advance of the storm. Worse, he found out that there was no way for him to get out because, by the following morning, the bail bondsmen, the judges, and the lawyers had all closed up shop and evacuated. He figured that he would have to wait the storm out.

He was housed in Templeman III, a section of the central lockup with two open tiers, one stacked above the other. On Sunday night, he and the other prisoners heard the wind whipping around outside. They had received a meal that afternoon, but no dinner. They went to sleep hungry and worried.

The following morning when they awakened, the water had begun rising in Templeman III and Dan heard yelling from the men below on the lower tier. The guards were gone. The only inmate whose cell was not locked was the "tier rep," who went down to the first tier to try to pry the cell doors open with a mop ringer. Dan and his cellmate took turns kicking the bottom of their cell door until it bent out enough from its hinges to allow them to squeeze out underneath it. It took an hour of constant work. Each of the men in the other cells did the same. As people escaped from their cells, they helped others get out, including those in the rising water on the first tier.

By the time Dan got downstairs, the water was chin-deep and people in the lower-tier cells were climbing on their beds, hollering for help. He said that they sounded like kids screaming. The inmates attempting to open these doors would take turns holding their breath and going underwater to pry up the cell doors from the bottom. Dan recalls that there were a "bunch of guys" whom they couldn't free, and that one older man had a heart attack and just lay motionless on his bed. He still doesn't know what happened to these men.

Along with a group of men, Dan made his way out of flooded Templeman III. Reaching what had been the reception area, they ran into a group of about ten police officers who were putting the prisoners who had made it that far onto boats. As Dan explained,

"Whoever got out, got out. If you got out and made it there, they'd put you on a boat." He didn't see any of the officers enter the prison, where men remained in flooded cells.

Dan was taken by boat to the Broad Street overpass, which crossed over Interstate 10. He described a chilling scene: hundreds of inmates, thirsty and hungry, guarded by a handful of angry and exhausted guards in uniforms from cities all over the state and country, who kept order with shotguns, tasers, and menacing dogs. As the rest of New Orleans sank into chaos and citizens were stranded at the city's evacuation point without food and water, it is not surprising that these inmates, almost all of whom were pretrial and thus legally presumed innocent of the charges against them, some as minor as traffic infractions, were treated with even greater indifference.

The men were given neither food nor water for the four days that they were kept on the overpass in the hot late-summer sun. Many resorted to drinking the polluted flood water as they watched the guards giving bottled water to their dogs. During this time, a several-story scaffold was erected from the highway below up to the overpass. When it was completed on Thursday, the inmates were ordered to climb down to buses waiting to transfer them to Hunt Correctional Center, forty miles upriver.

Dan told me that there was an initial sense of optimism among the inmates that they would soon get food, water, and clean clothes, but these hopes were dashed upon their arrival at Hunt. The buses deposited the inmates directly into a large, fenced-in football field surrounded by armed guards. "We went from worst, to worser," he commented.

Inmates were thrown together on the field without regard to the type of charges against them or whether they were in protective custody. Men being held on everything from public urination charges to murder charges, including dishonored police officers and known snitches, were all penned in together. The only water came from a pipe in the ground. Food, such as it was, was thrown over the fence by the guards. As Dan explained, "If you get a sandwich, you get a sandwich. If you don't, you don't. They were treating us like wild animals. Everyone was treated equal on this field."

The men slept on the wet ground at night. Some had blankets that the guards had thrown over the fence but, according to Dan, "the weaker guys were gonna get their sandwich or blanket took from them if they were lucky enough to get it." He said that the guards would laugh at them as they called for help through the fence.

Just as on the overpass, there were no bathrooms or anyplace to go to the bathroom privately. Men were forced to urinate and defecate in front of hundreds of other men. Dan felt that the men were being disrespected from every possible angle.

After four days, buses arrived again. The men were told to form lines and were taken to different prisons across the state, with no idea where they were heading, based simply on which line they happened to be in. Dan was taken to Rapides Parish Prison in Alexandria, Louisiana.

Unfortunately for Dan, this was not the first time he had been required to bide his time in prison while the justice system creaked forward to sort things out. He had spent years at Angola State Penitentiary on death row before becoming America's 118th death-sentenced prisoner to be exonerated by evidence proving his innocence. A protracted battle in the courts led to his release in 2004.[3] Friends and colleagues at my law office had represented him throughout this process, and I had watched them struggle incrementally to obtain his release.

That drama began on Superbowl Sunday in 1995, when a man was murdered outside Creola's Bar on Laussat between Press and Montegut streets in New Orleans in the Ninth Ward. He had just left the bar with a thousand dollars in winnings from a betting pool when he was accosted, and then shot in the back, by a man wearing a gray sweat suit. The victim returned to the bar, where he died on the floor, "his lucky day having come to an abrupt and tragic end," as the Louisiana Supreme Court remarked in its initial opinion in the case.[4]

Dan's luck went south several months later, when he was charged in the killing on the basis of a shaky eyewitness identification. The following July, an Orleans Parish jury convicted Dan and sentenced him to death. The jurors at his trial, however, had not heard all of the evidence, as became clear years later when, pursuant to a Freedom of Information Act request by his lawyers, an FBI document was turned over to Dan's lawyers that read, "The source further advised that DANIEL BRIGHT, aka 'Poonie,' is in jail for the murder committed by [BLACKED OUT]. The source stated that he/she has heard [BLACKED OUT] bragging about doing the murder and how he is confident that BRIGHT will be able to beat the charge because they don't have enough evidence against him."[5] As usually happens in such cases, this manifest statement of Dan's innocence was not enough to free him immediately, but it became the centerpiece of litigation that ultimately exonerated him in 2004, after more than nine years in prison on death row.

Following Dan's release, I met him at a party for his lawyer, Ben Cohen, who was moving from New Orleans to Cleveland.

Dan still seemed young, and was handsome, charming, and eager to begin his new life with the pretty woman he had on his arm at the party. He met many other lawyers that night who knew him from Ben's passionate work on his behalf and from the well-known case that bore his name, *State v. Bright.*

When the Rapides Parish Prison officials found out that one of their new inmates had been previously convicted of first-degree murder and had been sentenced to death, they took an altogether different view of Dan. Some of the jailers believed that he was still under sentence of death, and, taunting him, "nigger, death row killer," placed him in isolation.

According to Dan, the "country" guards derided all of the inmates, calling them "city slickers" and expressing their hatred of New Orleans. He told me, "You have to remember, in this state, no one likes New Orleans. It's like an outcast to other places."

Luckily for Dan, a close colleague of Dan's lawyer who lived in Alexandria had begun surveying the damage that Katrina had rendered to New Orleans's criminal justice system. Coming to the prison as a "monitor" and to begin to assess who, exactly, had ended up there, she saw Dan's name on the rolls. She asked to see him and recognized him immediately from the office party. She got word to Dan's lawyer, who drafted a habeas corpus petition for Dan and a number of the other prisoners charged with minor offenses. The petition was forwarded to me in Oxford, signed, and then filed in Alexandria.

This group of prisoners was brought before an Alexandria judge. Dan remembers the increased security during the proceedings in response to the small-town fears generated by having New Orleans inmates in the courtroom. Deputies carried shotguns and pistols in the courtroom, which was almost unheard of.

The assistant district attorneys who had come up from New Orleans to argue against the release of the group focused on Dan, saying that he shouldn't be released because he was still charged with first-degree murder. Dan's lawyer at the hearing, however, was prepared for this and had brought documentation of Dan's exoneration. The judge released the whole group.

Dan's friend John Thompson picked him up at the Red Cross center where the men were deposited by the deputies following their release. Dan had met Thompson, whom he calls "JT," when they were on death row together. JT had also been exonerated for a murder in New Orleans and had found temporary housing in Alexandria since the storm. Dan stayed with JT for a few hours until his father and brother could come get him and bring him to Texas, where his family had ended up after evacuating from New Orleans.

Dan knows that he was lucky, and that if it weren't for his relationship with Ben from his previous harrowing experience in the criminal justice system, he could have remained in jail for much longer or he could have been treated far worse.

Indeed, others who were transferred to different facilities did have it worse, as they found themselves in an overcrowded and impromptu patchwork of existing state prisons, parish jails, and facilities opened just to accommodate the evacuated prisoners. The unluckiest among them, mostly from Jefferson Parish, found themselves at Jena Correctional, a former juvenile prison owned by the Wackenhut Corporation that was closed after the Juvenile Justice Project of Louisiana, Human Rights Watch, and the Justice Department exposed widespread beatings of incarcerated children there in the late 1990s.[6] That spirit was kept alive in the new incarnation of the prison: Evacuated prisoners were routinely and viciously beaten by their jailers, guards from other facilities who were without a chain of command and for whom there was zero possibility of accountability. Rachel Jones of the Louisiana Capital Assistance Center, a pro bono attorney who was working at Jena at the time, told me that after being a public defender in Brooklyn and a capital trial attorney in Louisiana, "I have never seen anything like it."

Jones said the inmates were bruised all over their bodies. They passed her little notes when the guards weren't looking saying "help" and reported that guards were calling them "nigger" and "boy." When she returned to follow up, they had been brutalized even more; some reported having received beatings from guards as retaliation for having told her about their treatment.

As bad as it is that adult inmates were treated this way, it is shocking by any standard that, among the thousands of prisoners in OPP during Hurricane Katrina, there were nearly 150 children.[7] These children drank contaminated water, ate food that they found in that water, and were thrown in with older, stronger adult inmates during the ordeal. Among the children were fifteen teenage girls, two of whom were pregnant and who received no medical care during the entire ordeal despite their exposure to contaminated water and the lack of food and water.

Since the storm, there has been little reckoning—Sheriff Gusman won reelection in Orleans Parish by a wide margin—and many issues remain uncertain. Among them is whether any prisoners died during the flooding or evacuation. Although officials deny that any bodies were found, many prisoners who were there insist that they saw floating bodies. The fact that no one has been identified as missing among the prisoners supports the officials' contention but scarcely clears them of their role in this debacle.

What is clear is that the evacuation was neither "safe" nor "orderly," as maintained by Sheriff Gusman. Further, as prisoners' rights and human rights advocates have maintained, the tragic stories of the OPP inmates are not anomalous but rather the "logical outgrowth of a flawed system," as evinced both by OPP's long history of violence and indifference to the needs of prisoners and its specific failure to create a meaningful evacuation plan for its seven thousand wards.[8] One report noted that OPP officials were on notice of potential flooding, as everyone in the city was, and had done little to anticipate the obvious hazard that became manifest during Katrina.[9] When pressed by the American Civil Liberties Union, which had a long-standing prisoners rights suit against the prison, officials were finally able to produce their evacuation plan. For one of the country's most populous prisons, the plan was a page and a half long.[10]

The fact that OPP failed to create or institute an evacuation plan for its prisoners is reflective of a broad cultural disregard for the lives and well-being of incarcerated people. This lack of commitment to the lives of prisoners is important by any measure but takes on a new dimension in light of the national trend toward incarceration as a catchall response to broad societal problems ranging from unemployment to poverty to failing public education. Louisiana is at the razor's edge of this broad American trend toward incarceration, leading the nation with 824 sentenced prisoners per 100,000 residents.[11] Among the state's 1.5 million blacks the numbers are even more disturbing, with 2,251 sentenced prisoners per 100,000 black residents, or more than 2 percent of the black population in prison, not even counting the many thousands more in jails across the state.[12] By contrast, European democracies incarcerate at a rate of about 100 people per

100,000 residents, or .01 percent of their populations, 88 percent less than Louisiana and 86 percent less than the United States as a whole.[13] These numbers make the United States the world leader in incarceration, with Louisiana as the most rigid adherent to policies of mass incarceration, so matters concerning real lives affected by incarceration here, and the success of these policies in creating safe communities, are of international significance.

Sadly, despite all the public and private costs of these policies of mass incarceration, we do not appear to have made any real gains in either reducing our staggering crime rate or reforming and rehabilitating our citizens.[14] We incarcerate people at tremendously high rates, but the great majority of them have committed only nonviolent offenses and thus incarcerating them can be viewed as merely discretionary and not necessary to protect public safety. Meanwhile, we are not addressing the needs of the communities that absorb these prisoners upon their return home to their families, nor do we provide prisoners with the tools for successful community engagement, tools that impoverished schools and communities failed to instill, and the lack of which generated crime and hopelessness in the first place. Far from providing meaningful possibilities for education and rehabilitation of prisoners, our prison system is failing and our prison officials seem not to care. This was horrifyingly demonstrated by the fact that nearly 2 percent of the city's population, disproportionately poor people and minorities, were left to die in Orleans Parish Prison in a manner that reflects callous indifference to prisoners—an indifference that, if uncorrected, we will live to regret.

Despite the terrible injustice Dan has suffered on two separate occasions in the New Orleans criminal justice system, he still loves his hometown. He explained, "New Orleans is where I'm born and raised. It's like no other place and has its own flavor. It's where my history lies. You can't go anywhere else to see a Mardi Gras."

Like Dan, scores of other former prisoners will also be returning home to New Orleans, and many thousands more will be making their way back to hometowns across the country after having served jail and prison time. Most of them will emerge from the criminal justice system more damaged, less skilled, and less able than when they went in to be punished or to be warehoused for trial. Their capacity to change and contribute to society will suffer from the failure of the prison, parole, and reentry system, as will the families and communities to which they will return.

CHAPTER 8

Bring the War Home

Zeitoun's Flooded Van on Earhart

ABDULRAHMAN ZEITOUN, WHO HAS lived in New Orleans for more than fifteen years, owns and operates a painting and contracting business whose sign, reading "Zeitoun's Painting" above a colorful rainbow, could be found on the front lawns of houses all over New Orleans before Hurricane Katrina. He is a hardworking businessman and tradesman whose reputation for honesty led his customers, many of whom owned the grandest houses in town, to simply turn over their house keys to him in anticipation of occasional odd jobs or continuing work. His values are grounded in an old saying from his native Syria, "small stones support mountains," which led him to stay in New Orleans during Katrina. He believed that he could help his friends, neighbors, and customers, almost all of whom had evacuated, take care of their homes and possessions if the worst were to occur. The worst did occur in the city, and Zeitoun rose to the occasion, showing the best of American resourcefulness and generosity before finding himself buried under an equally American mountain of prejudice and discrimination.

Zeitoun, which is what everyone, including his wife of twelve years, calls him, was born in Syria in the late 1950s and came to the United States in 1973 to get away from "too much politics, confusion." (This "confusion" was Syria's 1973 "October War" with Israel over the Golan Heights.) He headed directly to New Orleans, where a friend from home lived. He held jobs in construction and used-car sales, and once he had saved enough money, he fulfilled his version of the American Dream by starting his painting business. His hard work provided a modest home in safe and prosperous Uptown New Orleans for his wife, Kathryn, and their four children. Even with a hurricane barreling down on the city, he wasn't about to leave.

Kathryn had arranged a place to stay in Baton Rouge with her sister but delayed leaving until Saturday, trying to convince Zeitoun to join her. Before she left, she went grocery shopping to make sure that there was plenty of food in the house, and filled the freezer with meat. The storm kept coming and Zeitoun wouldn't budge, so she finally left late Saturday afternoon. Zeitoun summed up his feelings: "I wanted to stay and see what happened. Something that will happen will happen. Nobody can stop it from happening. But if you stay, you might minimize the damage."

He spent Saturday and Sunday boarding up some windows and moving things inside that could "fly away" from the yard. By Sunday night, the hurricane had arrived. Zeitoun described those hours: "And the roofs start blowing away—a few pieces here, a few pieces here, and the water starts coming in." All night long, he went around the house with containers, moving them about and emptying them, trying to catch the water running through the holes in his roof. When the rain finally stopped on Monday morning, he cleaned up all of the water and emptied the containers. He had been up all night.

After the wind died down, Zeitoun went outside for the first time. There was a couple of feet of water in the street and maybe a foot of water on his lawn, but none had reached the house, which was raised a few feet off the ground. He had seen water like this in his neighborhood before, following hard rains, so he wasn't alarmed.

It occurred to him that he had a canoe in the backyard. He had bought the canoe from a customer who had used it in the bayous. His wife had thought he was crazy for buying it, and she wouldn't go out in it. The couple of times he had taken his daughters out in it, they hadn't liked it. But he found paddling around relaxing. He decided he would use the canoe to check out his neighborhood and see how his neighbors had weathered the storm. He paddled around his block, saw some downed trees and power lines, nothing serious, and returned home. By nightfall, the city's pumps began drawing out the water, and by the middle of the night the streets were dry.

He lay down to sleep Monday night feeling tired but believing that everything had gone well and that the city had been spared. Before he fell asleep, he called his wife on his cell phone to say, "I think it's over," and they made plans for her and the girls to return home.

Having gone without sleep for two days and now feeling relieved that his home and city had been spared, Zeitoun slept late on Tuesday. Midmorning, when he came downstairs from his bedroom and looked out the window, he was surprised to find that the water had risen again. It was a couple of feet deep in his yard, still a foot short of his raised home, but seeing that it was still rising, he went around the first floor of his home elevating everything he could. He brought his daughters' clothing, and everything else he could carry, to the second floor. Things that were too heavy for him to lift he used as platforms. He explained, "I sacrifice one couch to save one couch. Like, put one couch on top the other one. Dining room table, I put all the chairs on top of the table. I lift the mattress, I put chairs between the mattress and the bed, and it comes up about four or five foot above the ground. I start trying to do things."

The water did not stop rising until the middle of the day on Wednesday; by then there was three feet of water in Zeitoun's living room. At that point, Zeitoun decided to go back out in the canoe and check on more of his neighborhood, as well as on his tenants at a house he owned about twenty blocks away.

As he paddled past submerged stop signs and through storm debris, a few blocks into his trip, he spied a friend on the porch of a house. His friend called out desperately, asking Zeitoun if he had a cigarette. Zeitoun responded that he did not smoke and joked that he would take his friend to the store but he didn't think that anything was open. With little else to do, his friend decided to ride along anyway. A few blocks further, past Fontainebleau Drive, they saw an elderly couple calling out from the second-floor window of their submerged house, "We need to get out of here, we need help!" Without space for two additional people in the canoe, Zeitoun called back that he would find someone and send help.

They paddled on and for several blocks there was eerie quiet, barely broken by a small voice that Zeitoun thought was coming from another submerged house. Worried that someone might be drowning, Zeitoun paddled toward the house, and when he heard the noise again, he jumped into the water, opened the screen door to the house, and swam in. He explained what happened next: "Inside, I see one old lady, remind me like my grandma. Her dress full like a big balloon, floating in the water, and she's on her back holding to her furniture. I drag her [by] her shoulder, and brought her outside through the door. No way to put her in the canoe because the canoe . . . to save her would be to drown her if I tried put her in the canoe, because it would flip, no question."

Zeitoun left her on higher ground and paddled to Claiborne Avenue, where he thought he might find other boats to help. Airboats flew past on Claiborne, just as cars had a few days earlier. Zeitoun used his boating skills, developed as a child on an island off the Syrian coast, to keep from capsizing in the wakes. Eventually, they flagged down two men in a fishing boat who were willing to come with them to the woman's house. When the four men arrived, the woman was frightened and reluctant to leave. Eventually, they carried her out but, as she was very large, they were unable to lift her into the fishing boat. When they found out that she had a ladder in her garage, one of the men from the fishing boat swam through the house, into the garage, and retrieved the ladder. They set it up next to the boat, but the woman was unable to climb because of a problem with her leg after so many hours in the water. "I mean it was a very tough situation," Zeitoun explained.

Eventually, Zeitoun figured out that if the woman couldn't climb the ladder, they might be able to raise the woman into the boat by lifting the ladder. Zeitoun submerged himself in the water and lifted the ladder from the bottom while two other men in the boat pulled the ladder up. Finally, they were able to get the woman into the boat. They immediately noticed another elderly couple—Zeitoun thought that they were in their eighties—in a house across the street. The group helped these folks into the fishing boat. Zeitoun directed the boat to return to the first elderly couple he seen earlier that day, and the four men helped these people get into the fishing boat as well. From there, the boat headed with its elderly passengers to a nearby hospital, where they could be evacuated to safety.

Zeitoun and his friend then paddled to his rental house. When they arrived at the house, his tenant, Todd, was shocked to see them. Todd exclaimed, "You're very good to come check on me. You're a very good landlord!" When Todd told Zeitoun that he did not have water, Zeitoun gave him a couple of bottles from a case of water he had earlier found floating in the flooded streets. Zeitoun was happy to hear that the telephone at the house was working, and he took the opportunity to call his wife, to whom he hadn't spoken in three days. She was worried, but he assured her that everything was fine.

It was beginning to get dark, and they had no light, so Zeitoun and his friend paddled toward home. Zeitoun dropped off his friend and then settled in at home. That night, through the quiet darkness, he began to hear the barking and moaning of dogs from neighboring homes.

Upon awakening the next morning, Zeitoun began to look for the dogs. He heard a dog barking at a neighbor's house. Unable to enter the flooded first floor of the house, he climbed a tree up to the second-floor balcony and opened the window, and the dog came to him. The dog ravenously consumed the water and sausage Zeitoun had brought from his house. After climbing back down the tree, he heard dogs in the house next door. Again unable to enter from the ground floor, he found a long plank of wood, and leaned it against the balcony from which he had just climbed down. He climbed up again, pulled up the plank, and then placed one end on the balcony rail on the adjacent house, forming a bridge. He crossed this bridge, spanning about twelve feet between the two balconies, as the flood water flowed below him. He said he was scared but felt compelled to help his neighbors. He explained, "When [you] feel like do[ing] something nice . . . you feel like you have the courage to do it."

When he got to the other balcony and opened the window, he saw two large dogs. One ran away, but the other came to him. He fed and gave fresh water to the dog that came to him and left food and water for the other dog. He then returned to the other balcony, climbed down, and returned to his house.

The following day, Friday, he returned to his rental house to make phone calls. Several neighbors had relayed requests through Zeitoun's wife that he check on their homes, which he did. As he paddled home after finishing his rounds, an elderly neighbor called out to him from a porch a few doors down. The man, in his eighties and in a wheelchair, did not seem well. He was desperate to leave and eagerly asked Zeitoun to evacuate him in the canoe. Zeitoun couldn't manage the wheelchair in the canoe but promised to find help. He paddled back to the hospital, thinking that he could arrange for help there.

When Zeitoun got to the hospital, he saw a group of heavily armed "military guys" and approached them. As he came toward them, they trained their guns on him. He explained to them, "Look, we have old man who needs help." They responded that they couldn't help or call anyone to arrange for help. Zeitoun commented that the men seemed scared of him and acted "ugly" and "very rude." They told him that he needed to go all the way down to St. Charles Avenue, which was many blocks away, to arrange help for his neighbor, and then they ordered him to leave.

Zeitoun was shocked, having never experienced this kind of indifference, either in America or Syria. He explained, "I expect from them to offer to help. I believe these guys are in the city to help. Not one, almost ten of them, more like, were there. I see boats back and forth. I come there. If I had known these people are not for this purpose there, I would never go to them. If you're drowning and someone says he want to save you, you give him your hand, and he never takes your hand, how you feel about it?"

The day had turned rainy and windy. Zeitoun paddled for a half hour into the wind before reaching St. Charles Avenue. He found someone from the Red Cross and explained the old man's situation. Zeitoun gave him the man's name and address and the man from the Red Cross said that they would send a boat. Worried that help wouldn't come fast enough, Zeitoun asked when they would go for the man, and the man told him that they would send a boat for him in an hour. Zeitoun felt confident that it would happen. He told me, "I believed he'll go do it. I'm not talking to someone who's just passing by. Then I might not take it serious. This coming from government. . . . It's something serious."

When he got back to his house hours later, the man was still sitting on his porch in his wheelchair in the rain, waiting for help. Zeitoun was furious. He went back out in his canoe, eventually finding a man with a fishing boat who was willing to help. They brought the old man onto the boat and then down to St. Charles. Zeitoun did not look for the man who had promised help earlier. "I don't want see him, maybe something ugly will happen."

The following day, Saturday, after feeding the dogs and making the rounds of the neighborhood in the canoe, Zeitoun threw a barbeque and grilled the meat that had thawed in his freezer. The people staying at his rental house came in their boat and other remaining neighbors and acquaintances came by to eat shrimp, fish, and chicken. Everyone took food home with them, and Zeitoun took the leftovers to other people in his neighborhood who had not come over. He fed the rest to the neighbors' dogs the following day. Otherwise, he stayed home, spending the day resting and listening to the news on a battery-powered radio that someone had given him. The news was bad, both on the radio and right before his eyes in his own neighborhood, where the water had not even begun to recede.

For the next couple of days, Zeitoun was joined by a friend, Nassir Dayoob, in his travels through the city. Nassir was a fellow Syrian who had worked for Zeitoun and whom Zeitoun had run into several days earlier. On Tuesday, more than a week after the storm, the two friends went on an epic three-mile canoe ride through the city to check on the house of another friend who had relayed the request through Zeitoun's wife. Upon returning to his neighborhood, Zeitoun went straight to his rental house to call his wife and report what he had seen so she could relay the report to their friend. His wife's concern over his activities was growing, but he felt that he was doing the right thing in helping his friends and neighbors.

After getting off the phone, Zeitoun discovered that the water in the house was working again, so he took his first shower in days. He felt cleansed. Sitting inside, he heard a motorboat approach. Looking through the window, he saw that it was a military boat with five or six soldiers aboard. The soldiers quickly came into the house with their guns drawn and demanded to know what Zeitoun, Nassir, and Todd were doing there. When Zeitoun tried to explain the situation, a soldier demanded to see his identification, which he produced. Before even looking at it, the soldier shouted, "Get on the boat." Zeitoun tried to argue, but the soldiers insisted. Before Zeitoun even realized what was happening, the soldiers had forced the three men, along with another man who had just stopped by to use the phone, onto the boat. Initially, Zeitoun thought the worst thing that could happen would be that they would force him to leave the city and everyone he was helping. This notion was dispelled, however, when the boat reached St. Charles Avenue, the same place where he had dropped off the handicapped man days earlier. There he was "jumped on" by soldiers, who threw him in handcuffs while a few reporters and photographers recorded Hurricane Katrina's first terrorism arrest in this newest front of "the global war on terror."

It became clear that Zeitoun was in for more than a bus trip out of the city and was facing something very serious. He told me that if he had known that they were arresting him, he would have jumped from the boat and tried to swim away. He was certain he had done nothing wrong and didn't deserve to be arrested. Escape was now completely impossible, as the soldiers began treating the three prisoners like a "big catch" and placed them under heavy security. Zeitoun could see what the soldiers were thinking: "I think he thought he catch a group of terrorists. I think that's the first thing that come to his mind. He thinks that's what he's got. I think this was the first idea to come to his head. He saw this, what he's seen on TV, what he's seen on the news and he got some kind of match."

When they searched the prisoners, the soldiers found twelve thousand dollars in cash in Nassir's bag, along with maps plotting routes to and from the airport. Nassir tried to explain that he had the cash because he had planned to leave the city and didn't have a bank account, and that the maps were for his job, delivering lost luggage to aggrieved travelers. No one listened. As far as they were concerned, this was the smoking gun. The men were transported in a military van to a downtown bus station that had been turned into an impromptu jail, dubbed "Camp Greyhound" or "Angola South" by prison officials, which took the place of the flooded Orleans Parish Prison.[1]

The four men, locked in a cage made of chicken wire that sat on the bus docking area, were isolated from other prisoners and under constant observation. They were forced to sit in a certain way, with their legs spread, for "security." This lasted for three days, during which they were interrogated by an official from the Department of Homeland Security and were called "Taliban" and "terrorists" by the guards, who threw things at them in their cage. Zeitoun was not allowed to make any phone calls to his wife (who he knew would think that he was dead or in danger because he had not called for days) or to an attorney. They were fed ham sandwiches and military MREs (meals ready to eat), which also had pork in them. Zeitoun, an observant Muslim, ate what he could. He looked around the camp, considered his circumstances, and was reminded of the prisoners held at Guantánamo Bay. He asked everyone he met—the guards, the man from the Department of Homeland Security, and police officers—to call his wife and let her know that he was safe. They all refused.

While he was at Camp Greyhound, Zeitoun's foot began to hurt from a large splinter of wood that had cut through his shoe during one of his canoeing adventures. Part of his foot turned black and he asked to see a doctor or a nurse, a request that was ignored. He then asked for a needle or razor to cut out the festering splinter, which was also ignored. Finally, when they brought a glass with his lunch one day, he broke the glass and cut into his foot with a shard. He now has a long scar on his foot.

After four days, buses arrived to move all of the prisoners to Hunt Correctional Center. Zeitoun figured that upon arriving at the prison, a real jail rather than a makeshift camp, he would finally be allowed to call his wife and get in touch with a lawyer. Again, these hopes went unrealized. He was placed with four other men, all strangers to Zeitoun, in a small cell with a single bed. The men would take turns lying on the bed as the other men lay on the concrete floor. The men were forced to use a toilet placed in the back of the tiny cell, with the others lying at their feet. "You go use the bathroom, there's somebody there between your foot. It's very ugly." For a week, the men were kept in the windowless cell twenty-four hours a day. Zeitoun continued to beg the guards to call his wife, but he was told that the phone didn't work.

After that week, Zeitoun was moved to another cell, this one with two beds that were shared by three men. It was a great relief. Around the same time, he heard that a judge from New Orleans had come to the prison to conduct hearings for the prisoners. A public defender met with a group of men and told them that they were not to say anything in court. Zeitoun recalled what the lawyer told them: " 'He will say what you're charged with, and how much your bond. There's no reason to talk to judge.' I mean, he did not want us to say anything, or try to explain, just to listen."

This is exactly what Zeitoun did when he was brought into the makeshift court—a big cinder-block room in the jail, containing a couple of tables and chairs—and heard, for the first time, that he was being charged with looting and possession of stolen property. The prosecutor requested $150,000 bail; the public defender asked that it be reduced to $75,000, to which the court agreed, and that was that. When they returned him to his cell, he felt as though the whole thing had been a joke. He hadn't really had an attorney. (The public defender, like everyone else, refused to call Zeitoun's wife for him.) There hadn't really been a judge. There wasn't really bail for him because, less than two weeks after the storm, there was no way for him to get seventy-five thousand dollars, even if he were able to contact his wife, which he had been completely unable to do anyway.

Even so, part of Zeitoun still believed that he would be released, that things would work out somehow. In his mind, every time he heard guards walking toward his cell, he could not resist thinking that they were coming to free him. The sound of footsteps would draw him to the bars in anticipation. It reminded Zeitoun of waiting at the hospital while his wife was in labor, years earlier: he became excited at the prospect of his daughter's birth every time he heard the footsteps of a nurse or a doctor. At the prison, these moments of anticipation happened with such regularity that one of the guards commented on it, joking that Zeitoun jumped up every time the guards walked by to hide that he was having sex with his cell mates. After everything that he had been through, this was the final straw. Enraged, he yelled back at the guard. Zeitoun's wife, knowing her husband's infrequent but explosive temper, later told me that Zeitoun was lucky that his outburst didn't make the situation much worse.

Having been insulted, treated like a criminal, and prevented from presenting any evidence of his innocence and wrongful imprisonment, Zeitoun for the first time began to despair. He thought, "I can't believe this is happening in this modern country. This thing might happen somewhere else, not here. I mean, we're talking about going to free other people, other countries. We have problems here. They say, 'How we going to go free other people's country when we have these kinds of problems?' "

Finally, someone did come for Zeitoun. He was called out one day to meet with a lawyer whom his wife had retained. She had heard several days earlier from Nassir, who called her at a telephone number that Zeitoun had given him on a scrap of paper weeks earlier. The lawyer told Zeitoun what he already knew, that he needed to produce seventy-five thousand dollars to be released. Meanwhile, Zeitoun's wife managed to get back to New Orleans to get the deeds to their property as security for a bail bond. The last Thursday in September, after Zeitoun had spent almost a month in prison, Kathryn brought the deed that she had found in their badly damaged office in New Orleans to a bail bondsman in Baton Rouge and the papers required for Zeitoun's release were faxed to Hunt. On her arrival at Hunt to see her husband at last, she found that she would have to wait another night. The secretary at Hunt had left work early, so the release papers couldn't be processed until the following day.

Zeitoun, completely unaware of his wife's efforts toward his release, woke up on Friday expecting that it would be like any of the other days since he had come to Hunt. Just after noon, a guard called out his name. He thought that he was going to have to meet his lawyer or go to court, but instead he was told to get ready to leave. As arbitrarily as it had been taken away from him and seemingly without reason, his freedom simply fell back upon him.

Back in New Orleans, living temporarily at a little house in Algiers neighborhood on the city's west bank while his uptown home was being repaired, Zeitoun was philosophical and stoic about the whole affair. He was happy to be back with his wife and his girls, and business was booming, with only a shortage of good workers slowing him down. The thing that made him saddest was that when he returned to his house, where he spent the hard days following the storm, he looked in on the dogs, his former companions, and found them all dead from starvation.

Kathryn was still angry about Zeitoun's arrest and felt that he was a victim of discrimination because he is an Arab man in post–September 11 America. Zeitoun took the long view, seeing the hurricane as something that brought people together. After the storm, he would have fought to save his worst enemy. He couldn't have cared less about people's backgrounds, and he felt that most people didn't care about his religion or what country he was born in. Zeitoun had come to terms with what happened to him and felt that it does not reflect on America, a country he loves and is proud to live in. "Each country, each house, has nice people there, and has dirty people there," he told me, offering another Syrian proverb: "Back home we say, 'Each home has a toilet.'"

CHAPTER 9

The Dry Run of the Apocalypse

Branded by Fire, Central City

AFTER A WEEK IN OXFORD, and with little hope that we would be returning home to New Orleans anytime soon, Nikki and I started looking for an apartment by posting signs around town, including an offer for a housing swap that we posted in the bookstore on the Square, thinking that an attempt at levity might evoke sympathy among the town's readers: "New Orleans Couple Seeks to Trade Downtown Greek Revival Townhouse for an Apartment Close to the Square." The ad failed to bear fruit but, in asking around, we heard of a big apartment near the Square above a shoe store that displayed a giant, six-foot-tall flip-flop outside the door during business hours. A handful of frat boys had just been evicted from the apartment, which was why it was available. It had drop ceilings and dirty carpet, but we didn't plan to live there forever and we needed some space to ourselves, so we took it after the landlord, a local lawyer and state legislator, gave us a break on the rent because of our refugee status.

On our last night before moving into our own place, Nikki, Siobhan, and Will were all curled up on the white couch in front of the television watching the dapper and charismatic Anderson Cooper offer the day's horrors on CNN. I was shuffling about behind them, listening as Anderson recounted Mayor Nagin's command that everyone remaining in New Orleans must evacuate the city and warning that those remaining must not drink the contaminated flood water. Anderson moved on to talk about the "tremendous pressure" on New Orleans's "first responders" and the extent to which they toiled to help save people while their own homes had been destroyed and the well-being of their own families remained uncertain. He then led into an interview with a "Tulane University psychiatrist [who] says there hasn't been enough help for the helpers, or protection for those who are helping," commenting that the doctor had gone back into the city "ready to protect himself."[1]

As our world had already shrunk so much and we had become used to seeing the familiar scenes of our lives on the news and in the papers as the backdrop for devastation, Nikki joked with me, "It's probably Jeff," the one psychiatrist in New Orleans we knew. And then there was Jeff Rouse, on the television screen in Will and Siobhan's living room in Oxford, Mississippi, standing on Canal Street, New Orleans's main drag, looking as if he were in a war zone.

The clip began with Jeff, looking overwhelmed and nervous in front of the camera, asking, "Where was the help for the helpers? And if a psychiatrist has to come in on his own with a gun and a backpack to do it, that's not a failure of an individual, that's a failure of the entire system."

Cooper responded, "That's what you did, you came in with a gun and a backpack of medicine?"

Jeff replied, "And a backpack of supplies for myself, including medicine, bandages, you know, scalpels, I mean, just anything I could get my hands on."

Unable to resist referencing the gun yet again, Cooper asked, "Are you carrying a gun—do you carry the gun with you?"

Jeff replied, sad and disheartened, "It's right here." The camera zoomed in on a shiny automatic handgun, a Glock, at his waist. "I was not coming back to this town without this. I was not coming back in this town checking my house without this. I have a sworn oath to help. And the last thing I want to do is hurt somebody."

I could hear Nikki start to sob on the couch, and I finally broke as the reality hit me of my friend—a psychiatrist, not an emergency room specialist—being the only doctor left in New Orleans, walking around with a bag of scrounged medicine and supplies, treating exhausted cops and sick, poor, desperate people. Could it really be possible that so few people gave a shit about the city and its people that our friends were showing up on the news? I began to cry for the first time since the storm.

SUBSEQUENT CONVERSATIONS WITH Jeff have given me a clearer sense of what he was doing in New Orleans during those sad days and what he has done since to help first responders and others who themselves live on the brink of collapse but are entrusted with serving the public.

Jeff came back into town on his own, with his gun and his bag full of drugs, and connected with another doctor with whom he established a health clinic in the downtown Sheraton Hotel gift shop. When word spread that they were there, people began pouring in—people foaming at the mouth from severe dehydration, confused and disoriented from untreated diabetes, the whole range of inner-city emergency care magnified by what Jeff called "the dry run of the apocalypse," Hurricane Katrina.

These two doctors, neither of whom provided emergency care in their normal practice, worked for days treating the poor, the elderly, and the left-behind, as well as police and other first responders who had literally been left to fend for themselves. Being there, serving others, Jeff and the few other volunteer medical professionals were defying government orders to stay out of the city, and yet there was no organized medical cavalry coming to relieve them. So Jeff stayed, and after sleepless weeks, he was given a bed by the police, who allowed him to stay on the Carnival cruise ship that the city had rented to provide housing for police and first responders.

Once the city was fully evacuated a few weeks after the storm, Jeff returned to his specialty, psychiatry for sufferers from post-traumatic stress disorder, on which he had cut his teeth working with Vietnam veterans and other trauma survivors at the New Orleans Veterans Administration Hospital prior to Katrina.

Jeff had found himself living among the New Orleans Police Department (NOPD), the most demoralized police force in America, which had scrapped its way through one of America's worst natural disasters. Unlike the New York police and firefighters after September 11, their efforts were not lauded and no one called them heroes. Two officers had committed suicide since the storm. The public face of the force had been marred by reports that hundreds of officers had abandoned their posts and deserted during the storm, and that officers had been involved in looting the city that they were charged to protect. The image worsened when Police Chief Eddie Compass was forced to resign in light of these failures.

The frayed and ineffective police department must be viewed in light of its history, which, according to Human Rights Watch and other groups, has been unique in that the NOPD leads the nation in both brutality (alongside Los Angeles and Chicago) and corruption (alongside New York).[2] Friends of mine represent two former New Orleans police officers, a man and a woman, who separately ended up on death row for crimes that sadly conjoined corruption and murder.³ In one case, police officer Len Davis had Kim Groves, a poor woman from the Lower Ninth Ward, killed by a drug dealer a few days after Groves filed a brutality complaint against Davis.

The brutality of the police force would reassert itself following Katrina in the early days of October, when a cameraman filmed three white police officers senselessly beating a sixty-four-year-old black man who was handcuffed and lying writhing on Bourbon Street.⁴ The video shows one punch driving the victim's head against a wall. To make matters worse, one of the officers then ran over to the cameraman and roughed him up for recording the event, which was then broadcast around the world as another instance of the city's depravity. After shoving the cameraman against a parked car, the officer yelled, "I've been out here for six weeks trying to keep alive. Go home."

The behavior of the NOPD during the storm became something of a perverse citywide joke when, poking fun at the fact that police officers had looted Cadillacs during the storm, the local Cadillac dealer, Sewell's, posted a huge billboard next to the Superdome along the main highway, stating, with cool irony, "New Orleans' Finest Drive Sewell."

To stem the bleeding, Jeff began to establish interim and long-term mental health services for police officers, who had experienced the trauma of Hurricane Katrina as citizens of the city and as first responders trying vainly to create order on the streets, and who, even in safe and sensible cities, have really difficult and complicated jobs. Initially, his clinic was set up either in the ballroom of a French Quarter hotel that acted as the temporary police headquarters or on the cruise ship, where he lived among the police. In an e-mail he sent at the time, he explained his situation: "I am living on the cruise ship with the NOPD and it has been fascinating to be given glimpses behind the Blue Curtain. Forget the worried well. I have found my population to serve and they are armed."

Though the need for trauma and mental health treatment for police officers was acute in the immediate aftermath of the storm, clearly there is a need for this kind of treatment and assistance to be available during the duller months of murder and violence facing law enforcement in this city. For that reason, Jeff folded his triage mental health services into a more expansive program that offers mental health services for officers. Jeff's program is distinct from the program that existed prior to Katrina, in which the doctors offering counseling were the same doctors who determined whether an officer was fit for duty, thus providing a clear disincentive for officers who needed help but wanted to keep their jobs from seeking counseling. Jeff is not in the business of taking away an officer's badge and gun; instead, his interest lies in restoring balance and mental health. Jeff is doing this work because he believes in treating people who are suffering, especially those struggling to help others. He also firmly believes, however, that offering meaningful treatment to police officers is a first step toward improving relations between officers and the poor and minority citizens who are most in need of their services.

Another step might be to pay officers a decent wage. Until the summer of 2006, when a modest raise was put in place in an effort to increase officer retention, the starting salary for a New Orleans police officer was less than thirty thousand dollars a year. Even with the raise, it remains six thousand dollars a year less than the national average, and among the lowest in the country for police officers in large cities.[5] Clearly, a low wage discourages some of the best candidates from pursuing the job. Furthermore, the ones who do take these jobs are forced, because of the low wages, to moonlight in uniform, providing security for many city businesses that cannot rely on regular policing to keep their facilities, employees, and customers safe. Thus, private businesses are forced to subsidize city policing, and police officers, who can't get by otherwise, are worked to the bone. Consequently, these officers are tired and aggravated on their difficult beats, and more prone to violence. The off-duty officer standing at the bar at a French Quarter restaurant represents a two-fold failure: the incapacity of the police force to adequately police the city, and a police workforce that is compelled to seek outside employment in order to support themselves and their families.

"Law and order" has been too easily swept up into the conservative "tough on crime" agenda, but in places like New Orleans, it is clearly the poor who suffer most from crime and who are least served by this approach. Too many in poor communities, understandably, and on the political left, less understandably, have developed a reflexive anti-cop attitude. In reality, poor communities, overwhelmed by crime, need police on their streets, but they need to be served by police who are treated with dignity as workers and who, consequently, are better able to treat the communities they serve with sensitivity and decency.

Although higher wages and mental health services by themselves are not going to cure the problem of urban crime in places like New Orleans, interventions like Jeff's give us a better shot at a model of policing that does not present poor communities with another group of thugs to fear.

CHAPTER 10

History Repeats Itself

Round Window, Lower Ninth Ward

Oh cryin' won't help you, prayin' won't do no good.
When the levee breaks, mama, you got to lose.
Memphis Minnie, "When the Levee Breaks"

IN NEW ORLEANS, history does not always seem so long ago. The old city streets don't look so different from seventy-year-old Walker Evans photographs, in which the city's nineteenth-century frame buildings, then as now, droop under the weight of cat's claw vines. The sadder aspects of our history are also with us. People casually talk about renting apartments and living in "slave quarters," small buildings that used to house slaves and the kitchens for the connected big house. Inmates, mostly black, are still sent to Angola Prison after conviction, a prison named for the country of origin of the slaves who used to work its vast fields. The inmates there still toil on the farm. The city's hotels contain racks of color pamphlets advertising tours of the antebellum plantations that dot the River Road between petrochemical plants that have sprung up along the Mississippi River. Congo Square, one of the only places in America where slaves were allowed to play African music and dance, is still a city landmark. With all of that history still very much a part of our present, I was not at all surprised when I began to hear people, most of whom were black, express their belief that the compromised levees that had allowed their homes to be destroyed had been purposely blown up for purposes of gentrification or genocide, or just because that's what happens to black folks at the hands of whites in this part of the world. Always has, always will.

Even before the water receded, the rumors of sabotaged levees had burst into the national media. The rumors had trickled in from survivors from the Lower Ninth Ward and other neighborhoods where residents had heard loud booming noises before the water came rushing into their neighborhoods. Of course, the national media did not pay attention to the voices of poor, frustrated, angry residents of these communities; initially, the public voice for this theory was Louis Farrakhan, the leader of the Nation of Islam, who said in a speech in early September, "I heard from a very reliable source who saw a twenty-five-foot crater under the levee breach. It may have been blown up to destroy the black part of town and keep the white part dry."[1] Of course, Farrakhan's words were used as fodder against him, and this view, actually shared by many people who had suffered devastating losses of family and homes in New Orleans's poorest neighborhoods, was ridiculed as foolish race-baiting. Not surprisingly, Farrakhan's words were given the most play on right-wing television news broadcasts, where it provided a paper tiger for pundits who wanted to argue that this was another instance of "black paranoia" and that the disaster that played out following Katrina had nothing to do with race.[2]

Despite being dismissed and ridiculed by Sean Hannity, Bill O'Reilly, and Tucker Carlson, the rumors of explosions in the Lower Ninth Ward levees persisted among former residents of that community.[3] More sympathetic voices followed, including several black women from flood-devastated neighborhoods who, during a congressional hearing in Washington, took issue with what one congresswoman referred to as a "breach" of the levee. Dyan French Cole, a strong sixty-year-old woman known in the Lower Ninth Ward as "Mama D," responded, "Can you define that word for me, please? What does *breached* mean? Bombed? I was on my front porch. I have witnesses that say [they saw people bomb] the walls of the levee. And the debris that's in front of my door will testify to that. So, what do we mean breached?"[4]

Ms. Cole went on to make an impassioned and forceful statement that, bombs or no bombs, she was coming back to New Orleans, "My grandma says she made fifty cents a day, you all, and she bought the house I live in now. My last breath—my last breath. Five generations, it will take that. It's not for sale. Please let whoever these people know, New Orleans is not for sale. We ain't going nowhere. Roaches and black folk, they've been trying to exterminate, eliminate us. We're still there. We plan to be there whatever it takes—tent city, no city, sleeping in cars, whatever we've got to do."[5]

As before, a chorus rose up in the media and dismissed these "conspiracies."[6] I remember hearing grumbling on the streets and in the coffee shops in New Orleans for the next couple of days following the December congressional testimony. People were annoyed that these women had made the city look foolish. These criticisms were well placed, as unsubstantiated claims of attempted genocide and comparisons to the Holocaust made during the hearing were needless distractions from the real critical issues facing the city, allowing continued avoidance of the unmistakable reality of a city laid waste by government negligence and inaction. But those women testifying during the congressional hearing weren't engaging in a well-thought-out public relations strategy. They were expressing their beliefs. In the rancor and civic embarrassment that followed, New Orleanians and Americans missed an opportunity to really delve into the meaning of the women's remarks and beliefs, as well as those that Farrakhan had coopted from people in evacuation centers across the

South. What we failed to see is that these people—and not just a fringe group, but community leaders and other everyday members of poor and minority communities—believed that their government had intentionally blown up the levees and killed more than a thousand citizens to effect a whitewashing land grab. Although you can argue with these beliefs, it is undoubtedly more useful to attempt to understand the underlying rationale, which is based on a history that remains as present for many New Orleanians as Mama D's grandma making fifty cents a day.

In April 1927, the Mississippi River was swollen to capacity from heavy rains that had drenched the Mississippi River Valley for almost a year. The first breach of the levee system that hemmed in the river from its mouth at the Gulf of Mexico to Minnesota occurred on April 16 in Dorena, Missouri, where more than one thousand feet of the levee succumbed to the water's pressure. Five days later, another breach occurred at Mound Landing, Mississippi, and water consumed the Delta where, for days, thousands of black workers were forced at gunpoint to fill sandbags in a desperate attempt by wealthy landowners in the area to prevent the inevitable. The water gushed in uncontrollably, and ultimately covered ten thousand acres, including areas as far as one hundred miles from the breach. The homes of almost two hundred thousand people were destroyed, and many people lost their lives in the fields or in their homes as the water rose. Similar breaches occurred along the lower Mississippi River in Missouri, Arkansas, Tennessee, Mississippi, and Louisiana, flooding twenty-six thousand square miles, an area about the size of Massachusetts, Connecticut, New Hampshire, and Vermont combined.[7]

As John Barry tells the story in his book *Rising Tide*, the river's threat to New Orleans, then the South's largest and wealthiest city and the center of commerce in the region, brought together men from the heights of the New Orleans business community— men who knew one another well from the network of private clubs and Mardi Gras krewes that still define the city's society— who met in the smoke-filled office of the president of Hibernia Bank, which was located in an elegant skyscraper that dominated the cityscape, the tallest building in the South, adorned at its peak with a miniature Roman temple. An engineer was present to explain to the men the situation the city faced: anticipated breaches in upriver levees would likely reduce the pressure on the city's levees and allow them to remain intact, but in the unlikely event that the upriver levees held, the pressure on the city's levees could cause a crevasse. As Barry tells it, then the engineer "suggested that they could eliminate any doubt about the safety of New Orleans by dynamiting the levee elsewhere, if the men deemed it wise."[8]

Despite the likelihood of a breach upriver, the men determined that dynamiting the levees below New Orleans was necessary both to guarantee that the city wouldn't flood and to build confidence in the city's businesses and financial institutions, which were under enormous pressure as people worried about the possibility of flooding fled the city in droves and as New York banks began to question New Orleans's viability as a center of commerce. The plan was to dynamite the levees in Poydras, several miles downriver from New Orleans in St. Bernard Parish. The breach would destroy all of St. Bernard Parish and the portion of Plaquamines Parish on the river's east bank, displacing ten thousand residents in the process. The plan was put in motion without input from a single local elected official or from the people whose homes and livelihoods would be destroyed. President Coolidge had already been personally consulted after the owner of the *New Orleans Item* newspaper made a trip to Washington to ensure federal support for the plan, and the approval of the Governor Oramel Simpson was obtained after pressure was applied by the city's elites, who coordinated these political efforts from their St. Charles Avenue mansions. The politicians had one condition for their assent—that the residents of the areas flooded by the breach be compensated for their losses. Caernarvon, the site chosen for the explosion, was thirteen miles south of the Ninth Ward, abutting St. Bernard Parish. On April 29, the dynamite was ready. St. Bernard and Plaquamines parishes were evacuated in advance, as it was predicted that the water from the river would destroy everything in its path.[9]

At the site of the explosion, there was a party atmosphere among the city's elites, who had received permits to witness the dynamiting. As recounted in *Rising Tide*, "New Orleans meanwhile was enjoying itself. The fine families, as if on a picnic, traveled down to see the great explosion that would send dirt hundreds of feet high and create a sudden Niagara Falls. Cars jammed the road down to St. Bernard, and yachts crowded the river." At 2:17 P.M., the first explosions were heard, beginning ten days of dynamiting that consumed thirty-nine tons of explosives and, when completed, allowed 250,000 cubic feet of water per second to flow into the poor, rural parishes. As predicted by engineers, the day following the completion of the dynamiting, a levee upriver from New Orleans burst and it became clear that others would soon follow, lessening pressure on the city's levees and rendering unnecessary the breach at Caernarvon, and the consequent destruction of the homes and livelihoods of thousands of people.[10]

Among these people were the Isleños, a group of Canary Islanders who originally immigrated to the area in the eighteenth century, making their living trapping animals in the area. In addition to the Isleños' hunting grounds, the small farms on which poor whites and blacks sustained their families were also destroyed. Despite earlier promises of restitution from New Orleans, the city rejected nearly all of the claims from the residents whose lives and homes were destroyed. Of the thirty-five million dollars in claims made, residents received less than three million dollars total, or less than three hundred dollars per resident in most cases.[11]

This history has never been far from the minds of New Orleanians and the city's neighbors, and fear concerning the lengths to which the city's wealthy and powerful will go in order to save the city is very real. As Hurricane Betsy approached the city in 1965, black residents in the Ninth Ward policed their levees with shotguns to insure that they would not be intentionally destroyed, no doubt urged on by old timers with a sense of history. Despite the precautions, and with no evidence to support the theory, some residents still believe that the flooding during Hurricane Betsy was a result of dynamiting those levees. As James Gill, a populist New Orleans columnist wrote, "The story of unscrupulous fat cats preserving their property by drowning the poor is too rooted in the New Orleans consciousness to brook contradiction."[12]

These ideas stem from a history that includes the flood of 1927 and also the ugliness that lurks in every corner of America's racial history, including atrocities such as the Tuskegee syphilis study, which began in 1932, in which hundreds of poor syphilitic black men were—without knowledge of their illness—studied as untreated guinea pigs so that the U.S. Public Health Service could observe the disease's progression. Finally, the study was exposed and forced to end in the early 1970s.

Never afraid of a fight, the hated and revered black filmmaker Spike Lee weighed in heavily on this issue in his documentary *When the Levees Broke*, providing a platform for the fears of black New Orleanians. Explaining his own views, he attempted to provide a context for the fears of black Americans:

> So, in the collective mind of African-Americans, it is not some science-fiction, hocus-pocus thing to say that the government is doing stuff. Even if it didn't happen, you cannot discount it and dismiss it as "Oh you people are crazy." It's what people think—talk to Jewish people. Because of the Holocaust, you know, anything that happens, it's like, "Oh! It's starting again." And I'm not going to fault someone of Jewish ancestry that feels like that because that happened! This is history. No one is saying to Jewish people, "Oh, you're crazy!" So if you use the same analogy, then it's not so farfetched. . . . [T]here are people who will swear on a stack of bibles that they heard an explosion down there.[13]

With many of New Orleans's white residents celebrating that the storm "cleaned up" the city's social woes of crime and poverty in the months following the storm, coupled with the abysmal treatment of the city's poorest residents in its immediate aftermath, as well as the city's failure to welcome home many of its poor and minority citizens, it is no surprise that people see history repeating itself.[14] If people are troubled by their view, they ought to offer these New Orleanians, and black and poor people in the places like the Lower Ninth Ward around the country, a reason to believe otherwise.

PART III

Personals

Departures and Homecomings

CHAPTER 11

Going Home

Grin and Bear It, St. Charles Avenue

It was such a fine spring day,
down Louisiana way,
with fragrance divine, oh baby,
and such magnificent regalia,
oh so fine, Azalea.

I've got to go back there
and find that blossom fair,
I always dream of,
cause with you who can be a failure.
My first love, Azalea.

Louis Armstrong and
Duke Ellington, "Azalea"

LESS THAN TWO WEEKS after the storm, I saw the sunrise over the Mississippi River from my roof on Carondelet Street in New Orleans. I was up there with Wallace Lester, a fellow displaced New Orleanian I had met the day before in Oxford.

I had vaguely recognized Wallace when I saw him in Oxford. We talked for a minute and he mentioned that he was a teacher and I was able to place him. He was the hip public school English teacher at George Washington Carver High School, a struggling, all-black school in New Orleans where I had taught street law one day to "at risk" kids. He had John Coltrane posters on his classroom walls and tried to teach his students radical history. He made an impression on me when I taught his class because his students, who didn't usually pay much attention, listened to him. Wallace, in turn, listened to his students, who weren't used to being heard.

After a short conversation, Wallace proposed that we attempt to drive the six hours down to New Orleans in his old white Econoline van—previously used on tour with his band—to assess the damage firsthand, to fix our homes if necessary, and to retrieve precious things we had left behind. We both had just received nearly seven hundred dollars in Wal-Mart credit from the Red Cross so, flush with cash, we stormed the hardware section anxiously buying anything we thought might be useful on our trip, a trip for which we had neither precedent nor foresight.

Wallace bought a set of battery-charged power tools, walkie-talkies for times we might be separated, canned pineapples, and water. I bought blue tarps, bungee cords, the biggest Maglite on the market, and energy bars. I searched in vain for rubber boots. We left Oxford just before 10:00 P.M., filled with nervous energy and hoping to slide into New Orleans just before dawn. Friends had informed us that the security checkpoints were not manned before sunrise. There was no traffic at all as we passed through Jackson and approached Hammond, Louisiana. We talked steadily through the night, sharing stories about our wives, progressive politics, and our hopes for and concerns about New Orleans. Occasionally one of us would note the possibility that our twelve-hour drive to New Orleans and back might be in vain if we were turned back at the city limits. Again and again we rehearsed the work-related pretext we intended to pitch if we were stopped. Maybe ten times on the drive, one of us said, "That's my story and I'm sticking with it."

We had a quarter tank of gas and two full five-gallon gas cans in the back of the van when we stopped for gas in Hammond, about sixty miles outside the city. We figured that it would be our last chance for gas before New Orleans, and we were not sure that we would make it the 120 miles back and forth with the gas we had. There was one gas station open in town when we got off of Interstate 55 at two in the morning. It was packed full of cars, and at first I assumed it was a gas line full of southbound New Orleanians like us. It turned out, however, that teenagers, mostly black, hung out at the gas station in their cars until late at night, playing loud, bass-heavy music, and talking to friends. Just as we approached, five police cars simultaneously converged on the gas station, lights ablaze, closing down the place and chasing off the kids. We pulled into the now-empty gas station after making the block and letting the dust settle. The pumps had been turned off, so I walked up to the little store. The glass door was locked and I stood staring in at the clerks until one of them came up to the glass and told us that the station was closed.

In the weeks since evacuating New Orleans with my wife and pets and no place to live, I had gotten used to asking for favors, begging, and saying please and thank you. Through the glass, I told the clerk my sad story. I told him that I was from New Orleans and trying to get back into town because I had seen a satellite photo of my roof that showed that it was damaged, and I wanted to repair it before it got worse. Then I played a trump card that works with most men in most situations. I told him that my wife had her heart set on my recovering her wedding rings and the diaries of her late sister, and it would break her heart if I didn't make it home to try to find these things and bring them back. I wasn't lying, and he could tell. He asked me if I had cash and when I said yes, he told me that he would let me fill up. I thanked him sincerely, not in the manner I do in my normal life, when people do little more than is required.

Within minutes of getting back on the interstate, we saw flares and a police roadblock. Wallace and I practiced our story once again and slowed to a stop beside a tired-looking middle-aged white police officer.

"How you doing, officer?" Wallace asked.

He asked us where we were going, and we explained that we were going to New Orleans, that I was a lawyer and that I had legal business related to the storm, a half-truth. We showed him our identification. He responded simply, "I'm too tired to care. You can do what you want." He commented that our car smelled of gas and chemicals, "What you got, drugs in there?"

We explained that we had cans of gasoline in the back of the van. He responded kindly, "Gas? You know that's not really safe. . . . Get out of here."

We drove through the checkpoint and up onto a causeway, an elevated highway that runs through the swamps toward New Orleans. On both sides of the causeway, we could see the glow of the massive plants, the cities of industry, spewing flames, back in action, devoid of life.

We were quiet and exhausted, eager to see our homes, our city. We both knew that everything had changed. We cut around the city to the south and onto Highway 90, the old highway into the city on the west bank. The west bank is part of Jefferson Parish, the white-flight suburb surrounding the city. It is the part of the city into which throngs of people tried to flee over the bridge, only to be turned away by armed sheriffs. Just a few days later, two white men in a van, we were trying to cross in the opposite direction.

The west bank was in remarkably good shape. We passed a bingo hall with blinking lights. The Burger King was opening up, getting ready to sell egg sandwiches and tater tots. All of this just minutes away from New Orleans. It seemed impossible.

As we approached the bridge, we reached another roadblock, manned by the Crescent City Connection Bridge Police. The officer standing guard was bleary-eyed and looked as if he was about to fall over. He hardly listened as we told him why we were traveling into the city. He had no objections. When Wallace asked him how he was doing, his pain poured out. He told us that he had lost his house, that the floodwater had risen to the roof and destroyed everything. The insurance adjuster had told him that his policy didn't cover floods. His wife and kids had gone to Florida.

He was worried about them and wanted to be with them, but he managed to talk to them for only a few minutes at a time because his cell phone service was constantly cutting out and roaming charges were high. He had just finished restoring a classic Bronco, only to have a huge tree fall on it during the storm. We asked him when he would be relieved so he could take care of his home and his family, and he laughed ruefully. He explained that there weren't many officers on his detail and they were all working eighteen hours a day, unsure if they were even going to get paid. When Wallace asked whether his union was doing anything to help him, he laughed again, saying, "Union—you're not even allowed to say that word around here."

We thanked him and drove off. As we pulled away, I saw him go back to sit with his fellow officers, none of whom, probably, could bear hearing one another's sad stories another time. Each, perhaps, waiting to tell his story to the next couple of guys trying to pass into town who were willing to listen.

The city was dim as we passed over the bridge. We could see a big military ship docked along the riverbank next to the Convention Center. Within minutes, we reached my house, five blocks from the Superdome. It was still dark outside.

I inspected the house with my flashlight and it looked the same as I had left it. I unlocked the door and walked into my living room. I could smell the aroma of home—slightly stale, a little sour, but distinct—filling the high-ceilinged rooms. No water had come in; the flood had not reached us. I drank some bottled water from the cooler I had left stocked with four five-gallon jugs.

I crept up the stairs, not knowing what I would find on the second floor, almost blind in the dark with my flashlight off, but knowing the steps by memory; I was finally home. At the top of the stairs I reached reflexively for the light switch, with no effect. I turned on my flashlight and saw that the ceiling had collapsed. From the right angle, I could see the night sky through the wound in my roof. Soggy sheetrock and wet bits of shredded newspaper insulation were everywhere. I wanted to start cleaning up then and there but realized that it was absurd, that there was still more to see. I crossed through my wife's studio, which was unblemished, with her paintings still on the walls, and then into our bedroom, where the ceiling had collapsed onto our new pillow-top mattress, which we had talked about with joy every night as we got into bed.

I climbed the narrow ladder up into my attic, walked carefully along the rafters, and then climbed through the door-sized hole in the roof that I had seen from below. I nervously walked up the back face of my double-pitched roof and could see with the help of the flashlight that large portions of the roof were damaged and exposed. Jitters passed through my body. I had been awake for almost twenty-four hours, I was standing on my roof in the middle of the night in my abandoned city, and I was nauseated. Even under the best of circumstances, I have no business out on a roof. But anticipating the damage, I had brought up a tarp, some screws, and Wallace's new drill. I tried to secure the tarp over some of the damaged areas but I began to feel my feet slipping on the remaining roofing tiles beneath my feet. I struggled to put the tarp in place.

Knowing that I was a danger to myself, I slid back down through the hole in the roof, made my way downstairs, and told Wallace what I had seen and what I had tried to do. He told me that he was good on roofs, so we made our way back up. He did most of the work, explaining as we worked that we weren't really accomplishing anything, but it was good to try—I could tell my wife that I had attempted to repair the roof in the middle of the night, and I would be a hero. I felt pathetic and scared, but comforted. Wallace looked at me and said, "Slim" (which is what he calls me), "I must like you to get up on your goddam roof, and I don't really know you at all." I thanked him.

Before descending into the house, we watched the city awaken. New Orleans never had the early morning hustle and bustle of other American cities but, instead, a few people heading to work and a few stragglers still trying to find their way home. In New Orleans, sunrise meant "go to sleep" about as much as it meant "wake up," even among many of us who live here. With the city empty of its citizens, however, sunrise signified only wake-up time to the soldiers who, that morning, occupied the high-rise apartment building on St. Charles Avenue, the great Mardi Gras parade route, a block behind my house. They wandered out of the building, absentmindedly gazed up at us on the roof, and then got down to the business of brushing their teeth and shaving with little cups of water in their hands.

Back downstairs, I cleaned up what I could, packed some things, and brought them down to the van. I found the rings and the journals, but I had lost the list my wife had given me of things to bring back. I panicked, knowing that I was in no state to make decisions. Everything seemed pointless by this time. Miraculously, I got through to my wife on my cell phone.

"Nikki, I can't find the list. I've lost it. All I can remember are the rings and the journals," I told her.

She could hear in my voice that I was not well, that I hadn't eaten, and that I was exhausted. She said, "Billy, you got everything that matters. Go downstairs, eat some beans from a can, and sit down for a minute. Promise."

She had said these kinds of things so many times in this house as we restored it from a shell and as I worked myself into the ground with my job. Her words pulled me back together—a little bit, anyway. I hung up the phone and grabbed as much as I could remember, neglecting her advice for the time being.

Before we left, Wallace handed me two garbage bags and told me that I should clean out my fridge. It hadn't occurred to me. I opened the door and began to retch at the smell. I tried to wrap a cloth around my face, but it kept dropping down. The worst of it was a package of chicken cutlets in the freezer that turned to mush when I grabbed it, and then leaked through the Saran wrap all over my hands. I dragged the garbage bag through my house to the curb. Immediately flies swarmed over it. Wallace sprayed bleach on my living room floor and wiped up where the bag had leaked. For that, I will love him forever.

When I got my bearings, Wallace introduced me to two dogs that had approached him while I was upstairs. Wallace had brought kennels with him in case we ran into strays, and these two dogs were already nestled peacefully in their new cages. They had been fed and given water and, knowing they had hit the jackpot, they weren't going to do anything to mess it up. Wallace had already named one of them. The black lab puppy was Sancho Panza, after Don Quixote's sidekick. Wallace asked the names of the cross streets on my block, as Carondelet, the name of my street, didn't seem like an appropriate dog name. I told him that they were the names of muses, Clio and Erato streets. He named the baby pit bull Clio, the muse of history.

We got into the car and drove to his house. On the way, we looked for my Jeep, which I had parked in a six-story garage in the business district to protect it from flooding. Near the garage,

Wallace parked the van next to the Liberty Monument, a tall white marble obelisk erected to celebrate the 1874 Battle of Liberty Place, an uprising of the White League, a group of white New Orleanians, against the biracial Reconstruction government and federal soldiers—a monument that still serves as a rallying point for racist right-wing extremists.[1] I ran from the van and up the dark corkscrew ramp. I went to the spot on the fourth floor where I remembered leaving the Jeep, but it wasn't there. I went to the identical places on the fifth and sixth floors, thinking that I was just confused, but it was definitely gone. It had been liberated. I hoped that whoever had taken it made it out of town with their family. I thought that maybe they would drop me a postcard from El Paso, or wherever they were, when they were done using it. No hard feelings.

We made our way down to Bywater, Wallace's neighborhood. His house was in much better shape than mine, and he made quick work of packing, cleaning out his fridge, and getting us back on the road. I could tell that he felt kind of bad that his house wasn't damaged like mine. I was just glad that I didn't have to go up on another roof.

As I waited for Wallace, I met two young guys from the Oregon National Guard who had come up to the house, thinking that we were holdouts and intending to encourage us to leave. They were very sweet and I offered them cigars, a recently acquired vice, which they initially declined. They had both signed up for the National Guard before September 11 to help pay for college. Although I could tell that they both had some hesitation about "the war on terror" and their pending deployment to Afghanistan, they were patriots in the best sense. The lieutenant told me about their temporary barracks in an old neighborhood high school. He told me that he was disgusted that kids ever went to school there, and that in Oregon the place would have been bulldozed and rebuilt so that kids could have a proper place to learn. He seemed troubled that all of this was happening in America. He realized that many of the problems he was seeing in New Orleans existed before the storm, and he wanted to know why people had put up with it and why they hadn't voted out of office the people who had let this happen. I told him I didn't know, but maybe we could change things in New Orleans in the future. He seemed hopeful. I felt less certain.

I introduced the guardsmen to our new dogs, who were happy for a little attention. One of them told me that dogs were dying everywhere and it made him incredibly sad. He explained that they had to shoot some of them because packs were attacking units of soldiers. He said blankly, "These starving dogs are the saddest thing . . . after the dead bodies." They quickly changed the subject.

After being yelled at by holdouts, the police, and their commanders, these guardsmen had made their first friend in New Orleans. I told them how to pronounce the street names properly and what each neighborhood was called and what they had been like before the storm. I stressed that Esplanade Avenue is pronounced like lemonade and that they should correct any of their superiors who said it otherwise. They both laughed when I explained how upsetting it was for locals to imagine that the city was occupied by an army of people mispronouncing the names of our streets and neighborhoods, with no one around to correct them. I offered the cigars again and this time they accepted.

As they were walking away, one of them accidentally bumped my leg with the barrel of his M-16. He felt terribly embarrassed, as though I might not have noticed the massive guns that both of them held as we talked. To break the tension, I said, "You're the only two twenty-two-year-old men to ever come to New Orleans and not get drunk or laid." They laughed hard and started walking away again.

"What we wouldn't give," they said.

As they walked away, I told them, "When you come back, go to the Circle Bar. My friend Mike will be at the bar. Tell him I sent you. He'll buy you a drink and set you guys in the right direction."

I didn't know if there was going to be a Circle Bar again and doubted that Mike would ever return from New York, but the thought of him in the late-afternoon light of the bar, serving drinks to people as they wandered in, was comforting. I hoped that these guys would see it some day.

Wallace and I got back in the van and started to head out of town. Before we left, we came across some scrappy-looking guys, and we pulled over to see if they wanted any of the water or food that we had left in the van. They introduced themselves, saying, "They call us holdouts."

They turned down the water and food, saying that they had plenty of canned food and they had gallons of water in their hot water heaters. They explained that they had been bathing in the Mississippi, but "it was beginning to get nasty." They wanted bleach to keep things sanitary, but we didn't have any. They settled for some orange-oil cleaner, cat food that we had brought for strays, and a five-gallon can of gas for their generator. They told us to tell others to come home: "Bring people back. Tell them that it is okay. That you can make it here."

We drove off and quickly passed out of our occupied city. I

slept most of the drive back as Wallace, still solid, drove. I woke up as we were approaching Oxford and told Wallace to pull into a convenience store so that I could get some beer. It was around eight o'clock at night and we had been on the road for a full day. I brought a six-pack of Budweiser to the register and the cashier told me that they couldn't sell beer on Sundays anywhere in Lafayette County. Broken-hearted and shocked, I told her my sad story, but she was inflexible. I thanked her and left, resolved to return home to New Orleans as soon as possible.

CHAPTER 12

Oxford Town

Tupelo Truck, Back in New Orleans

TOWARD THE END OF SEPTEMBER, I drove to the Memphis airport once again, this time to deposit my wife, who was embarking on a trip to Europe of indefinite duration. The trip had been planned, in a very different form, months earlier for Nikki to attend a friend's wedding in Leuven, Belgium. She had grown miserable in Oxford, felt incapable of producing art, and grew to believe that her unhappiness, which I was preoccupied with correcting and talking her out of, would only distract me from focusing single-mindedly on my work, work that she believed in more than I did by that point. I dismissed this selfless motive and, instead, insisted that this would be an ideal opportunity for her to travel and see friends abroad. I began acting the part of the beleaguered husband, left behind to sort through the details of our scattered life while my wife went on vacation. After growing tired of arguing with me over this view of her trip, Nikki resigned herself to allowing me my misunderstanding.

We arrived at the airport and shared a tearful goodbye. I held back my reluctance about her departure and my concern about whether I would be okay with every element of my life changed. She is always the stronger of the two of us in these moments. She offered words of encouragement about my work and its significance to our city, and promised that she would be back soon. She kissed me hard on the lips, and I got back into the car, driving off in a mild panic. I was alone in a strange place, my city had been devastated, and my friends and wife were dispersed. Naked.

I heard my cell phone ring through the chatter in my head. It was Nikki. Her flight had been delayed by five hours. Could I please pick her up? I was relieved, but I was angry that I would have to go through it all again. I turned the car around and we spent the rest of the afternoon together before I brought her back to the airport. The second goodbye was exhausted, numb.

I returned to Oxford and our ugly apartment, our dogs and cat, the few things that we had from home, and the many nondescript household articles that we had bought at Wal-Mart with our FEMA and Red Cross money. I attempted to gather myself, to figure out what held me together. I called Will and asked him to meet me for a Louisiana-brewed Abita Amber at a bar around the corner owned by an expatriate New Orleanian.

AROUND THIS TIME, rumors started circulating by e-mail, online bulletin boards, and word of mouth that residents from unflooded New Orleans neighborhoods were being allowed to return to the city and fix their damaged homes. With this in mind, I decided it was necessary to buy a cheap pickup truck to replace our stolen Jeep, so that I would have a work truck to haul sheetrock, plywood, and roofing tiles, from Mississippi if necessary, so that work could begin as soon as possible on my wounded home. I passed what looked to be a perfect prospect parked in the high grass on the side of the road just outside of town near the Beacon Restaurant, where, sitting among the town's old men, I had just filled myself with eggs and fried pork medallions smothered in white gravy.

The truck was a huge baby blue Chevy Custom pickup. The for sale sign said that it was a 1977 (the year of my birth), that it had less than 100,000 miles on it, and that it was only $2,900. I walked around it, inspected it, and saw etched into the rear chrome bumper in confident block letters, "RED HOAGLAND CHEV. TUPELO, MISS." The truck had come from Elvis Presley's hometown. It even had Mississippi "antique truck" plates. It was perfect. I called the number on the sign and arranged to give the truck a test drive that morning.

A neatly dressed man met me in the grassy lot by the truck at the appointed time. He worked in the education department of the university. He explained that it was a "good old truck" that his father-in-law had bought from his accountant, the original owner, who had used it sparingly for twenty-five years as a farm truck. He showed me a small spiral-bound notebook in the glovebox where the accountant had recorded a decade of gas purchases and mileage notations. The care required to jot all of those numbers, for all of those years, inspired my confidence.

I climbed high up into the driver's seat of the truck and got behind the large black steering wheel, and the man got into the passenger seat. There were several feet between us on the massive seat. I turned the key and the engine started right up, strong and self-assured. I drove around town, going fast and then slow, testing the brakes and then the signals and then the AM-only radio, until I was satisfied that everything was in good order. We got back to our cars and started talking price, settling quickly on $2,500, and we immediately set out to close the deal.

We drove separately in our cars to his bank downtown on the square, where I withdrew the money. He signed over the title and I had it notarized next door at my landlord's law firm. I took it a half block over to the Office of Motor Vehicles. Within minutes, I had Mississippi antique truck plates of my own, valid forever without reregistration. We drove in his car back to the truck, shook hands, and he drove off.

I was pleased with my purchase and eager to tell Nikki about our new truck. She grew up admiring and working on a similar old Chevy that her father, from whom she was now estranged, had souped up with a Corvette engine. Despite its connection with her father, or maybe because of it, the truck made me feel bigger, stronger, more put together.

I climbed behind the wheel again and turned the key. The engine coughed and wouldn't turn over. I couldn't believe it. I tried it again, without any luck. After trying unsuccessfully to find the hood release, it occurred to me that I had bought the truck without even opening the hood—not that I would have known what I was looking for if I had. I felt like a fool. I had bought a dead truck to replace my stolen Jeep.

Taking one baby step back from my panic, I noticed on the dashboard that the gas gauge showed an empty tank. Hoping that was all that was wrong, I set out on foot to a gas station I remembered seeing about a half mile back toward town. It was bright and hot as I walked.

I filled up a gallon jug that I had found on the side of the road, brought it back to the truck, and emptied it into the gas tank with a funnel I found behind the driver's seat. I tried the engine again but, after one encouraging moment, it still wouldn't turn over. I convinced myself that I simply hadn't added enough gas and set out once again for the gas station. While I was paying for the gas, the man at the counter asked if I had tried adding gas to the carburetor. I stared at him blankly and lied, telling him that I would try that, neglecting to mention that I didn't know what a carburetor was, that I couldn't even figure out how to open the hood. As I walked away, a man driving a banged-up 1980s American sedan pulled up beside me and rolled down his window. He was black, in his thirties, and had a sympathetic face. He asked me if I was having a problem, if I needed help. I told him that I thought that I was out of gas with a truck I had just bought, but I wasn't sure. He told me that he was a pretty good mechanic and would drive me back to the truck and help me out.

When I told him where the truck was parked, he asked if it was the "nice, old blue Chevy." He had seen the truck himself heading to the Beacon, where he worked as a dishwasher when he wasn't "ministering" or fixing cars. He told me that he had been thinking about buying it himself. "A pretty good buy," he said, brightening my mood.

As we pulled up to the truck, he asked me if I had added gas to the carburetor and I told him that I was thinking about doing that. When we got out, he told me to add most of the gas to the fuel tank but to save a little. Going straight to the hood of the truck, he found a lever behind the grill and pushed up the massive hood. I added the gas and brought him the jug. He deftly removed a wingnut holding down a black circular pan, revealing a white, corrugated cylinder underneath. He poured in a little gas and closed it back up. I got back behind the wheel. "What should I do?" I asked.

"Tap the gas a few times and turn the key," he advised. I did just that, and the engine turned over, to my enormous relief.

He escorted me back to the gas station, where he had pulled in a half hour earlier just to get some gas. I filled up the truck and paid for his gas as well. He tried to decline but I insisted, telling him that he was a hero. He accepted the gas but insisted that it was no big deal. "Pretty much anyone knows how to add some gas to the carburetor," he explained.

I omitted this episode when I drove the truck over to Will and

Siobhan's house later that night to show it off. They both loved it, and Siobhan insisted on driving it with me and Will in the back. We had talked about how sexy and empowering it was for a woman to drive a massive truck. With Siobhan, a small, pretty woman at the helm, this effect was realized as Will and I careened around the bed when she took hard corners. I looked forward to seeing Nikki, serious and self-confident, gunning the engine of the truck, her disinherited paternal bounty.

The next day I drove the truck to Taylor to show it off to Wallace. Because he was a musician and a Mississippi boy, I was sure he would love the truck and its Tupelo inscription. He admired its good looks, and then we walked over to the Taylor Grocery for their "meat and three" lunch plate. Full of greens and cornbread, we walked slowly back down the country road to his house. When we got back, I showed off the truck a little more, showing him the little spiral-bound notebook and a little feed store pencil that I had found in the glove box. I said goodbye and got into the truck. I turned the key and heard nothing. Nothing.

Wallace suggested that it might be the battery, given that the truck had probably sat a long time, so we tried to jump it from his van. Still nothing. He drove me back home and told me to buy a battery.

The following day, I returned to Wallace's with a new battery and a ratchet set. A drizzle that had begun on the drive over had turned into a driving rain by the time I got there. When I turned on the radio, the announcer explained that the remnants of Hurricane Rita, which had battered western Louisiana a few days earlier, were starting to pass through the area. I calmly got out of the car, undeterred by the rain and wind. Within a second, I was soaked through as I knowingly released the hooded and propped it up. I loosened the connections on the old battery with the wrench and replaced it with the new battery. I got into the driver's seat of the truck, dripping wet, and turned the key in the ignition. It started right up.

HAVING NO ONE around to rally and convince of my exuberance at this difficult time, I became aware of my sense of isolation and sadness in Oxford. At this point I had no reason to be there, and though it was possible to return to New Orleans, I know myself just well enough to perceive the dangers of returning alone to the sick and depopulated city. I had recently received an e-mail from the parents of an old friend, who had become friends in their own right, offering to let me stay indefinitely in their small New York City apartment. Shortly thereafter I received an invitation to travel to New York to speak about social justice issues facing New Orleans. The organization sponsoring the event was willing to pay for my transportation. The final piece fell into place shortly thereafter, when Chris Radcliffe, a friend and neighbor from New Orleans, contacted me to say that he was gathering a crew of workers from around the country and he would get work started on my house if I picked him up at the Jackson, Mississippi, airport and then loaned him my truck to get down into the city. Chris was a gifted and resourceful builder who had rebuilt a house around the corner from my home when all that remained of the structure was a crumbling shell of three exterior walls. Perhaps not unrelated, he was also a speed freak—and often, when high, a cross-dresser—and his workers were always a ragtag crew, resembling dust bowl carnies. I could see the limitations of the arrangement but also felt that this would be a fitting workforce for my postapocalyptic city. I was also eager to hand off the overwhelming, complicated responsibility for repairing my house to anyone willing to take it, even my fifty-year-old garbage-head, evil genius friend.

I drove the three hours to Jackson to pick Chris up at the airport, finding him at the pickup area wearing a leather motorcycle jacket, a gray felt porkpie hat, and jeans and cowboy boots, and holding an army rucksack. He jumped into the car ready and energized, talking a mile a minute and chain-smoking Camels. We headed back up to Oxford, where Chris was to spend the night before starting for New Orleans in my truck the following morning. On a desolate stretch of highway about halfway back to Oxford, the engine began to sputter as we climbed a small hill, and then died completely as I pulled onto the shoulder. Fully stopped, with night falling fast, I looked down at the illuminated dash board and apprehended the problem. I had run out of gas.

Hours later, in my borrowed bed, after waiting forever for the AAA truck to bring us gas, I stared at the drop ceiling, following the metal strips with my eyes and imagining how much effort someone had spent to mar the high-ceilinged room, before finally succumbing to a sleeping pill.

THE NEXT NIGHT was my last in Oxford before setting off for New York. A recent acquaintance, Jasmine, was having a farewell dinner at a terrific restaurant located several doors down from my apartment and invited me to join her large group of friends. Having gotten Chris under way and finished most of what I needed to get done before departing, I accepted. I walked through the door of the restaurant—a salumeria whose chef had worked curing meats at one of the most famous Italian restaurants in New York—ready to enjoy soppresata and red wine in anticipation of my trip. I joined the group at a large table in the rear and was introduced to the people I hadn't already met. One of the women, seated across from me, was originally from New Orleans, so we exchanged details of how our families and friends had weathered the storm. Her childhood home had been destroyed, her family's business was in jeopardy, and she was clearly distressed about all that had occurred. I endeavored to be optimistic and supportive until the conversation moved on.

After we ate, someone asked for my views on what had happened in New Orleans and I responded, criticizing the role of the government, before and after the storm, in its failure to assist poor people and minorities in New Orleans. The woman with whom I had just connected, based on our common feeling for the city, was incredulous. "I don't know why people keep saying that," she responded. "The fact is that black people were warned and chose to stay in the city."

Now I was shocked, shocked to be breaking bread with a living embodiment of the Fox News version of my city's disaster. I sprang into a caricature of the opposite view. "You can't really believe that," I snapped back. "No one would choose that! Everyone who could get out, got out. Everyone who couldn't, ended up at the Superdome being treated like animals."

"That's the problem. Everyone wants other people to take care of them. My parents grew up poor. But they worked hard, started their own business, bought their own home, and didn't take anything from anybody. I didn't grow up rich either, but I finished school. I didn't get pregnant when I was sixteen."

We were at a standoff and our conversation, initially political, had become personal. Everyone at the table was uncomfortable, but I couldn't let go. I stabbed back, guessing, "You didn't go to public school in New Orleans. You have no idea what it would be like to have grown up poor in New Orleans."

Things deteriorated from there, and the conversation ended with her getting up and walking away. We had found little common ground in the interim.

Months later, I found out that her family's business was a venerable New Orleans establishment in a severely damaged, almost exclusively black, neighborhood. Following the storm, it was one of the first places in the neighborhood to reopen owing to her family's tenacity, and it served as an anchor in reestablishing the viability of a neighborhood whose future people had questioned.

By the end of the night, I wanted to be back in New York more than ever, among my friends and family, in an apartment on the Upper West Side of Manhattan, where I wouldn't have to argue about things that appeared self-evident to me, but that I couldn't explain to the people whose opinions were most crucial.

When I got back to my apartment, I called Chris to check on his progress. He answered with a tense voice and told me that the truck had made it to just outside New Orleans. The engine was dead, he thought. He had used my AAA account to call a tow truck and, although New Orleans was beyond the towing range, he had traded a few bumps of meth to the road-weary driver for the additional miles. My dead truck was being towed to my dead city, and I was eager to head in the opposite direction.

CHAPTER 13

I Do Believe I've Had Enough

Queensbridge Houses from the Bridge, New York City

I WASN'T ACTUALLY ON the road until late in the afternoon, after handing off the keys to my apartment to a New Orleans couple who needed a place to stay and agreed to take care of our already fed-up cat. My departure had been delayed by complications in posting a petition for a writ of certiorari to the U.S. Supreme Court for one of my capital cases before the deadline. The petition was a shot in the dark, although I file one in every case, believing that even when I lose an appeal to the Louisiana Supreme Court, the Court has gotten it wrong. I also know that the several months the Court takes to consider the petition and deny it will delay my clients' executions by at least that long, if their later appeals are denied. The petition had to be postmarked that day and, as always, photocopying nine copies of the thirty-five-page petition, one for each justice, hadn't gone as smoothly as I'd hoped. When I finally got under way, it felt good to be moving again, to be leaving behind Oxford, New Orleans, prison farms, death rows, and the rest of the South that I loved, hated, and scarcely understood.

Using figures corresponding more with my hopes than with reality, I figured I would cover the eleven hundred miles in about fourteen hours, arriving at my father's apartment at around five o'clock the following morning. That would leave plenty of time to sleep for eight hours, pick up the keys to my new digs, and settle in before heading down to my speaking engagement among the liberal elite, such as New York City's former public advocate and Democratic mayoral candidate, and the editor of the country's longest-running weekly magazine, *The Nation*, the "flagship publication" of what remains of the American left.

The sun was still up when I reached Jackson, Tennessee, and I thought of the playful but slightly sad Johnny Cash–June Carter duet about the city, which I found and played on my car stereo.

> Well now, we got married in a fever, hotter than a pepper sprout,
> We've been talkin' 'bout Jackson, ever since the fire went out.
> I'm going to Jackson, and that's a fact.
> Yeah, we're going to Jackson, ain't never comin' back.

Johnny Cash always reminded me of Nikki, who grew up listening to his songs as a kid in Maine's poor mountainous interior along the New Hampshire border. From those days, she learned one of her mottos, "Country is country," summing up her notion of the way in which rural poverty across the nation buried other more clearly defined regional characteristics. In her experience, whether you were a poor Yankee from Maine or a redneck from Alabama, life didn't look too different aside from the weather and the accents.

Hearing Johnny sing with or to June Carter also reminded me of the tangled, usually inadequately expressed, but searing love I felt for my wife, now so far away. Johnny destroyed himself and succumbed to his weaknesses, and June lifted him up, but with open eyes. After all, she was the one who wrote "Ring of Fire."

I had written Nikki a poem when Johnny died, just a few months after his wife's death. The poem ended, "I have sat drunk in bars / playing 'I Walk the Line' on the jukebox / to show my wife / asleep in our bed / how much I love her." I knew Johnny would understand what I meant and believe my sincerity, even if no one else did. As always, though, Nikki got it.

As I passed out of Jackson on the interstate, Nikki called. She spoke in a low voice, thousands of miles away in a city where the sun had long since set, where her hosts were asleep in the adjacent room. She wanted to know if I had gotten on the road okay. My anxieties poured out to her. I wanted to know whether she thought that I was doing the right thing by heading to New York, by leaving our foothold in the South, leaving our truck and our house with Chris. She responded, calmly, "Of course." It made me furious. For me there was no "of course" about it. I snapped, "If it was of course, why would I be worried? And, anyway, why do you always call me when it's so late that you can only speak for a few minutes in hushed tones?" She became angry and I recip- rocated, upset that she wasn't listening to me. "You left me here to deal with all of this crap by myself. I am alone in this fucking car with two dogs driving all night to New York because I had to take them and couldn't fly. I am supposed to speak at this thing to- morrow and will be staying at the home of people I haven't seen for a decade." I started to cry. I felt impossibly alone and out of place, as though I had been forced to become a nomad after a life- time as a farmer, or vice versa. Nikki no longer offered comfort, which was just as well because I wasn't going to feel it. The con- versation ended coolly, summing up my alienation from every- thing that I had cared about only a month earlier.

As night fell, I stopped just outside Nashville to walk the dogs, to grab something at Sal's Pizzeria and Restaurant, the lone non- chain restaurant just off the interstate, and to buy five cartons of Camels for Mike in New York, where cigarettes cost four times as much. This is a singular embodiment of a mode of governance that actually seeks to encourage citizens to live better and avoid a wheezing death, which I was circumventing with the assistance of the laissez-faire state of Tennessee's respect for human autonomy and self-determination.

It was very late by the time I finally left Tennessee and entered the more familiar state of Virginia, which borders on Washington, D.C., and Maryland and whose northern suburbs could easily be transplanted to Long Island or Connecticut. The area along the stretch of Interstate 81 just over the Virginia state line, however, made a convincing argument that the Old Dominion is still very much a part of the South, with service station t-shirts, hats, and shot glasses emblazoned with the stars and bars. After stopping for a Starbucks espresso in a can, a beverage that has apparently shed its image of effete Northeastern liberalism and that had been fueling me for the past few hundred miles in my tear out of the South, I filled up my gas tank. As I pulled away from the pump, I heard a loud metal clunk. I stopped the car and got out to see what I had hit. A middle-aged white man filling up his pickup yelled, without condescension or irony, "You gotta take the pump out before you drive away." Red-faced and slightly more awake for the moment, I nodded in his direction, removed the nozzle, and drove off.

Without fail during this stretch of the drive up north, my astonishment at the distance across Tennessee is rivaled only by the maddening length of time required to cross Virginia, as the drive cuts diagonals from the farthest-flung points of both states and offers little amusement or variation in the massive in-between spaces. I had been saving a big, dark cigar that Will had sent me off with, which I figured would provide some stimulation after more than twelve hours in the car. As I lit the cigar and began smoking, the entire car filled with thick, sugary smoke. I hadn't anticipated this sweetness and nearly gagged. But I pulled again, and this time, with accurate expectations, I enjoyed the sweetness on my lips as I played with smoke, blowing out strong, heavy rings that hung for a moment in the light of passing headlights before disappearing out the windows that I had opened a crack. For an hour I smoked and took smalls sips of my sweet, cold, canned espresso, and I imagined that I was sitting at some funny, cramped café, hurtling past the homogenized American highway landscape.

As the sun began to rise, my playfulness and good humor left me entirely. My mouth tasted like an ashtray and several cans of espresso had rendered peaceful contemplation out of the question. I was unable to focus on anything, even driving. When I realized that I wasn't paying attention to what I was doing, I stopped at another service station west of Washington. I had begun to notice an increasing stream of cars on the road heading in the opposite direction.

At the gas station, I looked at a map that hung near the bathroom. The "you are here" mark put me about twenty miles past where I was supposed to turn off onto a highway running south of Washington that led to Interstate 95. Turning around now seemed impossible, especially with the heavy traffic heading south. I plotted a route that seemed just as good, cutting through the Pennsylvania rust belt and heading into New York City from the west. I started pulling out of the station, thinking that I would still get into the city by nine or ten o'clock, four hours hence, as that was about the time it took to drive from Washington. I again heard the metal clunking sound and was shocked not by the noise but by the fact that I had now twice pulled out of a gas station without removing the nozzle from my gas tank. In what was by now a rather active interior conversation, I told myself to be careful as I replaced the nozzle and got back into the car.

Four hours later, I was nowhere near New York or any of the familiar rest stops on the Jersey Turnpike—the Vince Lombardi, the Woodrow Wilson—that normally measure my approach into the city. Instead, I was in a hilly stretch of Pennsylvania farmland that was occasionally punctuated by withered rust-belt towns. I started nodding off despite the bright sun hurting my eyes, the open window bringing cool, dry air rushing uncomfortably into the car, and water squirting into my face from my water bottle. I pulled off at an exit in Bethlehem when, in a moment of clarity, I recognized that the situation was genuinely dangerous. I had to drive through town to find a gas station. The modest old Volvo seemed big and awkward off the interstate on the smaller streets of the small city. I pulled in when I found the gas station. I considered sleeping but worried that I would sleep too long and miss the engagement for which I had driven so far and which was paying for my gas.

I peeled myself out of the car and walked the dogs for a block or two. Initially, I felt braced by the movement in the chilly air, but after passing people on the street going about their lives, I began to feel like an alien and quickly returned to the car. I filled up the car and then went into the convenience store, looking for sun glasses and something solid to eat. The only thing that didn't make me ill just looking at it was chocolate milk, so I bought two, along with some ridiculous-looking sunglasses, and got back into the car. As I pulled off, I heard the now familiar sound of the nozzle reluctantly pulling out of the tank and clanking against the ground. There was no longer any shame in it, just concern. I replaced it and got back into the car, confident at least that I wouldn't need to stop for gas again (thus repeating the mistake a fourth time) before getting into the city.

As I approached the city on Interstate 78, I was able to tune in the New York public radio station, WNYC, on its AM frequency. The voices that had emanated from my clock radio, voices that had for years lifted me into waking with their soothing, insightful tones, now grated on my ears. Even WNYC's even-handed and thoughtful morning show host, whom I was always eager to listen to when I was in town (and even listened to on the computer when I especially missed New York), sounded brutal. I turned off the radio, resolved to drive in silence.

As I approached the Lincoln Tunnel, I called my father. Using a tone that would only be tolerated by a parent whose unconditional love has eclipsed his need for respectful treatment, I told my father that I would be arriving at his apartment in a half hour. That I would pull the car up to his apartment and double-park. That I needed him to be waiting for me, to park the car for me, to walk the dogs. That I believed that I could make it up the four flights to his walk-up but I would almost certainly collapse at the top, hopefully right into his bed. He offered breakfast, which I declined with disgust, and he agreed to my requests without hesitation. "I didn't think that you could possibly make it in the time you expected," he told me. "But I didn't want to discourage you. You're wearing your seatbelt, right?" For once, it felt good to hear his concern. It seemed well placed.

The city looked glorious to me after I passed through the tunnel, as it always does after a long absence. I felt, reluctantly, that I had come home after a great ordeal, one which, in that moment, seemed no less arduous than Odysseus's voyage back to Ithaca from Troy. When I pulled up in front of my dad's apartment building, he was waiting for me. I pulled over, put on my hazard lights, and got out of the car. The dogs in the seat behind me were ecstatic, sensing that we were going to be stopping for awhile. My dad gave me one of his big, enveloping hugs. I handed him my keys and told him to wake me up by five o'clock. I made it up the stairs and, within seconds, fell asleep. It was one in the afternoon.

MY FATHER WOKE me up a few hours later, and I took a shower. My face felt hard and leathery from fatigue. I sat on his bed with a yellow legal pad and attempted, through my haze and anxiety, to pull together my thoughts about all that had befallen New Orleans.

I arrived at the university auditorium, the site of the event, at the appointed time. I introduced myself to someone who appeared to be in charge and was invited to the "green room," where I was introduced to the woman who was to moderate the event, the host of the morning radio show on Air America, a smiling woman with short hair—a haircut I had as a kid, parted to the side and pushed back—and a bright collared shirt that reflected a frenetic and welcoming manner.

I grabbed a sandwich from a big spread of wraps and salads, and toyed with it, not quite able to eat due to nerves and lack of sleep. Through the door came an olive-skinned young man with a narrow mustache, close-clipped hair on the top and sides of his head and a ponytail that streamed down the back of his enormous white t-shirt. He sat down next to me and introduced himself. "Ryan Bourgeois, from New Orleans. I am supposed to speak at this thing."

I told him that I was in the same boat. "Where you stay at?" he asked. We exchanged details about our missing lives in New Orleans. He had lost his home and all of his belongings to the flood. He hadn't yet been able to find out what had happened to his son. In his manner, his stoicism, and his words, he was of New Orleans. It felt like home. Gesturing to the food, he asked, "You think I can have a cookie or a sandwich? I haven't been getting enough food at the Red Cross hotel."

"I think that you can have whatever you want. It's all for you," I assured him.

RYAN WAS the first speaker and, unlike those who followed, he did not rise from his seat to address the couple of hundred people in the audience but instead spoke into a microphone from his seat. He seemed nervous and began by saying to the audience, and to himself, "It's hard, it's hard." He explained that he had made it to New York City because of the generosity of New York University, where he had been given free tuition for a semester and where the calculus was "kicking [his] ass." He was clear that, without the bus ticket from NYU, "I would still be sleeping on the floor of a shelter in Texas." He explained that for people like him there was no safety net beyond the generosity of private groups and individuals, and he worried aloud about the coming weeks, when he would be put out of his hotel without money to get a place of his own. As a consequence, despite his best efforts, he wouldn't be able to finish school and make a better life for himself. He complained that the hundred families from New Orleans in the hotel with him in Queens were going hungry because they couldn't always be at the hotel when meals were served by the Red Cross, and they couldn't prepare their own food because they didn't have refrigerators or microwaves in their rooms. He explained that people tried to keep milk and other perishables cold by leaving them on the air conditioner and setting it as cold as possible, which didn't work too well. About the food that was served, with a distinct sense of New Orleans flare and priorities, he said, "The food is so nasty. I wouldn't let someone I didn't like eat it. It horrible." He elaborated, to laughter from the audience, "A lot of people just starve themselves because they don't want to eat that food. I'm from the South. I like seasoning. Put some seasoning on it, you know?" There was little to laugh about, however, as Ryan explained that he, and all of the people from New Orleans, felt forgotten and that at the hotel, people were living on pennies. He ended by thanking people for their generosity, but wondering aloud, "What is the government doing?"

The next speaker, from the National Priorities Project, attempted to answer Ryan's question and explained that of every tax dollar spent in America, thirty cents went to the military and nineteen cents went just to pay interest on the nation's debt. He explained that our military spending was so inflated that our nation's military budget was the biggest in the world and, in fact, was just slightly less than the military budgets of all of the rest of the world's militaries combined. Given the extent of military spending, he noted, fewer cents of the federal dollar were being spent on social programs than at any time in the last fifty years. So while the war in Iraq was costing the country seventy to eighty billion dollars a year, and tax cuts for the richest Americans were costing the country sixty billion, the government could not afford the tens of millions of dollars requested by Louisiana's congressional delegation to shore up New Orleans's levee system *before* Hurricane Katrina. Nor could it afford the billions necessary to provide health care to the nation's children, to hire enough police to keep our cities safe or teachers to teach the country's children to read, or to provide its neediest citizens with the tools to break out of intergenerational poverty.

The ironically named Katrina vanden Huevel, the editor and publisher of *The Nation*, spoke next, emphasizing the extent to which the Republican-run government had gotten out of the business of the "common good" and how the Great Society dreams had collapsed as a consequence. She characterized Bush's "ownership society" as a way of telling the country's citizens, "you're on your own, Jack," and she urged that "the aftermath of the hurricane provides an obvious opportunity for progressives to state an alternative."

Next, feeling very much on my own, I began speaking unsteadily at the podium. I was jittery but wired from anxiety and felt compelled to explain that I had driven up from Oxford that day and spoke without any real sleep, given my miscalculation as to the distance to New York and the time required for the trip. First, I took issue with the media's characterization of post-Katrina New Orleans as resembling the third world as its poor citizens clamored for a way out. I suggested that my experience in New Orleans working with the city's poorest people in the years before the storm had reflected the reality of third-world conditions in New Orleans, and that Katrina had not turned New Orleans into a third-world city but had only revealed it to the world as such. I explained that my work, running Reprieve, a charity that brought lawyers and volunteers to the Deep South from abroad to work on death penalty issues, had made it clear to me that much of the world had perceived this third-world reality, even if it was unnoticed by our own citizens.

To try to answer Ryan's question, I attempted to use my own

experience to explain that for many people in New Orleans, and in poor communities around the country, the government was merely an antagonist, a terrible landlord, a jailor, and a prosecutor. As a lawyer assigned to indigent people under sentence of death and paid with tax dollars, I explained the difficulty of working with clients who stand to be executed and who are provided my services by the state, not because they deserve them, but because the Constitution requires that certain appeals be filed before these people can be killed. The state is providing my clients with my assistance, maybe the first real assistance they have ever received from the state, so that the state can kill them.

I explained my view that the country had grown complacent before Hurricane Katrina, believing that the civil rights struggle had been fought and won, as though having a national holiday for Martin Luther King, or an annual march by politicians over the bridge in Selma, Alabama, or a prosecution—forty years too late—of Edgar Ray Killen for the murder of civil rights workers in Philadelphia, Mississippi, were any more than gestures. Even though President Bush celebrates his birthday, wouldn't Dr. King cry if he could see how little things have changed since his death? If politicians or journalists went to Selma any other day of the year, they would see that it is a crumbling city suffering from all of the woes of the era before civil rights were won as well as new woes that have come about since. And does anyone really think that the Mississippi criminal justice system could possibly be a vessel of social change when it incarcerates a greater percentage of its population than almost any place in the world, other than Louisiana and Texas, and then compels those prisoners, most of whom are black, to work prison farms that their ancestors worked as chattel of other men?

In spite of a laundry list of disappointments, I explained my continuing hope that the turning points of history happen in the face of horrific events. I recalled attending law school thirty blocks to the south and walking past the building on Washington Square that used to be the Triangle Shirtwaist factory. I remembered imagining women falling from the sky there, their dressing billowing up as they streamed through the air before hitting the ground with a thud. They had died because their bosses, wanting to get as much work out of these poor immigrant woman as possible, barred the doors against their taking unauthorized breaks and trips to the bathroom. The deaths of these women galvanized an American labor movement and led to substantive changes in labor laws that protected future workers from a similar fate. Although I imagine that, at the time, there were some who pressed for "market-based solutions" to workers' rights issues, who claimed, as now, that everyone needs to take "personal responsibility" for their actions, and maybe even decried these women as the "welfare queens" of that era, the reality of that fire had pulled back the curtain on their language and revealed it as a fraud.

I hoped, out loud, that the post-Katrina experience could be a similar moment, in which the American people could act like the child in the story and declare that the emperor has no clothes, and hasn't for a long time. That, in light of Katrina, we could be visionary and bold about what people deserve. We could say straight out that there are people in this country who are racist, that minorities are still not getting a fair shake, and that Republican policies heartlessly disregard the needs of individual citizens and betray the common good. As I stood there, exhausted, in front of the thinning audience of New Yorkers, it seemed possible that New Orleans's destruction and the suffering of its citizens hadn't been in vain.

After the event ended, I was approached by a gentle middle-aged woman with the concerned eyes of a mother. She looked at me and touched my arm, saying, "You need to take better care of yourself. If you don't take better care of yourself, how are you going to help anybody else?" I quickly withdrew, found some friends who had shown up to see me, and went out for a beer in the big city, where things seemed fine, just as I remembered them.

CHAPTER 14

Everyday Reminders

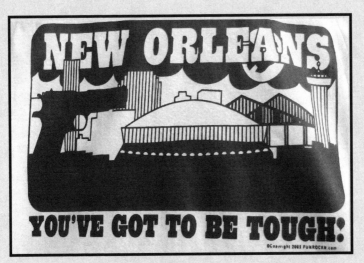

T-Shirt through Magazine Street Window

I FOUND MYSELF in a small apartment in a gray, prewar building near Columbia University in Manhattan. The building sat high above Morningside Park on a quiet street that snaked ninety degrees around the building, recalling the fast and loose city plan of an old European city more than the rigid, geometric grid of New York. The apartment belonged to a couple, a historian and the former university chaplain, whom I hadn't seen in nearly ten years and who years earlier had helped me avoid going to prison after police raided their home in Massachusetts, where I had been selling drugs while living with their daughter, Elsa. Since that time, I've led a life predicated on and made possible largely by that singular act of kindness and generosity, and now they had reached out to me again and opened their home to a virtual stranger who was already immeasurably in their debt.

The apartment was small but smart, elegant, and crammed with worn antique furniture and rugs that, when I was a kid, suggested the simple good taste of left-leaning professors, a sort I was then entirely unfamiliar with. I recognized my New Orleans home in their apartment. My home was similarly stuffed with books and mismatched antiques, a place that had perhaps derived from a long-forgotten affectation that had begun years earlier, from looking at the same dining room table where I now sat, drinking cold Lillette that I had found open in the fridge.

In the hallway, I found a basket of photographs that I glanced at, not sure if looking through them would be snooping. Sitting on the top were pictures of small children that, from the gloss of the photo paper and the vivid colors, seemed to be of recent vintage. Looking closer at the pictures, I could see Elsa in the faces of the little boy and girl and, as hard as it was to believe, it was clear that the kids were her children. I looked beneath the photos on top of the pile and saw other pictures of Elsa, her parents, her brother, and the children, in various combinations. Despite the passage of time and Elsa's becoming a mother, living a whole life of which I knew nothing, I easily could have picked Elsa out of a crowd, as her eyes were entirely unchanged, looking out at a world that she understood and of which she was weary, the same look she had when I met her, when she was seventeen.

I sat down with the basket of photos on the bed and got a sense of the history of this family, a family I loved but of whom I knew little, a history that touched my own for a moment, but changed my life forever. Toward the bottom of the basket, I found a picture of a boy with thin features and long, curly brown hair under a colorful hat. With a passing view, his adolescent visage could easily have been mistaken for a girl's. I stared hard at the picture. Is this me? Uncertain, I put the picture back in the basket, piled the other, easier, photos on top, put the basket back where I found it, and tried to find the present.

I RAPIDLY BECAME a New Yorker again while living there, waking up each morning and going around the corner to the deli for a copy of the *New York Times* and an egg and cheese on a roll, with salt, pepper, and ketchup, before heading a few blocks downtown to the Hungarian Café, where I drank espresso and attempted to maintain office hours among the graduate students fighting for tables. I rode the crowded subway downtown every day to see friends and family, and stop at bars where other displaced New Orleanians were now playing music or tending bar, before I headed back uptown, slightly bleary-eyed, on empty late-night trains. Every day, I took my dogs to a popular dog run in the lovely park, designed by Frederick Olmsted generations earlier for the peaceful edification of the city's poor. My dogs became overjoyed when we descended the granite steps into the park, and as I looked up at the sky through the branches of the trees, I glimpsed something of the peace that had been missing from my life for what felt like forever. Every time I left the front door of the apartment building, the big sky above Morningside Park opened up before me, reminding me of the possibilities of each new day.

Each of these things appeared as a contrast to my life in New Orleans, which, even long before the storm, failed to provide much of anything to its citizens. In New Orleans one was rarely on the streets at night, because walking around the city seemed prohibitively dangerous. New Orleans parks, some as large and smartly designed as those in New York, were crumbling from neglect. The prospect of something like a dog run, in a city that couldn't adequately provide housing or education for poor people, seemed an impossibly bourgeois fantasy in New Orleans. By contrast, New York, despite flaws and inequities that I knew well, appeared to offer material benefits to its citizens, and the sense that its well-funded government was invested in the welfare of its citizens seemed woven into the city's fabric. For all the "if I can make it there, I'll make it anywhere" tough talk, life seemed easier in New York.

This sense of ease was compounded by my daily talks with people on the ground in New Orleans who sought advice and kept me posted on the continuing indigent defense crisis and on their own personal hardships. One lawyer called me repeatedly to help create a media strategy so that his cases, which addressed the suffering of people in the criminal justice system in New Orleans, might rise to the surface of our national conversation about Hurricane Katrina's myriad victims. As I advised him on the best way to approach the *New York Times,* or some other venerable old publication, he would interrupt me to apologize for having breakfast while talking to me on the phone, and then laugh to himself as he banged ice cubes against his highball glass. These were heady days in New Orleans, in which those few New Orleanians who could get anything at all done were unlikely to be called out for morning drinking, self-promotion, or lack of focus.

At the same time, my father, a New York City–based mold remediation specialist, had made his way down to New Orleans. He was training homeowners how to clean out their homes without poisoning themselves or leaving behind dangerous material that would poison their families in the coming years after sheetrock was again tacked up to the studs, and to pursue business opportunities in New Orleans's only growth sector in the past century—disaster recovery. He asked me to call the *Times-Picayune* to find out about rates for advertising his business, and before I could even get a quote on an ad, the ad salesperson asked me for my dad's number so she could arrange for him to take a look at her flood-damaged home near the lake. It took me ten minutes to refocus the conversation on getting an advertisement in the paper.

Driving into New Orleans each day from a small town just south of Picayune, Mississippi, to work on people's homes, my father gathered a disturbing array of photos of mold growing out from walls in columns, having already covered the entire surface of the sheetrock; mold consuming hospital nurseries that had been readied for newborn babies; and, most jarringly, mold consuming Christ in a station of the cross in a flooded Catholic Church. He e-mailed me pictures, stressing that they didn't represent isolated buildings but summed up the state of the majority of the city, in which entire neighborhoods had sat for a month in fetid water. When I asked him whether he thought that New Orleans was a place where my wife and I could live again anytime soon, he told me he couldn't answer; I would have to see for myself. I wasn't in any rush.

I kept busy conspiring on the phone to use the storm to somehow abolish the death penalty in Louisiana, writing about the disaster, and speaking regularly at law schools, colleges, and events around the city where I was invited to speak as a voice from New Orleans, however inadequate my accent. (Incidentally, a New Orleans accent does, in fact, sound much more like an old Brooklyn accent than a Southern accent, but, although I grew up listening to transplanted Brooklynites, I did not pick up the accent.)

In early October, I started receiving a series of disturbing voice mail messages from my friend Chris, who had returned to New Orleans in my truck to begin work on a number of homes, including mine. He was requesting payment for the temporary blue tarp roof that he had put on to protect my home until a permanent roof could be put on. He was frantic about being able to make his payroll, and it seemed that living in an emptied New Orleans was wearing on him. Although he wanted the money transferred directly into his account, I was unable to do that without access, in New York, to a local branch of my bank. So I called to ask if I could send a check by Federal Express. When I reached him, he was at the bar around the corner from our homes, the Circle Bar, and he called across the bar to a woman who worked at the FedEx a few blocks away. He said that she confirmed that he could pick up the envelope there. "She likes me. She'll make it happen." I rushed to the FedEx store on 116th Street, getting in just before the 8:00 P.M. cutoff, and posted the envelope to Chris.

The following day, he left a message on my voice mail late in the afternoon. "While you are up in New York making fucking speeches, I am down here holding *your* hand, taking care of *your* fucking house. I came down here with money and now, if I am going to pay my workers to fix all of these fucking places, I am going to have to pay for it myself? No one does what they say they are going to do. I need the money, Billy." The message went on and on in the same vein. Apparently his friend at the bar wasn't able to help him get the envelope in the city, and he would have to drive fifteen minutes out of town to get it—which, despite having transportation, he refused on principle to do. More significantly, it appeared that he was losing his mind, he had unfettered access to my home, which I had charged him with the responsibility of rebuilding, and he had my truck, which, despite his panicked diagnosis, was running fine after a minor repair. Shortly thereafter, I heard about other friends to whom he had made similar calls, with little provocation, threatening to destroy the work he had done. Aside from Chris's intended meaning, his message made me understand with great clarity that if I was ever going to go back to New Orleans, I had to go back soon to take care of my home and my responsibilities. My life down there couldn't be handed off or dealt with over the phone.

A few days later Nikki returned. I picked her up at Newark Airport. Things were chilly between us. There was no question in her mind about returning to New Orleans. A few days in New York, a city that was always too big, impersonal, and showy for her to love, only strengthened her impression. Despite the distance between us, we were soon on the same page: we would leave New York and return to New Orleans by Halloween, where we would throw a big party for whoever was around, and in doing so, try to breathe life back into our home, despite its condition.

I hated getting back on the road. I hated leaving my little sister, my stepmother, my brother, my old friends, the corner stores I remembered going to as a kid, the first bar I got drunk at, everything. As much as I hated it and as indistinct as our destination was in my mind, I drove toward it as fast as I could through the early evening twilight. Near the Walt Whitman rest stop on the Jersey Turnpike, I saw the flashing lights of a state trooper behind me and I pulled over. He approached the car. "Driver's license, registration, proof of insurance."

"Officer, here they are," I said, handing them over, and in case he didn't notice on my license, I continued, with a lilt at the end as though it were a question, "I'm from New Orleans. I am trying to get home."

His chin dropped and he looked up. "Is that right? How things down there for you?" I gushed that our house was damaged, that we were going back to fix it up and to try to rebuild the city. He went briefly back to his cruiser, then returned, smiled, and handed me my papers with only a warning. "Well, try to make it down there safely. Good luck."

As we pulled back onto the highway, Nikki laughed at me for the speed with which I blurted out my non sequitur New Orleans excuse, but it had worked and, above all, it was honest.

After going the wrong way around the Washington, D.C., Beltway and then heading west on Interstate 66, we slept in a small-town motel in Front Royal, Virginia, at the head of the Shenandoah Valley on the Blue Ridge Parkway. We continued into the South after eating at a small diner where everyone but us knew everyone else. As we were crossing over the Appalachians in West Virginia, in the late morning, out of nowhere, snow began to fall steadily. As we descended the western slope of the mountains, the snow stopped and hours passed.

We reached Jackson, Tennessee, very late that night and pulled off the interstate onto Tennessee Highway 18, which, I had discovered, cut straight down to Oxford, where we planned to spend the night. After fifteen hours on the interstate, I cut through Jackson's small downtown too fast and was caught in a speed trap, with the blue lights of a police cruiser pulling behind me from behind a blind at a small burger joint. This was only my second time ever being pulled over, and my second in slightly more than twenty-four hours. Nikki and I guessed at whether my earlier warning would appear in the computer. The police officer came to window. "You were going awfully fast through town." I nodded, trying not to appear overeager. He had likely seen more folks from New Orleans than the New Jersey state trooper had, and perhaps felt less sympathy for the South's pulsing capital of vice. I also wanted to play it cool to avoid further ridicule from Nikki. After a couple of days of caffeine and driving, however, a moment's pause seemed an eternity, and having waited that long, I explained that we were on our way home to New Orleans, and that I was sorry for going too fast. "Can I see your driver's license?" he responded.

When he got back to the car, I was sure that he was going to give me a ticket and call me out for using my city's tragedy twice as an excuse for my bad driving, but he returned with a concerned and sympathetic look on his face and sent us on our way with only a warning.

We drove out of town onto the dark country highway, past the Mississippi state line and then down to Oxford, arriving after midnight. In the morning, it was plain that our place in Oxford had been nothing more than a sad imitation of a home for us and we eagerly packed up our things there, unwilling to suffer any more delay or transition before returning to the home that we had built from a shell in New Orleans.

Retracing my steps from my drive down to New Orleans with Wallace the previous month, everything I saw seemed pregnant with meaning, from roadside gas stations to causeways that I had passed over. As we got closer to the city, Nikki grew quiet and I became concerned for both of us. This was to be her first time seeing New Orleans since the storm. I had resolved to come into the city on the interstate and then take an elevated highway that exited only two blocks from our home, thus avoiding the flooded parts of the city in our initial entrance, but that plan was thwarted by a detour near the Orleans Parish line that routed through Lakeview, a low-lying upper-middle-class suburb near Lake Pontchartrain that took many feet of water during the flooding. It was already dark and there were no street lights. We drove down Canal Boulevard, formerly a busy street with nice houses on either side, but now a wasteland lined with grim, dark homes and flooded cars that were momentarily illuminated in our headlights. The eerie quiet of the city grew as the road turned into Canal Street, a grand old thoroughfare where newly planted palm trees and street cars had shared space on the neutral ground (the local term for the median) as the street ran through densely populated neighborhoods down to the French Quarter. Now it was dark, with no street cars to be seen and the palms bent at crazy angles as though set for a junior high geometry exam assessing protractor skills. Also, in pockets, we smelled "that smell," the indescribable odor of rot and decay that New Orleanians would bear for months as people put their refrigerators and the remains of their pre-Katrina lives on the curbs.

When we reached neighborhoods closer to our home, ones that did not flood, the faintest pulse of city life became detectable, reflected by street lights and occasional illuminated windows in homes and buildings. We reached our own block with great relief, with our dogs in the backseat recognizing that we were home. The house looked great. We parked on the street and brought the cat carrier and a few things to the door. As I walked past a mountain of trash that had risen in the street immediately in front of our front door, I recognized things. I saw the thick wooden frames that had surrounded our windows, the twelve-inch baseboards that we had salvaged when we rebuilt the house, and the painted quarter rounds that ran along the baseboards. I recognized these pieces of wood in the trash because I had bought, salvaged, painted, and admired them in the process of restoring our house. Rage filled me as I ran to the door on the side of the house where people had been gutting out water-damaged sheetrock. When I opened the door, I saw that in their enthusiasm they had simply discarded much of what I loved most about my house.

Without paying attention to the dogs, unloading the car, or taking a moment to enjoy the fact that, for better or worse, I was home, I began angrily digging through the trash pile until I had retrieved every bit of salvageable wood. It took me an hour, and by the end I was filthy, but I had done something for myself and for my home, to try to make it whole again—something that, clearly, no one else cared about. Before I went inside, where Nikki was in a similar frenzy of cleaning a house with collapsed ceilings that had been boarded up for months, I grabbed a chair and reached up to light the flames on the two brass gas lamps flanking our doors. It had saddened me to extinguish them as we left prior to the hurricane, imagining how beautiful they would look in a city otherwise without illumination, and I was happy to see them elegant and alight again in our sad and dimmed city.

The mountain of trash, minus our moldings, stayed there for months, growing at some times and diminishing at others, until just before Mardi Gras, when it was cleared once and for all. Until then, it greeted me each day when I left my house, reminding me that I lived in New Orleans, a city ravaged by storms and built below sea level.

PART IV

Against the Ropes

New Orleans's Unlikely Recovery

CHAPTER 15

Second Line

Street Dancer at Black Men of Labor Second Line

In this place, there's a custom for the funerals of jazz musicians. The funeral procession parades slowly through the streets, followed by a band playing a mournful dirge as it moves to the cemetery. Once the casket has been laid in place, the band breaks into a joyful "Second Line," symbolizing the triumph of the spirit over death. Tonight the Gulf Coast is still coming through the dirge, yet we will live to see the second line.

George W. Bush, September 15, 2005

WORD SPREAD IN BARS, coffee shops, and New Orleans's independent radio station, WWOZ, that there was going to be a second line on Saturday morning, starting at Sweet Lorraine's on St. Claude Avenue at ten o'clock. The parade was with the Black Men of Labor, who second-line annually on Labor Day. There were to be two brass bands, the Hot 8 and a group of teenage musicians, To Be Continued.

By the time I arrived at 10:15, an odd assortment of recently returned city residents was milling about on the sidewalk and the trash-strewn neutral ground in front of the closed bar. Amid duct-taped refrigerators and piles of moldy sheetrock, residents of the surrounding neighborhoods, where the second line culture has lived for generations, watched with anticipation the unfolding preparade drama that had seemed so distant a few months ago. Mixed into the crowd were gutter punks with their faces tattooed and pierced, dressed for a postapocalyptic ball, girls in tutus, men in top hats, and middle-aged music aficionados in vintage "Jazz-fest 88" t-shirts, testifying to their long-standing love of New Orleans music. A hundred cameras and a dozen video cameras were recording the scene and the moment for posterity.

One documentarian, who had a large movie crew, was conspicuous in his Yankees hat. The storm had blown in Spike Lee, a genuine national celebrity, to a city that prefers to revere its own local celebrities, such as Mister Quintron, an indie musician and the inventor of the Drum Buddy; rock-star celebrity chef Susan Spicer; and the late Ernie K-Doe, singer of the 1960s R&B classic, "Mother-in-Law," and self-proclaimed "Emperor of the World." Spike attracted little more attention than the rest of the many cameramen as he worked on his new documentary, *When the Levees Broke*. No one had come to Sweet Lorraine's to gawk at stars other than the dozen or so men in yellow shirts who were to perform their distinctive dance up and down New Orleans's streets.

While we waited for the parade to start, an off-the-cuff press conference began, as cameras converged around the dapper men and people asked questions about the meaning of the second line after the storm. As New Orleanians are rarely at a loss for words these days in explaining their plight and the significance of their lives and culture (nothing like being left for dead to make you realize that you have to speak up for yourself), Fred Johnson, one of the founders of the thirteen-year-old Second Line Club, wearing a black fedora and dark glasses, responded at length, linking New Orleans's black cultural traditions with his ancestors, who were slaves in Louisiana. "Slaves created gumbo from the scraps off the table out of what no one else wanted," he said. "The big house didn't know what the little house was doin', but when they found out, it became a cuisine." He enunciated *cuisine* with slight mockery and derision but also with understanding, because, of course, who wouldn't love gumbo?

Not everyone was eager to listen to talking. A lanky middle-aged black man interrupted the monologue, announcing, "I came here to dance! Where's the music at?" He was soon placated by the booming moan of Bennie "Big Peter" Pete tuning up his tuba. A heavy black woman with a tiny Nike backpack, big gold earrings, and a faint tattoo of an M on her hand, was ecstatic at the sound, "Bring me back home. Waah, waaah, waah, waaah. I been waiting to hear that. I been hearing it in my sleep."

As the Hot 8 tuned up, the Black Men of Labor disappeared into Sweet Lorraine's and the excitement of the promise of real New Orleans culture after months spent in the monocultures of Jackson, Houston, or Pensacola spread through the crowd.

The Hot 8 began playing "E Flat Blues," and tears came to people's eyes as they gathered around the doors of Sweet Lorraine's, waiting for the second-liners to emerge. Then they burst through the doors, one by one, like hometown players coming onto the basketball court at the beginning of the game. Each man, dressed in the same yellow and black outfit, expressed an individual character as he came through the darkened doors. Some sauntered, some strutted, and one particularly inspired dancer walked and danced in a squat with his butt almost on the sidewalk. Cheers for each of them were barely discernible over the loud brass band.

When the last man was through, we began to walk, en masse, down St. Claude Avenue, a street that runs from the Seventh Ward down to the famously devastated Lower Ninth Ward. The parade turned up St. Bernard Avenue, where the brown, chest-high waterline was evident on the facades of people's old wood-frame, shotgun houses.

As the band finished up "Paul Barbarin's Second Line," the dancers quickly headed into Mickey's Next Stop Bar. About fifty paraders, all wanting a quick beer, followed them in. It was unclear whether the bar just happened to be open at 11:15 A.M. on the parade route or whether these were normal hours in this nearly vacant, crumbling neighborhood but, certainly, the few late-morning drinkers inside must have been surprised at all the company.

As sometimes happens here, we got sidetracked at the bar. This time the delay was justified by the fact that two critical components of the second line—beer and hot sausage po'boys, typically sold from the beds of pickup trucks following the parade—were absent.

The band got going again with a slow dirge as the parade resumed slowly up St. Bernard into Treme, one of the oldest black neighborhoods in America, where free people of color built homes in the mid-nineteenth century. We passed Circle Grocery, the old neighborhood grocery store, which, submerged in deep water, had become an emblem of New Orleans's post-Katrina chaos that was shown with nauseating frequency on CNN. The sad music captured the feeling that so many of us had as evacuees while looking at elements of our everyday lives turned upside down and projected to a national audience to tell the story of this terrible natural disaster.

The band, however, refused to dwell on this mood for long. It commenced a rousing rendition of "I'll Fly Away" just as it passed under the interstate. With the sound trapped beneath the highway, the acoustics exploded. The band stopped marching and played even harder, as everyone cheered ecstatically.

When the song ended, the parade turned onto Claiborne Avenue, which runs under the highway, and which served for generations as the center of commerce and social life for Treme. It had a wide neutral ground with elegant oaks under which families often picnicked. But the oaks were cut down and the neutral ground was paved for parking when the highway was built above Claiborne Avenue in the 1960s as part of a backward "urban development" plan. Recently, the oaks have reappeared as murals on the massive concrete cylinders that support the highway, providing imagined shade to the many persistent families who still picnic there on lawn chairs just as their great-grandparents did.

On the corner of Claiborne and Columbus, the parade turned left, and then lingered for a moment under the interstate once again while the band and the second-liners scurried over to Antoinette K-Doe, who was sitting on the corner in front of the Mother-in-Law Lounge, which she opened with her late husband as a venue for New Orleans music and tradition. Even before Ernie K. Doe's death in 2001, it had become a museum of artifacts from his career and even contained a life-sized K-Doe in one of his old 1960s outfits. Almost all of the many images that adorned the walls featured K-Doe, with rare exceptions, including a painting of Christ himself. Since his passing, Antoinette is more open about the fact that the lounge is, and always was, a shrine to her legendary husband.

Miss Antoinette is a revered figure in New Orleans among musicians of all stripes, from brass bands to indie rockers. In addition to her years as K-Doe's "wife, his manager, his secretary, his bartender, everything," as she described it to me recently, she is also a cousin of Lee Dorsey, the writer and singer of the New Orleans anthem and 1960s R&B hit "Ya-Ya," as well as being a singer and dancer in her own right.

All of the musicians and dancers stopped to chat with Miss Antoinette, offering condolences for the extensive flood damage that the lounge and K-Doe's old black limo suffered in the storm. She remained smiling, optimistic, and proud as she sat against the brightly colored murals of musicians on the exterior cinderblock walls of the lounge. In sharp contrast, everyone could easily see past Miss Antoinette, through the doorway, into the gray and gutted lounge. As Empress of all of this, Miss Antoinette greeted Spike Lee as she did everyone else, as she posed with him for a picture taken by one of his crew, apparently a memento for him to hang on his office wall.

We got going again, down Columbus Street, a block that three months earlier had been an open-air drug market but now was abandoned to flooded cars and garbage, including a flood-darkened Ziploc bag with "pickled lips" handwritten on its white label. The next block down, in the fenced-in schoolyard of the McDonough 35 High School, the parade approached a group of young black men in orange jumpsuits with "OPP" stenciled in black block letters on the chest. These men, prisoners of the Orleans Parish Prison, which only three months earlier had left hundreds of men to drown in their cells in the rising water, ran to the high chain-link fence and, with their fists in the air, danced to the rhythm of their home, their neighborhoods. Cute women in pigtails and hand-painted "Make Levees, Not War" t-shirts, danced in the sunny street on the other side of the fence, framed against the burned-out shell of an old Creole cottage.

The Hot 8, no strangers to urban criminal justice, stopped to give a special impromptu performance of "Let My People Go" for the men behind the fence. This act of solidarity reminded me of the band's own loss: a year earlier, only about five blocks from the schoolyard, the Hot 8's trombone player, Shotgun Joe Williams, was shot by police.[1] (Although the media made much of his nickname in justifying the shooting of this unarmed man, anyone familiar with local jazz would explain that *shotgun* is a colloquialism for the trombone.) The band was to play to a mostly white, upper-middle-class crowd in the French Quarter later in the day, but it is unlikely that audience received as passionate and personal a performance as the Hot 8 gave for the men in the orange jumpsuits.

The parade wrapped up its tour of the Treme in front of the Back Street Museum, a museum of New Orleans's black cultural history that stands in the shadow of the old St. Augustine Church, where generations of Treme musicians were baptized. The museum staff was giving away homemade red beans and rice, first to the dancers and musicians, and then to everyone else. Some activists circulated a petition for Category 5 hurricane levee protection, and others informed the crowd of a march the following week to protest the city's lack of commitment to rebuild poor neighborhoods. They passed out flyers with the South African anti-apartheid anthem "Nothing about Us without Us" and details of the march. Everyone seemed optimistic and at home, and unlike almost any other place where New Orleanians congregate, no one talked about moving away.

We had, for a moment, lived up to the president's prediction, triumphing over the spirit of death with a second line through a city that had been left to die as he watched from the big house, while his wife no doubt explained to him that what we have down here is "culture."

CHAPTER 16

Gideon's Blues

Criminal District Court, Tulane and Broad

Without a change in priorities, the state might well have to spend the money for the welcome center to forewarn citizens: *Bienvenue en Louisiane: You Might Spend Months in Jail without a Lawyer.*

From a motion filed in *State v. Fleming*
in New Orleans District Court

WHEN THE MEN AND WOMEN held at the Orleans Parish Prison—essentially a county jail—were finally evacuated following Hurricane Katrina, they were scattered to prisons around the state, some more than four hundred miles from their homes in New Orleans. They were safe from the flood but, without access to any means of communication, could not find out about the safety and whereabouts of their families and loved ones. Just as bad, the system that had provided lawyers for poor people in New Orleans, already anemic and failing before the storm, had totally collapsed after the storm. This left thousands of pretrial detention prisoners—none of whom had been convicted of crimes and, thus, all of whom were entitled to be presumed innocent of the mostly minor crimes with which they had been charged—without access to counsel, despite the clear guarantees of the Bill of Rights. Consequently, many prisoners across the state were treated like animals by jailors who believed, correctly, that they could act with impunity while their charges' cases languished, without the prospect of a trial or release.

The human impact of the crisis hit me in mid-September, when I received an e-mail from a woman who had found my address by searching the Internet. She wrote, in a message that no doubt was sent to every address she could find:

my husband is in phelps correctional center in dequincy, la due to hurricane katrina and i am facing all this alone. i have

not recieved any help from fema or red cross as of yet. i have
been in lafayette for 3 weeks now and my husband was only
waiting to go to court on a rape charge that is totally a lie. i
was in contact with his lawyer before the storm and gave him
proof of my husbands innocense. . . . can someone please
help us. i need him with me. i am homeless and afraid, and
also sick!! and broke!! my husband's entire family has been
evacuated to arkansas and i would like for us to join them to
start a new life but i cant leave him in dequincy. i'm sure no
one cares about my husband and i but i do and im begging
anyone who can help us to please do so!!

I called the woman the next day, and the desperation obvious
in her note was even more acute in her voice. She explained that
she and her husband were both HIV-positive and that, when she
spoke to her husband the previous day, he told her that he hadn't
received any treatment for his disease in the weeks since the
storm. She offered details of the case that corroborated her claim
of innocence and suggested that the district attorney might not
even pursue the case. Since her husband had neither a lawyer nor
the means to pay for one, she had no idea when, if ever, her husband was going to get his day in court. She knew the system
wasn't supposed to work like this, but although she was horrified,
she wasn't surprised, because it hadn't worked much better for
poor people before Hurricane Katrina.

For more than forty years, since the U.S. Supreme Court's
landmark 1963 decision in *Gideon v. Wainwright,* state governments have been bound to provide an attorney for a poor person
who is at risk of losing his or her life or liberty as punishment for
a crime. This is the quid pro quo of the criminal justice system—
the state is entitled to deprive its citizens of their freedom, but

only after providing a meaningful process for establishing their guilt, including a genuinely adversarial process in which every defendant is represented by a lawyer dedicated to zealously defending his interests against the immense power of the state. In the absence of such process, there is little to distinguish our criminal justice system from the Stalinist show trials of the old Soviet Union or, closer to home, the effectively unreviewable detentions of terrorism suspects held at Guantánamo Bay and secret CIA prisons since President Bush commenced his "war on terror" following the September 11 attacks. Even before Hurricane Katrina, New Orleans's criminal justice system, like many across the South, tread dangerously close to these latter models in administering the thousands of cases against indigent defendants—cases that were often humdrum but life-altering—that passed through the courts' dockets on a daily basis.

Before Katrina, the criminal justice system in New Orleans ran along two tracks, beginning with the arrest. If the arrest was for something relatively minor, such as drunk driving or minor drug possession, and you could afford a lawyer, you would make your phone call and retain a private criminal defense lawyer, who would then contact a district court judge to request that you be released on your own recognizance or that bond be set to secure your release based on your community ties and your likelihood of appearing in court for future hearing and trial dates. In other instances, this would occur in open court, rather than over the phone, but with the same result—release based on your lawyer's argument that you, as an individual, could be trusted, with or without bond, to return to court so that you could continue to live your life, go to work, and pay your bills in the interim.

The situation was far different, however, if you were poor and couldn't afford a lawyer. In that case, you would have to wait until your initial appearance for the purpose of setting bail, up to seventy-two hours after your arrest, before you could even see a lawyer. Prior to the hearing, that lawyer, appointed only for the purpose of the bail hearing, at which it would be determined whether you would be released while your case was pending, would not have even talked to you—the person whose life and liberty were at stake—to determine if you had a job, a home to return to, a family to support, or any of the other issues relevant to determining whether you should be released while awaiting trial. Because these critical details would be unexamined by the court, your bail would be set at the amount requested by the prosecutor, which would, of course, be out of your reach as someone who couldn't even afford a lawyer. Unable to make bail, you would then sit in jail for a month and a half or two months, depending on whether you had been charged with a misdemeanor or a felony—time during which you would have no lawyer to represent you, find witnesses, or file motions—before the prosecution had to decide whether it would even accept the charges and actually prosecute you. If the prosecution accepted the charges, you would then, finally, be charged with a crime and appointed an attorney, who is assigned to work exclusively before the judge who would preside over your case and whose professional performance would be assessed chiefly by that judge. After the lawyer submitted your not-guilty plea, you would be unlikely to see him or her until your next hearing brought you before the court, nor would you be likely ever to see your lawyer outside of court. Consequently, all of your communication with your lawyer would occur in court, with you handcuffed and tethered to the man next to you. More distressing, except in the moment your case is called, your lawyer would be unlikely to be doing anything on your case—filing motions or talking to witnesses—because he or she would have more important cases than yours, cases that pay.[1]

This is how things have worked in New Orleans for years because, unlike big cities around the country, New Orleans does not have a true public defender system. Instead, indigent defense has been provided by attorneys paid less than thirty thousand dollars a year by the Orleans Parish Indigent Defense Board (OIDB) for representing all the defendants whose cases arise in a particular division of the criminal court. This was a choice job for lawyers, who routinely finished up before noon and typically worked only every other week, depending on the court's docket. For the balance of their day, they were free to pursue paid legal work, ranging from writing wills to taking private criminal cases. Not surprisingly, these jobs had become patronage positions doled out more on the basis of fealty to the political players in the criminal justice system than on the real skills and abilities required of lawyers in these difficult jobs. For years the system had been recognized as failing to provide the representation promised by *Gideon v. Wainwright* and the Sixth Amendment and, like so many other things in Louisiana and New Orleans, was considered among the worst in the country.[2]

This house of cards collapsed following Hurricane Katrina, leaving completely unrepresented five thousand men and women, ostensibly still clients of the OIDB, people who needed the assistance of counsel more than ever. By the end of 2005, hundreds had begun doing "Katrina time," time beyond either the end of their original sentence or beyond the maximum sentence for the charges against them—often for crimes as minor as fishing without a license or public drunkenness (the latter a prohibition more honored in the breach than in the observance in New Orleans). The OIDB, which had shrunk from thirty-nine lawyers before the storm to five afterward, lacked the capacity, the will, and the institutional ethic to attempt to protect the rights of these thousands of people. When asked about the situation, Tilden Greenbaum, the head of the OIDB, who led by example in the area of adversarial vigor, said that his clients were patient. He commented, "Sooner or later, we're going to have to start to make some noise about it. But given the magnitude of what everyone's been through, now is not the time to push."[3]

Thankfully, in his stead, a handful of lawyers, some of whom had lost everything in the storm, entered the fray, insisting that the hurricane had not suspended the Constitution. They began filing habeas corpus petitions at jails and prisons across the state where prisoners from Orleans Parish Prison had ended up, and attempted to identify people doing Katrina time who were entitled to immediate release. My colleague Meg Garvey was among those lawyers. She had talked to too many prisoners and their family members to feel remotely patient with the system's progress. She explained, characteristically at full tilt, "So many of these guys were in there for minor stuff and when the storm came their communication with their families was cut off. They couldn't be part of keeping their families safe or together. Now the world is changing dramatically while they are in prison. Babies are born. Their grandma dies. Their family resettles in Texas. And they are in for nothing."

Although the fact that lawyers like Meg Garvey volunteered to fight the good fight should be heartening to anyone who believes that the Bill of Rights should be applied to everyone under all circumstances, it should also disappoint that it was made necessary by an institutional failure that could have been anticipated even by casual observers of the system in place before Katrina. Steve Singer, a former colleague who is heading up the effort to create a new and genuine public defender's office, likened the indigent defense crisis in New Orleans to other governmental failures after the storm: "I compare it to the levees. They were always substandard but nobody realized until the hurricane came. The same thing with the criminal justice system. It was always substandard."[4]

Neal Walker, my old boss and a veteran criminal defense lawyer of national repute, went a step further, declaring the situation for indigent defendants in New Orleans "Guantánamo on the bayou" and noting that if their situation "existed in Mexico, the State Department would issue a blistering human rights report."[5]

If New Orleans's recovery is to make the city more civilized for its citizens, if it is to begin to reflect the promises implicit in our national identity, undertaking the monumental task of fixing the levees and rebuilding homes will not be adequate by itself if the city continues to fail to fulfill the basic constitutional rights of its citizens.

CHAPTER 17

Live from the Circle Bar

Happy Talk, Circle Bar

Gunshots down on Franklin,
11:45,
two boys from the Lower Ninth,
the coroner arrives.
There's a blind man reading tarot cards
over there in Jackson Square.
He says the future is uncertain
but he don't really care.

Everyone is drowning here
and everyone is free.
God protect these fools who build
their homes below the sea.

   Happy Talk Band, "Ash Wednesday"

AT NEW ORLEANS'S CIRCLE BAR, a few months after the storm, Luke Allen, the front man of the Happy Talk Band, welcomed people back to New Orleans: "Thanks for coming back, folks. It's a great city. Everything else is a strip mall. We will lose in the end, but have fun while it lasts."

With his postpunk imperfect pitch and his cigarette jammed in the tuners of his guitar, he proceeded to sing his songs of New Orleans: having a broken heart at the Huey P. Long Bridge, Collins mix and methadone, and the melancholy jealousy of dating a stripper. He has a strange idea of "fun." A lot of people here do.

In the previous months, many of us traveled the country, missing this town and despairing at both the low point to which the city had sunk and the narrow lens through which the rest of the country was seeing New Orleans and its culture. People watching TV across the country had grown used to seeing musicians like Wynton Marsalis, the members of the Preservation Hall Jazz Band, and Harry Connick Jr., the son of a famously racist New Orleans district attorney, as the sole representatives of New Orleans culture. This version of the city's culture is so narrow that people outside New Orleans seemed shocked when I told them that locals at the Circle Bar don't sit around listening to Louis Armstrong and the Hot Fives on the jukebox all night long. Although the Circle Bar's jukebox (the best in town, in my estimation) wasn't afraid to look back into the city's past, with Irma Thomas's "Drip drop, Drip drop, It's raining so hard, Looks like it's gonna rain all night," pouring out of the speakers occasionally, the live music at the Circle Bar had a decidedly less anachronistic tone.

There have been few honest assessments of local music tastes in the press. The Associated Press did get something right, however, in an article that mentioned the looting of the music section of the hated Lower Garden District Wal-Mart: "They took everything—all the electronics, the food, the bikes," said John Stonaker, a Wal-Mart security officer. "People left their old clothes on the floor when they took new ones. The only thing left are the country-and-western CDs. You can still get a Shania Twain album."[1]

It is true. There is not a single "new country" fan among any of my friends and neighbors. There may be more traditional jazz fans per capita in New Orleans than anyplace else in the world; nonetheless, New Orleans has many great musicians of all stripes—from rockabilly to alt-country to klezmer, and many hybrids in between.

For the past five years, the Circle Bar has played host to and embraced this smart and eclectic scene that reflects the city's music roots and its current life. The bands that play there respect the city's musical heritage. They know the music of Kid Ory, Louis Armstrong, Professor Longhair, and other patron saints of New Orleans music, but they are making music that is new and different, reflecting the city that was laid waste by the storm. Lefty Parker, who runs the bar, books the bands night after night, and played bass in the thumping indie band The Interlopers, is a big booster of the city's rock music, inasmuch as he is earnestly encouraging about anything. In explaining what is special about the new music coming out of New Orleans, he said, simply, "Music comes from the poor. It always has. This city is poor. And we are poor."

New Orleans has struggled for generations with the poverty and racism that hides at the margins throughout this country. What Luke describes as the city's "dilapidation and entropy" fed his songs, almost all of which reference the city. "Ash Wednesday" sings of flooding and murder in the Lower Ninth Ward. In "Forget-Me-Not," he sings of losing your mind, getting picked up by the police in the Bywater for murder, and waking up on the third floor of Charity Hospital, the mental health ward of New Orleans's public hospital.

When do you ever hear New York's "it bands" singing about Bellevue Hospital or East New York?

According to Luke, the city's cheap rents and drink-to-forget atmosphere were a draw for many musicians: "The bars were open twenty-four hours a day and I didn't want to go home, so, along with a lot of other musicians, we got drunk, pipe dreamed about music, and worked at bars, and it was possible because my rent was only $250."

For other bands, like the raucous Morning 40 Federation, which provided a rhythm section for the Happy Talk Band after Katrina, when two of Happy Talk's original band members evacuated to New York City and Peachtree City, Georgia, the city's decay had long provided the backdrop for a postapocalyptic bacchanal, a party on a precipice. That party appealed so much to Dave Neupert of M80 Music, a new Los Angeles record label, that he decided to sign the 40s and let them practice at his house in the Faubourg Marigny, another downtown neighborhood. He explained, "This is underappreciated music that the rest of the country should hear."

As in other cities, music is a lifestyle as much as an art. Perhaps because of the city's long tradition of music and its veneration of music, musicians and music lovers have license to allow their fervor to take full bloom. In many instances, the scenesters are not content merely to wear the clothes of their favorite American cultural period. At the Mod Dance Party on Saturday nights at the Circle Bar, boys in bowl haircuts and polyester pants dance the fish and the swim to their favorite 1960s soul alongside facially pierced and tattooed punks. Linzey Zaorski, one of a number of local Billie Holiday–esque jazz chanteuses, each of whom would make Nora Jones blush, has affected not only the 1940s starlet dress of the era but even the tinny sound of an old 78 rpm recording in her inflection. Along the same lines, even the much talked about brass bands, full of kids steeped in hip-hop, incorporate their favorite riffs from Michael Jackson's *Off the Wall* album or the newest Dirty South hip-hop into their traditional songs. Unlike the water that flooded New Orleans for weeks, the music scene here is anything but stagnant or fetid, despite the press's simplistic depiction of it. Here, the cultural synthesis of past and present creates a vibrancy and originality in our music that defies simple categorization, makes life interesting, and locates the culture squarely in New Orleans.

This sense of place is echoed throughout the New Orleans music scene, filled with people who fell in love with the city as one enters a deeply dysfunctional love affair. Many came to this city like sailors drawn to the sirens and crashed against the rocks, but remain no less smitten.

Some musicians left the city for extended periods after the

storm, hoping to find opportunities that were hard to come by in a city with no real music business. Alex McMurray, who sang his strange and beautiful songs in gravelly tones at the Circle Bar every Wednesday for years, played on the Lower East Side a couple of times a week after the storm. I never heard him there, but it's hard to imagine that he found a tubaist or washboard player with an ear for his sound in New York, or that New Yorkers understood the drama of selling your plasma, of which he sings. Not surprisingly, before long Alex and his perfect tuba-washboard-rock made their way back to New Orleans for good.

My old friend, Mike, who resettled permanently in New York City after the storm, was the original upright bass player for the Happy Talk Band. For his part, he is proud to have played on bills with Liquidrone, Bingo, the 40s, and the many other bands that make up the New Orleans music scene. He likens it to other great music eras and thinks that history might look back on it more fondly than the present has.

Shannon McNally, whose amazing album *Geronimo* came out in 2005 on Back Porch Records, and her husband Wallace, a New Orleans teacher and drummer, and my companion on my first trip back to New Orleans, have settled comfortably in Holly Springs, Mississippi. They miss their Bywater neighborhood desperately, but Shannon is touring and needs a good home base and Wallace has settled into a life of catfish, creek walks with the dogs he rescued from the streets in New Orleans post-Katrina, and a weekly gig playing with the Thacker Mountain Band. Shannon describes her indie/alt-country music as "songs for people who are fighting and struggling against shit." As nice and peaceful as Holly Springs is, I predict that they'll head back to New Orleans, the city of struggle, before long.

Before the storm, everyone was always talking about leaving New Orleans for some other city to find work, decent public schools for their kids, or a music business that might allow them to stop singing first-person nonfiction narratives about being a medical guinea pig for money. These bands and musicians don't make much sense living anywhere else because the real, sad, vibrant New Orleans fed their art at the same time it was eating its young.

For my part, I have spent too many nights sitting half-drunk in the Circle Bar staring up at the old florescent clock from K & B, a defunct, nostalgia-prompting, local drug store chain, and listening to music about floods, poverty, and urban decay. It broke my heart that for months there was no one left in New Orleans to play these heart-rending, beautiful songs, and that the rest of the country was forced to learn about these same horrors on television while politicians claimed that what unfolded was unforeseeable.

Too bad that Bush hadn't spend more time in places like the Circle Bar when he visited New Orleans in his wild youth. Maybe he should stop by the Circle Bar sometime soon, listen to the Happy Talk Band, and get a much-needed education in the realities of life in this city. Not that he would listen. Or get served.

CHAPTER 18

Corporate Limits

They be home in a . . . , Central City

MANY MONTHS AFTER Hurricane Katrina, my New Orleans neighborhood remained a shambles. There were square blocks without a single inhabitant and scores of large nineteenth-century houses teetering at the edge of collapse with no prospect of repair. Although I have heard of people driving through Central City, and other old neighborhoods like it, and commenting that the damage from Hurricane Katrina was worse than they had imagined, it is a sad reality that this neighborhood looked little better before the storm hit and had little of the catastrophic flooding that did destroy many of the city's neighborhoods. The story of Central City's decay has less to do with the specific and dramatic story of Hurricane Katrina than with the much more universal American story of white flight and urban decline that has rotted cities from here to Detroit and from Newark to Oakland. The postdiluvial realities in New Orleans, however, must drive the revival of neighborhoods like Central City, Treme, New Marigny, and other blighted but dry neighborhoods if the city is ever to come back to life.

In the nineteenth century, New Orleans was one of the biggest cities in America, with a population of nearly three hundred thousand at the century's close.[1] Central City and the other neighborhoods along the Mississippi River bustled with people and commerce. The areas to the east and north of the city were wetlands, so, without the possibility of modern drainage, the entire city was compressed into a narrow strip of land above sea level, built up by millennia of silt deposited by the Mississippi as it curved along its crescent.[2] With the development of water-pumping technology in the early years of the twentieth century, developers such as the powerful New Orleans Land Company began to get notions of creating residential neighborhoods to the north of the city's core, in areas of cypress wetlands north of Bayou Metairie, a bayou that runs roughly parallel to the shore of Lake Pontchartrain out to Lake Bourne.[3] The development of the Lakeview and Gentilly areas achieved critical mass in the 1940s with the completion of the first phase of a development called Lake Vista. Soon, the entire expanse from the parish line at the 17th Street Canal to the west, to the Industrial Canal to the east, between the Mississippi River and Lake Pontchartrain, was developed despite elevations as low as ten feet below sea level in the lowest-lying areas of Gentilly and Lakeview.

However shortsighted the development of this area, it pales in comparison to what came next. The remaining undeveloped area of the city, a seventy-seven-thousand-acre wetland—an area larger than the total landmass of San Francisco and Boston combined—comprising 65 percent of New Orleans's land, came into the hands of developers in the 1960s and 1970s, just as the city's population peaked at more than six hundred thousand.[4] The swamps were drained and tens of thousands of homes were built, despite fierce opposition from scientists and environmentalists concerned with the destruction of this vast urban wetland. Opponents argued that the wetlands served to protect the city from storm surge and flooding from hurricanes, and that building neighborhoods on the filled-in swamp, many feet below sea level, and on land that was rapidly subsiding, was dangerous to prospective residents.[5] Their Cassandra's call went unheeded, and by 2005, ninety-six thousand residents lived east of the Industrial Canal, hemmed in like island dwellers between the Mississippi River Gulf Outlet (a man-made channel that acted as a "funnel" for storm surge from Lake Bourne into New Orleans East, the Lower Ninth Ward, and St. Bernard Parish) to the south, Lake Pontchartrain to the north, and remaining wetlands running up to Lake Bourne and down to the Gulf of Mexico to the west.[6] Though the area, referred to as New Orleans East, was initially conceived as a white-flight suburb, by the 2000 census it was 81 percent black (mainly middle- and upper-middle class), and 5 percent Asian, with whites fleeing farther out to surrounding parishes and the city's overall population plummeting to less than five hundred thousand.[7]

Predictably, the vast majority of this land flooded catastrophically following Hurricane Katrina, destroying homes and displacing nearly all of the residents. With the country's focus fixed on the viability of the city, calls were immediately made to place a moratorium on the rebuilding of this and other low-lying areas of the city that had been destroyed by the storm. These calls were formalized in the Urban Land Institute's recommendations to the Bring Back New Orleans Committee, a committee established by New Orleans's mayor to guide the rebuilding of the city.[8] The recommendations failed to articulate a plan for bringing the displaced residents of these neighborhoods back to their city. Understandably, these calls were met with outrage by citizens and groups who saw this as a massive effort to disenfranchise the city's minorities perpetrated by development interests that were set on creating a newer, whiter, gentrified New Orleans.[9] Faced with this criticism, and in a tight reelection campaign in which every vote counted, Mayor Nagin balked at the plan but failed to provide any genuine leadership, telling New Orleans East residents that they could return to work and live in their homes regardless of the elevation or the extent of flooding, but they were rebuilding at their own risk. He offered no assurances that their homes would not be flooded again in another hurricane or that they would receive basic government services.[10] In the subsequent months, people trickled back to areas throughout New Orleans, poured their lives back into their homes, fixed roofs, and gutted moldy sheetrock on ground that never should have been developed in the first place.

Before New Orleans East was built, the huge area it encompasses was essentially two massive land tracts. The easternmost tract, thirty-two thousand acres of wetlands, was "the largest singly owned tract of land within the corporate limits of any major city in America," comprising a fourth of the landmass of the city.[11] Perhaps due to the fact that it was an unimprovable swamp, dense with disease-carrying mosquitoes, this land had been in the hands of only a few men since the arrival of Europeans in the New World.

The tract was given to Chavalier Gilbert Antoine de St. Maxent, one of the earliest colonists in the Louisiana territory, by King Louis XV of France in 1763. In 1796, St. Maxent's heirs sold the tract at public auction to Lt. Louis Bronier deClouet, scion of another prominent Louisiana colonial family. DeClouet sold the tract to Bartolene Lafon, a well-known surveyor and architect in New Orleans, in 1801. He owned it through the Louisiana Purchase. Lafon's heirs sold his plantation to Antoine Michoud of France in 1827. The land remained in the Michoud family until 1910, when it was sold to the New Orleanian John Stuart Watson, who unsuccessfully attempted to develop the land before selling it to a Chicago bank. The land was subsequently purchased by Colonel R. E. E. deMontluzin of New Orleans, who renamed the tract Faubourg deMontluzin and held the tract, undeveloped, through the Depression. In 1959, Colonel deMontluzin sold the land to New Orleans East, Inc., run by a group of Texas oilmen, including Clint Murchison, the owner of the Dallas Cowboys, along with Ladybird Johnson, in much the same state it had been in when it was granted to Chavalier St. Maxent two hundred years earlier.[12]

The majority of the western tract, closer to the city, had more varied ownership, but plans for the development of the area were begun by the New Orleans Lake Shore Land Company in the early part of the twentieth century. The company's plans went unrealized after it went bankrupt following a large hurricane in 1915 and a severe freeze in 1917. The land passed through the hands of several other development companies with little change until it was purchased at a sheriff's sale by Samuel "The Banana Man" Zemurray in 1934, who pieced back together the original tract.[13] (Zemurray was a Russian immigrant who as the president of the United Fruit Company made his fortune selling bananas and overthrowing the Honduran government.)[14] In 1954, Samuel Brown, a Las Vegas casino owner, bought the vast tract, which was sold after his death in 1959 to the LaKratt Corporation, whose parent company, National Equities, formed the subsidiary Lake Forest, Inc., which ultimately drained and developed the tract, and whose name much of the area now bears.[15]

Despite the flurry of economic activity, much of the area remained undeveloped through the 1970s but, because of the promise that this relatively cheap land held for its affluent and powerful owners, the seeds of development had long been planted. The development of Interstate 10, at the urging of the powerful New Orleans East company, from downtown through the swamps of the east, opened the area up and provided quick transportation into the city. Simultaneously, the developers, working with the Army Corps of Engineers, devised a series of levees and pumps that would drain land well below sea level. The federal funds that financed these projects were a bonanza for the developers, whose tens of thousands of acres increased in value from two hundred dollars an acre to fifteen thousand dollars an acre as the land became ostensibly suitable for development (and values increased even more for the land running along the new interstate).[16] Although early development was confined to relatively high land, at sea level and above, along the ridge of the old filled-in Bayou Metairie and the natural levee along Lake Pontchartrain, the draining of the swamps left developers projecting that New Orleans East's population would skyrocket from 39,024 in 1970 to 170,000 by 1980.[17]

The developments were not without critics. Peirce Lewis, a professor of geography at Pennsylvania State University and a well-regarded expert on the city's history and geography, cautioned at the beginning of the chapter on "The Menace of Hurricanes and Storm Surges" in his 1976 book *New Orleans: The Making of an Urban Landscape*, "Such developments are raising serious questions about the wisdom, much less the safety, of the new New Orleans."[18] He went on to explain that tidal surges from hurricanes were the "main danger" in New Orleans East and that storm surges during the then-recent hurricanes Betsy in 1965 and Camille in 1969 had been extensively documented by the U.S. Army Corps of Engineers but, though the Corps was "too polific to say so in plain language, the reports make it clear that extensive building in the marshes of eastern New Orleans is inviting serious trouble." He closes the chapter with a sad and prescient note, citing advertisements from real estate developers along the new interstate that "wax eloquent about marinas, golf courses, and fun-in-the-sun, but remain strangely quiet about hurricanes."[19] He summed up: "It was a real estate speculation by people who were unwise or dishonest."[20]

This is not to say that early residents were entirely unaware of the realities of living in a swamp. A 1975 *Times-Picayune* article about the New Orleans East development, headlined forebodingly, "Drained Wetlands: How Infirm a Foundation," begins with the questions posed by out-of-state attorneys general who visited the neighborhoods built on drained wetlands: "How can the developer get away with it? Why don't the homeowners sue the developer? Why don't they throw the city administrators out for allowing it? Are there no laws to prevent it?"[21] The attorneys general were responding to the clear evidence of subsidence in these neighborhoods where, months after purchasing perfect new homes, the buyers would find that their yards had sunk around them, their garage doors had buckled, and they needed to bring in dump trucks full of earth and shovel dirt around their homes so that their foundations would not be exposed. Sherwood Gagliano, who gave these attorneys their tour of the neighborhood and who was one of the first scientists to note that Louisiana's wetlands were being eaten by the sea owing to levee construction, and that these wetlands were necessary to protect the city from storms, was quoted in the article explaining that only the natural ridges in the area were fit for development but the developers "usually tell the homeowner their lot is just on the edge of a levee ridge on high ground and good soils." On the basis of this deception, people were lulled into believing that their bit of reclaimed swamp, where their families slept and where they had invested all of their savings, was safe, high ground. The attorneys were incredulous at the residential developments built on dangerous ground; one muttered, "These people down here must be a bunch of nuts."

The then-nascent environmental movement also became active in opposing the development of New Orleans East. A group called Save Our Wetlands was formed in 1974 after its founding members discovered that developers in a neighboring parish were illegally destroying a fifty-two-hundred-acre tract of wetlands with, according to the group's Web site, "the aid and assistance of the Army Corps of Engineers."[22] The group began an all-out assault on the development of sensitive wetlands, working against a "Hurricane Barrier Project" proposed by the Corps and authorized by President Johnson after Hurricane Betsy. The project would have created a concrete barrier at the mouth of Lake Pontchartrain, intended to minimize waves coming into the lake from the gulf.[23] According to the Save Our Wetlands lawyer Luke Fontana, the barrier was "pure pork barrel" and would have created environmental devastation of the lake while reaping "windfall profits" for New Orleans East, Inc., which needed the barrier for the "land enhancement" of the remaining undrained thirty-two thousand acres of wetland at the eastern end of New Orleans East.[24] In 1977, Save Our Wetlands, along with the Environmental Defense Fund in New York, was able to obtain an injunction in federal district court to prevent the construction of the barrier, on the basis of apparent deceptions in the environmental engineering plan offered by the Corps that the judge denounced as "legally inadequate" science, in that it understated the risks to the environment.[25]

After years of legal wrangling, the Corps dropped the plan in 1984 when it became apparent that, even aside from the litigation, the barrier would cost nearly one billion dollars. At the same time, oilman Clint Murchison was having problems of his own, including an oil-bust bankruptcy in 1985, that sent New Orleans East, Inc., into receivership, with its sprawling acreage of wetlands still undrained and undeveloped.[26] Merrill Lynch, the land's new owner through its subsidiary South Point, Inc., facing a set of development problems created by a host of new environmental and building regulations for wetlands development, struck a compromise with the city and environmental groups and agreed to turn more than twenty-two thousand acres over to the federal government to create the Bayou Sauvage National Wildlife Refuge, while retaining another several thousand acres for development.[27]

Since Hurricane Katrina, right-wing antienvironmental pundits at Fox News, the *Weekly Standard*, the *Wall Street Journal*, and other publications have been quick to blame Save Our Wetlands' obstruction of the barrier for the flooding in New Orleans, but the U.S. Government Accountability Office exonerated the group in a September 2005 report that indicated that the barrier would not have prevented flooding and likely would have made it worse.[28] Save Our Wetlands has also been quick to point out that the injunction on the barrier prevented the development of the Bayou Sauvage Refuge, keeping many thousands of additional people from living in harm's way and creating the nation's largest protected urban wetland in a city where wetland erosion is a leading problem threatening its future viability.

In the aftermath of Katrina, it is now clear that the "nuts" were the Army Corps of Engineers and the government officials who allowed massive development in a floodplain that resulted in multimillion-dollar profits for out-of-state developers out of the pockets of New Orleans citizens who had been lulled into a false sense of security.

New Orleans East was one of the worst flooded areas in New Orleans following Hurricane Katrina, with significant areas under ten feet of water and virtually no dry land except for the natural ridges along the lake and old bayou that were nature's products, not man's.[29] As late as September 19, three weeks after the hurricane's landfall, large areas were still under water in the lowest-lying areas.[30] After the hurricane, nearly one hundred people were found dead in this area, where until fifty years ago almost no one lived.[31]

Driving through New Orleans East nearly a year after the storm, devastation was evident everywhere and there were few signs of progress. Most of the destroyed furniture, moldy sheetrock, and mildewed photos and mementos appeared still to be as they were left by the receding water. I noted to a friend with pleasure that some optimism could be found in sunflowers that appeared to grow wild on the lawns in various areas, brightening the day with their large yellow faces. My wife had taken photos of the flowers to reflect the area's recovery. My joy rapidly dissipated, however, when I was told that they had been planted to absorb heavy metals left by the flood, and then learned that after the accident at the Chernobyl nuclear power plant in Ukraine, similarly sunflowers had been planted near the ponds around the site of the accident to remove radioactive wastes.

The extent of the flooding in areas like New Orleans East, and the expectation that New Orleans's population, which had already dropped by nearly one hundred fifty thousand in recent decades before the storm, would drop as low as two hundred thousand after the storm, forced discussion of the fact that the city could no longer sustain such a large urban footprint if it was to survive. The Urban Land Institute's (ULI) city plan split the city into three "investment zones," with the city's unflooded historic core in the first rung, and New Orleans East and the other hardest-hit areas at the bottom.[32] The ULI recommended that people in areas such as New Orleans East be compensated for their homes at pre-Katrina values, and that rebuilding be prohibited there lest "scattershot redevelopment" occur and "homeowners will begin to rehab houses on partially abandoned streets, creating shanty towns with little to no property value."[33] A backlash followed, which has been echoed in the left-leaning press, where characterizing the rebuilding plan as a effort to turn the city into a "minstrel show" version of its former self for the benefit of wealthy developers and city elites has become de rigueur.[34]

The residents—either potentially displaced victims of the redevelopment plan who have been denied their right of return, or citizens protected from living in neighborhoods of questionable safety and widespread blight, depending on whom you ask—are left in the middle. Some have settled elsewhere for want of services such as flood protection, proper schools, health care, and garbage removal, and others clearly want to return home, but the issue is bigger than individual citizens' desires and resources.

Sadly, away from the world of individual desire (to return home or, more insidiously, to recreate the city as whiter or richer), the scientists and academics most familiar with New Orleans's urban landscape, its topography and geography, and its susceptibility to future disaster, appear to speak with unanimity concerning the environmental viability of areas like New Orleans East. The realities of post-Katrina New Orleans have pushed scientists to call for a denser, more historic city, not for the sense of community eloquently described by the late Jane Jacobs in *The Death and Life of Great American Cities* or for the real estate, lifestyle, and aesthetic leanings of the New Urbanists or preservationists, but for the very survival of the city.

Peirce Lewis, whose book has been selling briskly because of the sudden interest in New Orleans geography, told me the same thing that he has been saying for thirty years: "No responsible person would propose building or rebuilding anything in the environment where New Orleans East was located." He elaborated on the future of the city as a whole: "Putting off-limits rebuilding of heavily flooded areas will prevent more death. If you restore New Orleans as it was ten years ago, you are just inviting a human disaster of catastrophic proportions." He is quick to point out that Katrina was not nearly as bad as it could have been; if its eyewall had been just fifteen miles farther west and it had remained a Category 5 storm, the damage would have been "unimaginable." Regarding concerns that a smaller footprint would prevent poor people and minorities from returning to their homes, Professor Lewis was adamant that allowing people to return to homes in flood-prone areas was neither "particularly humane" nor in accord with civil rights, when "you know that they could drown there."

Craig Colten, a professor of geography and anthropology at Louisiana State University, who has written extensively about environmental racism in the development of New Orleans, links the susceptibility of minority areas to flooding to a lack of political will to serve minority groups, explaining that, prior to Katrina, "minority populations who have endured the worst flooding in the suburbs [had] been unable to mobilize an effective political response," whereas white areas were better served because there was greater political receptiveness to their concerns.[35] Without regard to the racial characteristics of the neighborhood, he has advocated suspending the redevelopment of catastrophically flooded areas such as New Orleans East (and mostly white Lakeview), explaining, "I don't think we should make any decisions based on race or class in rebuilding. . . . I think we need to look at New Orleans as a whole and look at the lowest areas—the areas that would be hit the hardest in any future flood—and think about converting those to green spaces, to wetlands, to flood retention basins, so that waters can stand in those areas without damaging property in the future."[36] Sensitive to charges of racial discrimination and to people's right to return, Professor Colton explained, "I realize it will be an insult [to former residents], but it would be a far bigger insult to put them back in harm's way."[37]

To illustrate his point, Colten summoned a postapocalyptic vision of what these neighborhoods would look like if people were allowed to rebuild as they pleased: "If you have low-density neighborhoods, you'll see that there will be a lot of houses deteriorating, which will lead to problems with rodents, vandalism and squatters, which all make urban life a bit dicey. Houses will be falling down, there will be fires. It just becomes a kind of uncontrolled landscape, a landscape of chaos."[38]

Professor Oliver Houck, an old-school New Orleans environmentalist and Tulane University professor of environmental law, summed up southern Louisiana's development pattern over the past few centuries in a few sentences: "For a long while, we tended to build elevated homes, on ridges, and kept the boats handy for what we knew would come. Then we raised levees. When they didn't work we got the federal government to raise levees and built out back into the swamps and put in pumps. Before long we were building on slab. And still we flooded. We lead the nation in flood losses. No reason not to. The federal government pays us for it."[39] He points out a potential deal breaker, however, in the form of global warming, which could raise temperatures enough to unleash a series of intense hurricanes over the coming century, fed by warmer waters and potentially more devastating due to higher seas resulting from the melting of the ice caps, which would, in turn, further erode Louisiana's already struggling coastal wetlands. He notes with concern that although city planners are trying to fight "the momentum to rebuild everywhere," they are unlikely to be heeded because building bigger levees and avoiding the hard decisions "is what we have always done, it is what the Corps of Engineers knows how to do, it avoids the need to plan, it sets up killings in real estate, and it is the easy path for politicians. Of course, it will be increasingly hard to maintain for even this century, the costs in trying will be enormous, and when there are failures more people will die. But those consequences are for another day. We are living now."[40]

Each of these experts recommends turning the low-lying areas of the city back into wetlands or water retention basins that will assist the city in preventing future catastrophic flooding. This view is summed up in Professor Lewis's comment: "If you're planning on having more hurricanes, the most sensible thing is to return to the areas that existed before the pumps drained the back swamps."[41]

If this is the universal prescription of scientists and environmentalists, who correctly predicted that all this would happen, and who predict that it will happen again if people rebuild as before, it is difficult to argue against the expert consensus, regardless of our clear understanding of and sympathy for those whose homes were in areas where no one should live again. Assuming that science is right and the Corps cannot fix everything, the question then becomes whether it is possible to shrink the city, as proposed by the ULI and some of the city's conservatives, in a manner that achieves justice for the people displaced and a better, safer, more functional city for everyone.

Whether or not the city comes up with a plan, it appears that federal dollars will begin trickling in, and the state's "Road Home" plan will begin compensating residents who want to move from catastrophically flooded neighborhoods, based on their homes' pre-Katrina values. In the absence of assurances that their neighborhoods will be safe and that services will return, or a plan to welcome residents back to other areas of the city, it seems clear that many families will take the buyout and invest their money and futures in places where jobs, good schools, and clear prospects for their family await them—probably not New Orleans.

On the other hand, city planners and other city housing experts have indicated the city's old "high and dry" core has the capacity to house everyone who wants to return, and that underpopulated areas in those parts of the city are ripe for redevelopment, giving all New Orleanians a place to come back to and giving the city a better chance of concentrating resources in a manner that will allow it to improve its decimated public schools, health care for the poor, and other city services. In various quarters, there have been suggestions that the city could use its existing blighted house and land program to distribute property to residents of flooded neighborhoods at below-market values, giving people an incentive to come back home to rebuild, and thereby creating jobs here.

While the mayoral campaign was underway, neither the mayor nor the challenger, competing for votes, were willing to indicate an ability to make the hard choices that could lead the city to higher ground. The candidates "refused to suggest the storm-ravaged city must shrink its footprint to provide affordable city services," yet neither offered viable plans for specific flooded neighborhoods.[42] Their positions were dismissed as "run-off politics." But long after his reelection, Mayor Nagin has not provided any real leadership on these issues, leaving people to cling to their homes, however flood-prone, as their only means to return to their city.

Many months after the storm, while others played politics with the city's future, Kim Watts, a black single working mother and a colleague at my New Orleans law office whose comfortable, middle-class, slab home in New Orleans East off the Michaud Exit of Interstate 10, the last before reaching the wetlands, had much of its roof submerged by the storm surge, was in limbo about what she should do with her home. While she was living in an apartment behind her mother's place in the recently gentrified but underpopulated Lower Garden District, where she grew up in the 1980s when the neighborhood became a frightening and violent victim of the crack epidemic, she was unable to put down permanent roots for herself and her son because she did not want to return to her neighborhood while it was unclear if services would return or if Hurricane Katrina's flooding would be repeated. Yet, without resources to start over from scratch, she spent thousands of precious dollars gutting and then renovating her home. Kim said, "If the choice is stay here, spend my money, and wait for another flood, or try to buy somewhere else without any money or savings, I didn't know what to do." She said she would have considered moving downtown for good if there had been a program for her to build in the Lower Garden District, where she would be closer to work and to her son's school, but nothing like that ever came to pass. With a lack of other good options and a ton of hope, she rebuilt and is back in a neighborhood that will likely see flooding from hurricanes again.

The choices presented to people like Kim and her son will determine the fate of New Orleans. The city's size, its future viability, and its safety in the face of environmental hazards and storms that are predicted to get bigger—many foreseen by the kings and chevaliers who put the city here in the first place, but ignored by twentieth-century developers and politicians—will turn on the balance of science and politics that is struck in creating those choices.

CHAPTER 19

Fat Tuesday

MAX Band, Muses Parade

For it is through the Muses and far-shooting Apollo that there are singers and harpers upon the earth. . . . Happy is he whom the Muses love: sweet flows speech from his mouth. For though a man have sorrow and grief in his newly troubled soul and live in dread because his heart is distressed, yet, when a singer, the servant of the Muses, chants the glorious deeds of men of old and the blessed gods who inhabit Olympus, at once he forgets his heaviness and remembers not his sorrows at all; but the gifts of the goddesses soon turn him away from these.

Hesiod, *Theogony*

THE TWO WEEKS leading up to Mardi Gras are always exhausting, with parades and parties scheduled almost daily. Living where we do, a block from the main parade route on St. Charles Avenue, the season is not something that we can opt out of or choose to ignore unless we leave town. In years past, I would sit at my desk on the second floor of our house, trying to work on one of my appeals as I heard the sounds of high school marching bands booming through my office window. Reluctantly, I would get up from my desk and look out the window across a parking lot, catching a narrow sliver of the action through a few degrees of perspective between a crumbling old shotgun house and a high-rise on St. Charles Avenue. I would see the bands, the dancers, and the floats speed by. I would sit back at my desk as long as I could, studying the details of a child's murder or my client's abuse on death row, and then, gradually succumbing to the sounds, I would walk out into the cool February air on my street, jammed with cars and foot traffic heading for the parade, and then join the mix of families, black and white, gathered at the corner of Erato Street and St. Charles, clamoring for beads and throws from the floats. As I stood watching the drum major proudly blow his whistle, or catching something special out of the air and handing it to a smiling kid, the troubles piled high on my desk in stacks of 8½- by 14-inch paper, though only a couple hundred yards away, seemed impossibly distant. After the year I had had, that all New Orleanians had had, I abandoned my ritual pretense of work for 2006, crossed Carnival off my work calendar, and lost myself in parades, music, beads, and cocktails.

Muses, a parade put on by an all-woman krewe a few days before the final weekend of Carnival, is the one part of Mardi Gras that my wife and I refuse to miss. The krewe, named after the nine goddesses of Greek mythology who evoke and inspire the arts and science, parades down St. Charles Avenue past our neighborhood, where each of the muses—Urania, Polymnia, Euterpe, Terpsichore, Melpomene, Thalia, Erato, Clio, and Calliope—appears in succession as street names. We mixed gin and tonics in colored plastic cups, walked around the corner, and stood on the neutral ground on St. Charles Avenue, with our backs to Popeye's Fried Chicken and Wendy's Hamburger, and watched the tail end of Chaos, the parade that preceded Muses. We waited, anticipating the parade but fearing that it wouldn't be as good as it had been in years past—when we had caught glass beads, flashing refrigerator magnets, and beaded beer cozy necklaces—but as the parade approached and we caught a glimpse of Muses' signature float, a giant, twenty-foot-tall stiletto high heel covered in fiber-optic lights, we relaxed, knowing that we wouldn't be disappointed.

After the shoe came a giant bathtub filled with women dressed in purple, and then a float filled with women first responders, who as cops, firefighters, doctors, and other emergency workers had attempted to keep the city alive through Hurricane Katrina. The next float, built to look like a giant Monopoly board, announced the parade's theme, "Muses Got Game, If We Don't Laugh We Cry," in large letters across its side. What followed were twenty parodies of games that, like the chapters of a book, summed up much of the city's experience during and after Hurricane Katrina.

The Barrel of Monkeys float depicted a monkey-faced President Bush telling FEMA head Michael Brown, "You're doin' a heck of a job, Brownie," as Brownie scratched his monkey butt while trying to choose a tie. The Blame Game float showed cartoon faces of Mayor Nagin, Governor Blanco, Brownie, and Bush all pointing fingers at one another. The Red Rover float depicted the Gretna police force in riot gear with arms linked across the Crescent City Connection, the bridge out of New Orleans into Jefferson Parish. The faceless officers were shouting, "Red rover, red rover, get your asses back over," written in a sound bubble below a "City of Gretna, No Entry," sign. The last game float, The Game of Chance, summed up what most people faced as they watched the float pass. While holding in one hand a suitcase decorated with Houston, Florida, and Alabama destination stamps, with his other hand a man was rolling dice, on the sides of which were written: "political corruption continues," "Blanco, Nagin reelected," "looters," and "criminals return." The man was exclaiming, as he rolled the dice, "I hope we don't crap out." Above it all, in bold letters was written, "It's worth the risk." We all hoped so.

. Throughout the parade, beads, doubloons, and other throws rained down from the masked riders on the floats, who were lost in the revelry of hundreds of people looking up at them and yelling, begging, for a string of plastic that would hold no value or interest in almost any other context. Interspersed among the floats were marching bands and other groups, including flambeaus, men who walked the streets with torches made from cans of gasoline lit at what appear to be large pilot lights. The flambeaus, who historically illuminated the parade route in the days before street lights, do their job in exchange for change tossed to them by the spectators. Whereas in years past this group was uniformly black, this year the majority of the faces beneath the dripping flames were Latino, another sign of the changing life of the city.

In anticipation of the MAX Marching Band, Nikki and I walked down to the highway overpass a few blocks from our house, anticipating the booming sound of drums and tubas trapped beneath the roadway. The band combined elements of the St. Mary's (M), St. Augustine (A), and Xavier Prep (X) high school marching bands, each of which was a musical powerhouse before the storm but none with enough students remaining after the storm to create a full band on its own. Majorettes dressed in bright yellow skirts and bearing flags were followed by dancers and then the drum majors, who wore white track suits with black shoes and jauntily thrust the band's standard into the air to the rhythm of the drums. The dancers stopped beneath the end of the second roadway, and the tubas and drums squeezed in under the first. The band stopped walking and began to play loudly, joyously, while the dancers—some looking as young as twelve, others as if they would easily get served in a bar—moved in perfect unison in a dance that, at moments, must have made the chaperones walking alongside the band blush.

I was happy. The kids in the band were happy. Everyone around me was happy. Nothing outside the drab confines of this spot mattered at all.

As the parade prides itself on incorporating New Orleans's ongoing artistic culture into the city's traditions, it also always has a healthy dose of the Ninth Ward, which contains the city's most cohesive independent art and music scene, as well as the city's other arts and cultural outposts. From these communities, as essential as any to the city's identity, sprang the Rolling Elvi, a hundred Elvis impersonators on mopeds cruising at chatting speed midway through the parade, as well as carnivalesque all-women step dancing troupes with bawdy, burlesque names such as the Camel Toe Lady Steppers and the Pussyfooters. This scene had its most clearly distilled expression, however, in the Ninth Ward Marching Band, which celebrated its tenth anniversary at this 150th Mardi Gras.

The Ninth Ward Marching Band was created by a bunch of artists and musicians living in Bywater, the upper and unflooded part of the Ninth Ward, in the mid-1990s. Bywater, an old Creole neighborhood of dusty, simple shotgun houses built right up to the sidewalks, was built on high ground in the mid-nineteenth century and then inhabited by successive waves of working-class immigrants—Irish, Germans, Italians, and then southern and eastern Europeans, who worked at the old cotton press and then the docks along the Mississippi River and attended the neighborhood's many Catholic churches. By the early 1990s, the neighborhood was predominantly black, down at the heels, with crack taking over, dead bodies appearing on the herringbone brick sidewalks, and gunshots heard more frequently than church bells. But there was beautiful light in the mostly treeless neighborhood and interesting, cheap old houses, so gays, artists, and musicians moved in, drawn downriver from the French Quarter and Fauburg Marigny, which had grown more expensive with the renovation of grand homes.

At the center of all of this were Mr. Quintron and Ms. Pussycat, the darling couple of this new bohemia. Quintron reigned with his Drum Buddy, a homemade piece of analog hi-fi on which an illuminated cylinder rotates like a record, with light peering through holes to sensors that moan at different electric pitches as he scratches like a DJ, saying earnestly, "The sounds and rhythms which you now hear are coming from my most recent invention, the Drum Buddy. The Drum Buddy is a five-oscillator, light-activated, mechanically rotating drum machine, the product of five years of research, development, and much experimentation with the photoelectric cell." Ms. Pussycat, his companion and, according to the *Times-Picayune*, his cousin, created a backdrop for his performances, shouting in a high-pitched voice, "Paris, New York, Chicago, New Orleans . . . " as her partner tore off his shirt in ecstasy.[1] (The newspaper article also noted that Mr. Quintron, who dances energetically on two legs while performing, was in a wheelchair from a roller coaster accident at Six Flags amusement park, throwing into question the veracity of the cousin claim.) Ms. Pussycat is at least as much in her element as he is, performing with her incredibly cute and lifelike hand-made puppets before or after their musical shows. Her art reached its zenith in a video titled *North Pole Nutria*, a film that works on several levels. It follows two New Orleans nutria as they travel to the north pole after winning a sweepstakes and are forced to battle there with the musically talented Virus, with the real-life voice of the racist Jefferson Parish sheriff Harry Lee, who is destroying Santa's toy shops but is ultimately defeated by—you guessed it—the grooving sounds of Quintron's Drum Buddy. My nephews enjoyed the film so much that we were compelled to watch it twenty-five times one Christmas after I gave it to them as a gift. Amazingly, it didn't lose its potency.

Quintron and Ms. Pussycat are certified local celebrities and the spiritual leaders of what was referred to as the Ninth Ward art scene before the Ninth Ward became nationally synonymous with the destruction and suffering of the mostly black community in the Lower Ninth Ward. They started the Ninth Ward Marching Band with a group of friends, with Quintron as the group's director and drum major and Ms. Pussycat as the head of the "gun girl team," which marches with the band carrying unthreatening white wooden rifles. She is also the chief designer and seamstress of the band's uniforms. Their music has only grown in authenticity over the years, with local brass and percussion musicians joining in. Fifty members strong, the band marched down St. Charles, following the band's banner held by men in white pants and shirts, red vests, and silver metallic helmets, each emblazoned with a red "9." Then came drums, brass, glockenspiels, cymbals, rifle girls, cheerleaders, batons, flags, and cowgirls (to thank Houston for its generosity to the city after the storm), trailed by the "team gong," carried on a huge yoke by two men and used sparingly.

The band played "House of the Rising Sun," the anthem of so many of the country's prodigal sons and daughters who found their way here, in a rousing, drawn-out rendition more in the manner of Lead Belly than of the Animals. This version hit its dramatic peak, with all members of the band giving their full emotional intensity, when the song reached the sorrowful lyrics, "Oh mother, tell your children / Not to do what I have done / Spend your lives in sin and misery / In the House of the Rising Sun."

As with so many things, the national press got the Ninth Ward Marching Band wrong. In the *New York Times*, Adam Nossiter, who lives here and therefore should know better, bemoaned "Hurricane Katrina's cruel demographic shift," using the band as fodder to make his point: "Another group styled itself the Ninth

Ward Marching Band, but it was almost all-white—clearly com-
memorative, rather than representative, of what had been a black
neighborhood, now gone. The band members wore military-
style helmets with '9' on them. The once-obscure Ninth Ward is
now a world-famous war zone."[2] Especially in an article that was
centered on the tragedy of the changing cultural landscape of the
city, it was disappointing and ironic to see the "national paper of
record" dismiss a cultural community of long standing simply because it did not correspond to a notion, born of ignorance, about
the cultural and geographic complexity of the city's neighborhoods.

But the *New York Times*, CNN, and other news outlets that
lazily misconstrued our odd and wonderful city were worlds away
as the Ninth Ward Marching Band played the world's first ever
big brass version of the Scorpions' "Rock Me Like a Hurricane,"
to the mad joy of the people in the city's streets, who knew just
what that meant.

The parade closed with one final ornate purple float that bore
the face of a beautiful woman at its front, her long white hair
flowing back and adorned with small white flowers, a tear falling
from her eye. She was Mnemosyne, the goddess of memory and
the mother of the Muses. In black letters, beneath a trio of deli-
cate flowers, a banner read, "We Celebrate the Life, We Mourn
the Past, We Shall Never Forget."

MARDI GRAS DAY is always hard. The day starts early and is preceded by days of parades and drinking. Furthermore, there are always too many choices, some of which exclude others. For instance, although it's possible to catch the two biggest parades of
Mardi Gras, Zulu, the one black parade that runs down St.

Charles, and Rex, the most historic of the parades, it requires missing the Saint Anne Parade, a more ragtag, satirical, and independent parade and the only one that runs through the old Creole neighborhoods into the French Quarter. Though once we opted for the bigger parades, this year, like most, we chose the intimacy of Saint Anne, a parade of no more than a couple thousand people in which there is no distinction between the parade's spectators and its participants as the mass of people moves along the route. Unlike the other parades, which are costly and exclusive, the only qualification for participating in Saint Anne is knowing about it and showing up.

I had been invited to a party near the beginning of the parade in Bywater, where there were to be grillades and grits, and where, as the host explained to me, costumes were not required but "de rigueur." Although I love grillades, tender pieces of veal served with gravy over grits, usually for breakfast, my feelings about costumes are much less straightforward. What I have learned from Mardi Gras and Halloweens past, however, is that my reluctance to wear a costume or "to mask," as people say during Mardi Gras, stems from a desire not to stand out—and by going without a costume, I draw much more uncomfortable attention to myself. So I gathered together a blue sequined fez, a full-body disposable hazardous waste suit, and a pair of black suede shoes and called it a costume. Nikki, who falls into childlike rapture at the mere mention of a costume, tied silk fabric into her hair and wore a black cloth mask over her eyes, like Zorro, and mosquito netting draped over a loose orange dress. She strapped wings made of Saran Wrap and wire onto her back and called herself, with an enormous, pretty smile on her face, a "litter bug." In our costumes, we jumped on our bikes, two old, restored, English-made three speeds, at nine o'clock in the morning and rode the five miles downtown. Our progress was slowed by wind catching Nikki's wings and her netting tangling between the bicycle chain and the gear, but we arrived unscathed.

We milled around with others, people dressed as mold, FEMA trailers, and discarded, graffitied refrigerators, ate grillades and grits, and steeled ourselves for the long day. From there we made our way on our bikes to the R Bar on Royal Street and awaited the procession. At the R Bar we found Richard Bourke and Christine Lehmann, friends and colleagues, dressed in marital garb, Richard in a dark suit with a small red tie and a black fedora, Christine, beautifully large with child, in a classic white wedding dress and veil. Their faces were painted white with black eyes and mouths in the manner of Dia de los Muertos. I shared a beer with Death, and we wandered a block closer to the river to Chartres Street, where we found Saint Anne, in full regalia, clearly identifiable from the long poles, carried by paraders, hung with rings of streaming brightly colored ribbons blowing in the early spring breeze. We were surrounded by people, the dressed and the undressed, the wigged, the odd-hatted, and the bald, a vast array of gay men dressed as cowboys à la *Brokeback Mountain,* and every manifestation of Hurricane Katrina from hurricane plotting maps and maggots to an incomprehensible Federal Emergency Marie Antoinette.

As we entered the narrow streets of the French Quarter, flanked on both sides by filigreed Creole townhouses, with loud celebratory music coming from the bands, I began to feel as though we had liberated our city and were marching through the streets of the Quarter as American GIs did through the streets of Paris in 1944. I looked up and saw pigeons above, and wondered what they made of it all, this carnival of butterflies, cowboys, mold, and maggots. I thought back to what I had heard about earlier days of the parade, especially during the height of the AIDS scourge in the 1980s, when paraders would carry urns containing the ashes of loved ones who had paraded before, and, after a last posthumous dance down the streets of the Quarter, the ashes would be scattered over the great Mississippi. That's a great way to go: in your hometown, after an amazing parade in the arms of a friend, into the river that defined our country.

Nikki and I scurried off to the side of the parade and made our way back to Frenchman Street, where we had stowed our bicycles. On the way, we ran into our friend John Howell, whose grandmother in Shreveport had tailored him a suit made of the same blue plastic tarp material that sheltered most of the roofs in the city. He looked grand in what was the best of many variations on that theme. We met other friends at a bar on Frenchman, Zack LeBlanc, who had planned his King Cake Baby costume at a sad remove from his native New Orleans in his evacuation home in Austin, and his fiancée, Ana Arrien, my first New Orleans roommate seven years earlier, who wore a cape and a large papier-mâché star on her head. We all sat down for a quiet drink at the Apple Barrel Bar. After a couple of drinks, one of which the bartender spilled down the front of my hazmat suit, we got on our bicycles and rode to Basin Street, in hopes of finding the lingering remains of the Zulu parade and the black Mardi Gras celebration beneath the highway on Claiborne Avenue.

Despite rumors of its demise, black New Orleans was there in full force. Blocks and blocks in either direction were filled with young, middle-aged, and old New Orleanians, dressed well and enjoying music and beer beneath the highway. As we approached, a man next to us swept the ground before a pretty woman, a stranger to him, as she walked toward the underpass and flashed him a smile. Alongside her, Nikki and I joined the crowd under the highway and watched the Zulu Second Liners strut up the street wearing gold and black outfits with matching umbrellas. The man next to us, a sharply dressed black man in his late twenties, wore a shirt with an overhead picture of throngs of people gathered near the recognizable Superdome. In bright letters, above the silk-screened photo, the caption read, "George Bush Doesn't Give a Shit about Black People." In this crowd, the message of the shirt was so self-evident that it seemed to evade comment or dissent. Two white people, however, one dressed as a hazmat fez boy and the other as a litter bug, stoked the interest of many, who asked to pose for photos with these intrepid folks who had come down to Basin Street and Claiborne Avenue. The revelry was cut short when the second line finished and the music was cut. The only sound that remained was the distinct voice of our mayor, Ray Nagin, who spoke with the relaxed, sometimes thoughtless, but well-intentioned manner of Huckleberry Hound, my favorite of the Hanna-Barbera cartoons.

Nagin began speaking about Tootie Montana, the "Chief of Chiefs" of the Mardi Gras Indians, who had died a year earlier at age eighty-two right after addressing the City Council on complaints of police misconduct at Indian events. He was a revered figure in the city, so much so that the huge crowd fell quiet and raised all variations of cups, cans, and bottles when the mayor proposed a toast to Tootie Montana. The mayor proclaimed, "He is the Big Chief, the Chief of All Chiefs," and—the biggest compliment one can pay a Mardi Gras Indian—"He was the prettiest." People yelled happily in agreement. The mayor paused, looking out at the faces in the crowd, and then said, "I'm glad to see that New Orleans is back." The crowd cheered. "Hail Tootie Montana," yelled the mayor, welcoming back many people whom the city had abandoned in a language that people in their Garden District living rooms five miles away would not understand.

WHILE THE MASSES were out on the streets enjoying a very raucous Mardi Gras, a different sort of Mardi Gras was underway in those Garden District homes and at exclusive gatherings and balls across the city. For the city's white elite, Mardi Gras is the culmination of the debutante season and an opportunity to show its gentility.

The celebration of Carnival in the days preceding Lent has existed in New Orleans almost since the beginning of the city, but Mardi Gras in its current form began in 1857, when a group of men from the city's finest families formalized the celebration and created the Mystic Krewe of Comus that paraded through the city. Comus took the motto *sic volo, sic iubeo*, Latin for "as I wish, I command." Other elites joined the party and created krewes of their own. The krewes of Rex and Momus were founded in 1872, and the Krewe of Proteus in 1882.[3] The men in these krewes belonged to the city's men's clubs—the Boston Club, the Louisiana Club, the Pickwick Club, all of which still exist today—and literally ran the city from their positions as bank presidents, lawyers, and power brokers of the cotton and agricultural markets. In those days, New Orleans was one of the biggest cities in the country and among the wealthiest.[4] Running the city meant something back then.

During Reconstruction, the krewes began the tradition of creating their own royalty: the men of the krewes would select one of their members to be king for the day and one of the wives or debutantes to be his queen. The royal court was made complete with maids and dukes. These men had lost the Civil War, and their interests had suffered with the emancipation of slaves and the Reconstruction governments that dominated postwar politics. A world gone wrong had taken their birthright and put scalawags and carpetbaggers in charge, so they created their own insular world in response, one that better reflected their antebellum reality.[5] For the next hundred years, these families harked back to the better days of the antebellum South, as they appointed pretend kings and queens while the city crumbled around them.

By the early 1990s, the city had become an economic backwater with few national businesses, and with high-paying jobs flowing out of the city during the oil bust. The elites had lost control of the city government decades earlier. They still owned their grand homes uptown and could brag at cocktail parties that Confederate heroes had slept there. They still sent their daughters to lessons to learn the proper use of a scepter or how to curtsy, and they still rode in parade floats as the people looked up from the street. But then even that was taken from them.

In 1991, New Orleans city councilwoman Dorothy Mae Taylor pushed legislation to ban unintegrated Mardi Gras krewes from using the city's streets and services for their parades. Her passion for integrating the krewes wasn't based on the Mardi Gras parades themselves, but on the belief that the social networks of the krewes and the related private clubs were where the real business of the city was done, and that racial and ethnic minorities were barred from accessing that business by the same walls that kept them from riding in the parades and appearing at the balls. Despite the opposition of the elites and their compatriots on the city council, the ordinance passed. James Gill, a muckraking columnist for the *Times-Picayune* and the author of *The Lords of Misrule: Mardi Gras and the Politics of Race in New Orleans*, commented, "I think you cannot deny that she is remembered among white people here as the vixen who tried to destroy Mardi Gras, and who to some extent succeeded."[6]

Of the four principal "old-line" parading Mardi Gras krewes, three—Comus, Momus, and Proteus—were aghast that the city council was involving itself in their "private" affairs and trying to pry open their societies, potentially compromising the secrecy that had defined these groups for generations. As their beneficence in providing entertainment at great personal cost was being questioned, these krewes met and decided that the city's streets would no longer be graced with their parades. As Gill reports in his book, the Krewe of Momus's official announcement typified the regal aloofness that the city's elites projected: "Momus, son of Night, God of Mockery and Ridicule, regretfully and respectfully informs his friends, supporters and his public that he will not parade on the streets of New Orleans on the Thursday evening before Shrove Tuesday, 1992, as he has customarily since 1872."[7] Similarly, Comus bowed out, explaining, "Comus finds Himself and His Mystical Krewe in a quandary as to whether or not their annual parade will be appreciated or indeed welcomed."[8]

By means of such pronouncements, the old-line krewes finally had themselves all to themselves, without the distraction of civic engagement, political responsibilities, or real business of any sort. They devoted themselves instead to maintaining tradition, holding grand balls, and reveling in fantasies in which they could be kings, their daughters could be queens, and everyone around them was the most select.

Rebecca Snedeker, a pretty, charming filmmaker in her early thirties, grew up in this set. Her family has long been a part of the old-line krewes, including those that no longer march because of the desegregation ordinance. Six generations of her family have been Carnival royalty, and her mother, grandmother, and great grandmother were Carnival queens. Her great grandfather was Rex, the King of Carnival, who receives the key to the city each Mardi Gras. Disappointed with the krewes' response to the ordinance, Rebecca rejected her birthright and resolved not to make her debut, thus giving up her chance at the queen's crown. Instead, she produced and directed the documentary *By Invitation Only*, about a Mardi Gras that very few get to see. In the film, she takes the viewer into balls, dressing rooms, parties, and dress shops to which she has access because "she's one of us."

Rebecca explained to me that little has changed in the community in which she grew up since she was a child. She told me that she could look through a list of second-grade students at the prestigious uptown private schools and guess with some certainty, from their last names, which little girls would be Mardi Gras queens eleven years later upon coming out as debutantes during their junior year of college. Conversely, she could tell me which girls need not apply, because things have changed so little over the years that if she didn't recognize your family name, your little girl was unlikely ever to be a Carnival queen.

While making the film and contemplating the culture in which she was raised, Rebecca alternated between believing that the Carnival tradition was racist and believing that the insular culture from which she came was no different from insular groups of like-minded friends and families around the country who simply don't challenge their own identities and narrow surroundings. When she found herself overly concerned about offending her elders, she would steel herself by looking at a recent ball invitation that mocked the idea of changing the names of New Orleans streets to honor civil rights leaders. Melpomene Street had been changed to Martin Luther King Boulevard. Dryades Street had been changed to Oretha Castle Haley Boulevard, named after a pioneering woman in the civil rights movement who led a boycott to integrate the workforce there. Dryades Street was the only commercial area in the city that would sell goods to blacks, in a mostly black neighborhood, but where blacks were offered nothing but menial jobs. The white elite preferred the name Dryades for a street they would never drive down, named after fragile fruit tree nymphs of Greek mythology, who would die if they left their tree.

The text of the invitation, a poem called "Fools' Names in Public Places," ridiculed decades of progress of the civil rights movement in clever, rhyming couplets, in which it is suggested that naming something after Jesse Jackson would be a "foul or cursed course of action." The poem managed to demean leaders of the black community as varied as Martin Luther King and Spike Lee. (The poem jokes that Lee Circle, named for Robert E. Lee, could be named after "our Brother Spike.") The drama of the poem is resolved, however, when the narrator of the poem realizes that New Orleans already has a black monument, Monkey Hill. It is located in Audubon Park near the zoo on what used to be the highest point in New Orleans. Rebecca was told when she was a girl that Monkey Hill took its name from the black children who played there. The poem ends merrily, "The cheers began, the bells did peel and everyone proclaimed, That no good reason did exist to anything rename. So with [this god], [this goddess], and their elves one and all, Let's dance and make merry at this [Mardi Gras] ball."

This was not a party that Rebecca would ever want to attend—that any thinking person would want to attend—but the invitation was accepted by a number of people whom Rebecca describes as "good" and "civic-minded," who enthusiastically dressed up in costume and suspended their disbelief. She is quick to point out that these people endorse the content of the racist invitation just by showing up, even if it isn't what they intended.

Rebecca told me that the majority of people in these clubs and krewes have a deep love of New Orleans, and, if not for their affection for the city, they could have moved to the suburbs years ago or to other cities where they could make more money. Her uncle so loves his home that he hired a team of Israeli paratroopers to come in by helicopter in the days after Hurricane Katrina to protect his block, Audubon Place, the toniest street in town. (Rebecca's father, responding to her distress at the prospect of losing her unfinished film to flood, fire, or looting in the days after the storm, suggested that she ask her uncle to have the paratroopers retrieve the only copy from her Oak Street editing studio, but she refused to ask, feeling that she would rather lose the work of six years of her life than exploit the troubling privilege that the film itself sought to understand.) Even if we believe that the elites really do love New Orleans, it is hard not to believe also that their self-love, expressed in their insularity, destroyed the city by resisting the natural changes and cross-pollination that would have brought fine minds and businesses to the city, that would have maintained a vital and energized commercial culture in the city that would have meant real jobs for working people and a tax base that could have paid for decent schools, housing, and other public institutions. Instead, after a century of culture in which you could get a business loan or a position in the boardroom of a New Orleans bank or corporation only if you were a member of the club, there are almost no New Orleans banks or corporations. As my friend commented in response to a local news report that suggested that New Orleans was back to business, "That means no business." At least there are still clubs and krewes for playing make-believe.

ON ASH WEDNESDAY, the day after Mardi Gras, I went to the Shrine of St. Jude, a little Catholic church named for the patron saint of hopeless causes. I walked into the shadowy church, past people kneeling behind the pews, no doubt praying for our city and for their scattered friends and loved ones whose lives had been destroyed. I waited in a short line as people peeled off to the sides with dark ash smudges on their brows. When I got to the front of the line, I looked up and saw the Virgin and Christ, before my view was blocked by the priest's hand. As his soft finger rubbed a cross on my forehead, he said in a low voice, "Remember, man, that you are dust and unto dust you shall return."

CHAPTER 20

Hard Lot

FEMA Trailer Park, Gonzales, Louisiana

DAN BRIGHT TOLD ME that to find his FEMA trailer, provided to him after his New Orleans home was destroyed by Hurricane Katrina, I should get on the highway toward Baton Rouge, drive about fifty miles to the first Gonzales exit, make a right, than another right at an Exxon station, go a few miles, and the trailer park would be on the right. "It's a long row of trailers in a field. You can't miss it." He told me that once I turned into the park I would pass about a quarter mile of trailers before I reached his, Lot 24. I knew he'd been having car problems, so I asked how he'd gotten by so far out of New Orleans, miles away from any town, without a car. "Things ain't been easy," he replied.

Early in 2006, Dan and fifty other New Orleans families were told that they were being given trailers by FEMA. They were also told that the only place they could put the trailers was in Gonzales, a town of about ten thousand people, nearly an hour's drive outside of New Orleans, that has grown in recent years as small suburban developments sprouted up in the green farmland, a short commuting distance from Baton Rouge. The town is just down the road from Hunt Correctional Center, where Dan had been held the previous September following a nightmarish experience in the Orleans Parish Prison. He tried to have his trailer placed in the yard of his mother's flooded Lower Ninth Ward home, but officials weren't allowing trailers in that neighborhood. Other communities closer to the city, including many unflooded

New Orleans neighborhoods, had successfully resisted efforts by FEMA to create trailer parks for evacuees. Hearing that Gonzalez, a place of bass boats and Dixie flags, was "nice and peaceful," and knowing that there was no affordable housing left in New Orleans, Dan accepted the trailer and tried to make the best of yet another imperfect situation.

The people of Gonzales, the Jambalaya Capital of the World, did not greet their new neighbors with steaming pots of the town's signature dish, but rather with a petition for a temporary restraining order to stop the placement of the trailers and to prevent families from moving in. The plaintiff named on the petition was Megan Bell, a white twenty-three-year-old mother and president of the homeowners association in Chase Court, a subdivision on a cul-de-sac with an etched stone sign and ye-olde-style wrought iron mailboxes that backs up against the Oak Place Trailer Park, which FEMA had rented and readied for trailers. When she was asked about the lawsuit by the *Gonzales Weekly*, she explained her position: "The ultimate goal is to shut down the trailer park. This started out as an emotional issue, a neighborhood security and property value issue, but the deeper we dig the more we prove that it is not supposed to be in existence."[1] She worried that the trailer park would make the neighborhood so unsafe that children would no longer be able to play there or walk down the street. She was not alone in this concern, as was clear when more than two hundred angry residents showed up to the normally sleepy city council meeting, "bombarded" the council and parish president Ronnie Hughes with "catcalls and insults," insisted on criminal background checks for the evacuees and a determination of whether any sex offenders were moving in, and demanded that the council revoke the permit for the trailer park.[2]

Hughes attempted to defend the trailer park on moral grounds. He appealed to the residents by pointing to the golden rule and asking, "If Katrina had been a direct hit on Ascension Parish, what would we expect neighboring parishes to do?" He asked the crowd what Jesus would do in the same situation, with so many faultless, needy people on his doorstep. The crowd had no patience for such reasoning. One resident exclaimed, "And what would Jesus do? Jesus tells me to help myself, and, Ronnie, if Ascension Parish got flooded, you know what I'd do? I'd go to work somewhere else, and I'd buy a trailer."[3] The crowd was so pleased at his remarks that everything he said from then on was drowned out by applause. Apparently, the uproar convinced Hughes that allowing the displaced families to move to town was a mistake. A couple of weeks later, he sent a letter to FEMA unsuccessfully attempting to revoke his previous agreement to allow the trailers to be placed in Ascension Parish, explaining that "this housing is causing an intolerable situation in our parish" and the parish was not able to take on the fifty additional families because it had "inadequate infrastructure."[4]

Unaware that Jesus was against providing housing for the victims of a terrible storm, a district court judge denied the request for a restraining order. The evacuated families moved in once FEMA provided plumbing, electricity, and air conditioning for the new trailers.[5]

Whatever people were so worried about was not evident when I turned past the "No Trespassing" sign off of Highway 621 into the trailer park. There was no one to be seen under the bright white, hot July sun along the dusty gravel driveway extending a half mile down, with fifty brand new identical trailers placed in a row, interspersed with freshly painted yellow and green fire hydrants, along the right side of the road that ended at a large, old live oak. The otherwise identical trailers were dolled up by their new residents with "welcome" wind chimes, plants, flowers, and trellises to make them feel more like home.

Standing on new wooden steps up to his trailer, Dan told me that he likes the peacefulness of the trailer park and enjoys seeing his sweet twelve-year-old twin girls playing in the woods next to the park when they visit. He is trying to see the positive and is grateful for the help he has received. When pressed, he told me, "I think that things could be better, but I'm not one to be whining and crying."

Despite his stoicism, difficulties do abound. For Dan, the hardest part of living in Gonzales is "not always being there" for his family in New Orleans, including his two little girls, who are attending school in the city while living with their grandmother. A close second is the fact that Dan's car has been on the fritz and, even after a loan that allowed him to make costly repairs, it costs him twenty-five dollars in gas to make it back and forth to New Orleans. So although Dan is eager to work, doing anything from gutting houses to helping his electrician father—the kind of work that is in great demand in New Orleans—he has been effectively shut out of these jobs since moving into the trailer. Especially before he was able to get his car repaired, his living situation had driven him into a forced dependency, reminiscent of his years of wrongful imprisonment: "There is a difference between having a home and living in a trailer temporarily. It's like I am back in the cell depending on everybody but myself."

Dan was aghast to hear that his trailer had cost FEMA approximately sixty thousand dollars. He was certain that he could have spent the money better himself, using some of it on a down payment for a permanent home back in New Orleans and the balance to start up a business in a town that will be booming with building needs for a decade.[6]

He isn't about to give up, however. He plans to move back to the city to be with his family as soon as possible. He has received some money from a charity and is using it to buy equipment for a tree service business that he is starting. He proudly showed off the brightly colored signs that he planned to post around town in New Orleans to drum up business for his tree service. After so much struggle, he is determined to make it work.

As I was leaving Dan's trailer, I met a young woman unloading groceries for her grandmother, who lived next door to Dan, and then some little girls tying ribbons in each other's hair as they sat in the grass in front of the door of another trailer, everyone biding their time until they can finally go home, or make a home elsewhere.

Beyond the half-built fence separating the Oak Place Trailer Park from the neighboring Chase Court subdivision, Megan Bell and other residents have conceded that their fears about their New Orleans neighbors were not realized. Kids could still play in their yards. Not one had been sexually molested. Bell admitted, "It's not as bad as we figured. It's not. I can't say it is."[7] She explained that she would like to have a picnic with her new neighbors if they are willing, but had been put off from going to meet anyone in Oak Place to make arrangements because of a recently posted "No Trespassing" sign at its entrance. Although the sign may have frustrated plans for a picnic for the moment, Megan should have plenty of opportunities to meet her new neighbors in court, where her lawsuit to close the trailer park was still moving forward.

CHAPTER 21

La Nueva Orleans

Waiting for Work, Claiborne and MLK

UNDER THE HOT LATE-MORNING SUN, men are gathered, waiting for work, occasionally talking but mostly still, in the shade of a row of trees running up the neutral ground on Martin Luther King Boulevard near Claiborne Avenue. Across the street, two stalwarts of New Orleans cooking, Ms. Hyster's Barbeque, a restaurant that doubles as a gospel music retailer and a de facto campaign office for local politicians, and Gloria's Place, an eight-foot-wide shed that has sold hot-plate lunches of meat, collards, and yams to workers under a highway ramp for years, have struggled to reopen in this crumbling commercial drag that took more than five feet of water during Hurricane Katrina. Another black-owned business, Alexis Fried Chicken, which used to serve amazing chicken cooked to order out of a cramped little storefront, still sits with its door broken open and a dark waterline across its windows. Meanwhile, closer to the neutral ground, a white box truck with "El Chaparral" emblazoned on its side in orange and yellow graffiti is doing brisk business selling tacos and tropical fruit juice. A block away, men wait in line at another truck with a piece of neon orange cardboard with "comida mexicana" written in Magic Marker above a list of offerings. A couple of blocks farther, the scene repeats itself at another truck with El Salvadoran, Mexican, and American flags painted on the side and a large neon "open" sign glowing on the inside of the windshield. Street life and business have returned here on North Claiborne Avenue, but the scene, the voices, and the smells of cooking food would have been hard to anticipate before the storm.

Since Hurricane Katrina, it is estimated that nearly thirty thousand Latino workers, almost all male, many illegal immigrants, have made New Orleans their new home.[1] They came with the promise of good jobs and high wages and brought their own cultures and ways into a city that, maybe more than any other place in America, has been fixed in its ways for a long time. But these men are not the first Latinos to call New Orleans home.

Fifty years ago, immigrants from Honduras began trickling into this otherwise black and white city. They were brought to New Orleans because of the city's historic ties to the Caribbean, and specifically to Honduras, through the fruit trade. New Orleans was the port of entry for nearly all of Honduras's exported fruit and the home of its two biggest fruit companies, United Fruit, later known as Chiquita, and Standard Fruit, later known as Dole. Combined with these ties, the city's historic Catholicism and its tropical climate made it an attractive environment for Hondurans fleeing fruit strikes and civil war (both, no doubt, caused in large measure by these corporations). These new immigrants settled into a community in New Orleans's Lower Garden District, only about ten blocks from the corner of Claiborne and Martin Luther King, which they named El Barrio Lempira, after a Lenca Indian chieftain who unified native tribes to fight the Spanish and for whom the Honduran national currency was named.[2] As these families found success in their new home, they followed other middle-class groups out into the suburbs surrounding the city. It is on otherwise soulless suburban strips like Williams Boulevard in Kenner that New Orleans feels most international.[3] The little shopping centers along this street are filled with businesses oriented toward Latinos, businesses such as CA$A DE ENVIO$, which transfers money back to "America Latina," and doubles as a "Latino American Barber Shop," where one can get a haircut from "Big Lenzo," an "International Barber," according to the neatly painted sign on the glass window. A few blocks down at the Kenner Grocery, a Latino food store and restaurant with "serviendo platos tipicos centroamericanos" painted beneath a setting sun and palm tree on its window, business was brisk, with a number of cars from Georgia, Texas, and Mississippi parked in its lot. Women perused the aisles, buying plaintains, limes, and fajita meat, while men, just off work, drank Tecate and ate big plates of carne asada, rice and beans, and other specialties. The grocery's strip mall neighbor, the Gigante Express, Central America's Western Union, is also doing well. In short, according to everyone along this strip, business is better than ever, as it is at other outposts of Latino culture in the metropolitan area. People who were initially in New Orleans as temporary workers are becoming settled here, bringing families and friends, and creating homes for themselves.

For the men at Martin Luther King and Claiborne, a stable home is a distant fantasy that comes only in dreams as they sleep, five or more to a room, in barely habitable motels that a year ago used to rent by the hour. Many even less fortunate live on the streets, including a handful of men living in an old, abandoned industrial site a few blocks off of Claiborne, their laundry hanging on lines between I-beams that support a rickety metal roof. In a city where most of the housing stock was rendered uninhabitable by the storm, rents have doubled, apartments are scarce, and people are forced to make do.

The lack of housing isn't the only obstacle facing these men struggling to make a living as they rebuild New Orleans. Wage theft, unsafe workplaces, a lack of health care, harassment from law enforcement, and the constant threat of deportation for those workers who are here illegally complete the landscape.

A workers' rights report illustrated these issues by explaining the struggle of twenty-eight-year-old Tomás Hernandez, a Salvadoran man who left a $5.50-an-hour factory job in New York after hearing on Spanish-language television about better job opportunities in New Orleans.[4] The work he found was dangerous, inconsistent, and not nearly as well paid as he had expected. He cleaned flooded homes, full of mold, toxic sludge, and dead animals, for bosses who rarely provided any gear—gloves, respirators, eye protection—to protect the health of the workers. But at least he was getting paid, allowing him to send what little he earned back home to El Salvador to support his mother and father. Many of his friends were not as lucky and had worked jobs only to have bosses disappear or refuse to pay them at the end of the day or week. He lived with several other Salvadoran men in a house without electricity, where he had been harassed by police. One night a group of officers came into the house while he slept, shined a light on him and his friends, and forced the group to raise their shirts to see if they had any tattoos of the Maras gang, the Salvadoran branch of MS-13 (which the FBI has named the most dangerous gang in the world). They did not. As the police were leaving, one of the policemen offered the men a job cleaning up his house and then picked them up the next morning. Tomás missed his family terribly, lived in fear of "la Migra" (immigration), and struggled to get by in his new home. Back in El Salvador, he used to do "many different things"—he used to be a radio personality, he used to sing in a tropical music band, he danced, he loved art—but he came to America so he could take care of his family. Now, life was different. "Mi vida es puro trabajo" (My life is just work), he explained.

For all of their toil and difficulty, and the ultimate necessity of their labor if the city is ever to make any real progress in rebuilding, these workers suffer not only the insults attendant on exploitation by greedy, untrustworthy employers and the lack of housing and services, but also must bear the official disdain of people like Mayor Nagin, who in his ugliest days of electoral pandering in the fall of 2005, asked a group of businessmen, "How do I ensure that New Orleans is not overrun by Mexican workers?"[5]

Nagin's voice is small and insignificant, however, compared to the shrill and powerful voices on the political right that are defining the national conversation on immigration. People like Jim Sensenbrenner, a Wisconsin congressman, and Tom Tancredo, a Colorado congressman, have staked out a hard-right position demanding that illegal immigrants, their employers, and the welfare and church workers who assist them all be thrown in jail as felons, and that anyone who comes here illegally never be given an opportunity to become an American citizen.[6] Legislation reflecting this position was passed by the House of Representatives in late 2005, setting the stage for declaring more then ten million people living in the United States to be criminals for their attempt to live the American dream, the same impulse for a better life that populated the United States with immigrants for four centuries. This radical proposal for harshly criminalizing illegal immigration comes on the heels of resurgent fears of immigrants following September 11 as well as highly publicized efforts like the Minuteman Project, gunslinging vigilantes who have taken the law into their own hands and patrol the southern border of the

United States to "protect the homeland." All of this activity ignores the central question in New Orleans, however, where worker shortages have already slowed a recovery that is expected to take at least a decade. According to the economist Tyler Cowen, the answer to Nagin's question about how to keep "Mexicans" and other Latino workers out of the city is clear and succinct: "Do not rebuild."[7]

Jihad couldn't be further from the thoughts of the men milling around one Sunday afternoon, eating complimentary pizza and listening to traditional Mexican music, at the "Safety and Health Fair for Workers" sponsored by the Hispanic Apostolate, a local Catholic organization founded by the city's Honduran population in the 1970s to assist a wave of Cuban immigrants to the city. The fair, publicized on La Fabulosa and Radio Tropical Caliente, the city's Spanish-language AM radio stations, and on flyers handed out at Latino lunch trucks and worker pickup corners around the city, brought hundreds of workers to a group of tents set up immediately next to St. Joseph's Church, a massive and imposing brick church standing several stories tall near the central business district. The men were drawn there to get free work gloves, rubber boots, hard hats, and protective glasses and masks—safety equipment necessary for their gutting, construction, and remediation jobs around the city, but hard to come by—and to find out about services available to help them with issues concerning immigration, housing, and workplace abuses. The social workers from the Apostolate were attempting to address various crises among these workers: people unable to find housing who were living on the streets, or some living with their families and children in cars or trucks; people being cheated by a new industry of opportunists who were selling worthless and invalid driver's licenses or other "services" to this emerging underground population; and people who were routinely being exploited out of wages earned with the sweat that is rebuilding the city. The social worker assisting workers with claims told me that of the hundreds of workers she had assisted, "I can count on the fingers of two hands the people who *haven't* had wages stolen." Simultaneous with the crisis among workers, however, there was also an emerging sense among the old-school Latino New Orleanians arrayed to provide these services that Latinos were finally being recognized as a socially and politically important group in this city that has existed under several different flags, but is perceived internally and externally as being culturally and racially binary—black and white.

My friend Alfredo Moran, who resurrected my house from the dead when we bought it several years ago and then again after Hurricane Katrina ripped off the roof, necessitating a wholesale replacement of the interior walls, has been in New Orleans for eighteen years and in the United States for more than twenty. He was forced to leave El Salvador when it became clear to him in the early 1980s that his schooling was going to have to end in his joining either the leftist guerillas in the jungle or the right-wing military. Finding both options unattractive, he set off on foot through Guatemala and Mexico into the United States. Alfredo, a respected craftsman who is well on his way to becoming a citizen, faced many of the horrors from which today's immigrants are suffering. He was bitten by a poisonous snake and nearly died in a Texas desert while attempting to evade the border patrol. He has worked for weeks, only to have his boss call Immigration once payday rolls around. But he is clear on why he came here, and why people still come: "We come here to work hard. Even more so when we come illegally." Alfredo is living the dream of many of those who have come to New Orleans following Hurricane Katrina. He is his own boss and owns a successful business. He is able to provide work for his brother, his brother-in-law, and a large crew of other workers, black, white, and Latino, whom he pays generously. He is married and has two small boys. He owns his own home, a nice car for his family, and a sleek black truck for his business.

Alfredo is used to people assuming that he is Mexican, and used to explaining to people he meets for the first time that he has lived in New Orleans for almost two decades and restored scores of classic New Orleans homes. He is also aware that people here tend to think that Latinos are all transients and that the recent influx of Latinos is merely temporary. Without question, Alfredo is here to stay. He boarded up many homes before the storm for customers who couldn't do so for themselves, and he has gutted and rebuilt homes since the storm, including numerous homes for which he charged less than his costs to elderly people in our Central City neighborhood whose lack of means meant that other contractors wouldn't even call them back. In the very best sense, Alfredo and the men he works with are New Orleanians, no less than the second liners, the debutantes, the jazz musicians, and the Mardi Gras kings.

The question remains open whether the many Latino men who have come to the city will stay, bring their wives and families, make this their home, and become New Orleanians themselves. If it is any indication, over at Martin Luther King and Claiborne, El Chaparral is moving out of its truck and into the brick and mortar storefront of an otherwise run-down and lifeless gas station. This is the new home of El Patio Chaparral, and business is booming.

CHAPTER 22

Yours in Struggle

Katrina Anniversary, Lower Ninth Ward Levee Breach

"The short of it is," said the knight, "whatever way you put it, these people are being taken there by force and not of their own free will."

"That is the way it is," said Sancho.

"Well, in that case," said his master, "now is the time for me to fulfill the duties of my calling, which is to right wrongs and come to the aid of the wretched."

Cervantes, Don Quixote

WHEN I ASKED NIK BOSE, a nineteen-year-old college student from Long Island who was working with the Common Ground Collective, an organization that has worked tirelessly on the recovery of marginal New Orleans neighborhoods since Hurricane Katrina, why she had come to New Orleans, she had two responses: "One, because I can, because of privilege. Two, because there was no reason not to." She had come to New Orleans five months earlier for a week. When I talked to her, she still had no clear plans to leave, finding personal and political meaning in her work gutting homes. She was looking for actors for a street performance of the play *I Am Rachel Corrie*, the story of a twenty-three-year-old American activist who was killed by an Israeli army bulldozer while trying to block the demolition of a home in Gaza. She thinks that people here would find meaning in it.

Like the other large charity groups working in the city, Common Ground has attracted tens of thousands of volunteers from around the country to gut homes, clean up neighborhoods, and attempt to assist residents recovering from Hurricane Katrina. Unlike most other organizations, however, Common Ground has a decidedly counterculture front, attracting mostly white progressives from across the country, including leftists, hippies, radicals, anarchists, and punks. It was born of the storm, finding its beginnings in the crazy days immediately following Hurricane Katrina, a tale that has taken on the character of a creation myth among its adherents. "In the beginning, after the Great Flood, there were two Black Panthers, two young Texans with radical politics, and fifty dollars," their gospel would begin, a story repeated in loops, several hours a day, on a pirate radio station established in the Lower Ninth Ward after the storm.

Recently returned from Venezuela, where he had been invited by Hugo Chávez's "revolutionary" government because of Common Ground's work for New Orleans's poor, Brandon Darby, one of the organization's founders, explained the origins of Common Ground at an outside table of a Faubourg Marigny café, where we sat in the hot summer sun as he chain-smoked. He is a broad young man in his twenties, with a soft, gentle, singsong voice.

"It started when I came back here to get my friend," Brandon began. He and his friend, Scott Crow, were living in Austin before the storm, and in the days immediately afterward they attempted to track down people in New Orleans they cared about. They discovered that their friend Robert "King" Wilkerson, a former Black Panther who had spent nearly three decades in solitary confinement at Angola Prison as one of a group of men called the Angola Three, remained trapped in his home in the flooded Mid-City neighborhood. Several New Orleans progressive activists began to "organize" to go back to the city to get King, a well-known personality in national progressive activist circles who has addressed the parliaments of several European nations and met with Bishop Desmond Tutu in South Africa. King was well known locally both for radical activism and for selling pralines—"freelines" he calls them—made from a recipe he perfected in solitary confinement. He sells the pralines to support himself and his activist effort to free the two other former Panthers who remain in solitary confinement in Angola for what he believes was a wrongful conviction for the murder of a prison guard in the early 1970s. Brandon and Scott eschewed the "process" and "meetings" the others wanted to have to determine the best course of action, instead traveling to New Orleans with a boat. After being blocked by the military in their effort to get downtown through the city, Brandon and Scott attempted another approach to King's house through Lake Bourgne, essentially a lagoon of the Gulf of Mexico that abuts eastern Orleans Parish and St. Bernard Parish.

In a flat-bottom boat and with little maritime experience between them, they took to the stormy and choppy gulf and found their way into Lake Pontchartrain and then down the Industrial Canal. They had heard of a gunfight on a bridge farther down the canal, where people on the bridge were said to have shot at and attempted to take other boats as a means of escape. Brandon thought that as "white men with resources and a boat" they were in danger, and although they were armed with a handgun and "delirious" about getting to their friend, they were frightened. So they holed up for the night in an abandoned warehouse. The next day on the radio they heard an order for all search-and-rescue boats to turn back because of the rising violence in the city. Reluctantly, they turned back as ordered, "leaving in shame" without their friend, and returned to Austin the following day.

Back in Austin, they received a call from Malik Rahim, another former Black Panther and New Orleans community activist, who had remained in his home in New Orleans's unflooded west bank. Malik put out a call for assistance, requesting food, water, and guns and ammunition to fight back "white racist militias" that, he said, were policing the streets of the west bank and terrorizing black men, whom they uniformly viewed as looters, cornering them on the streets with assault rifles and handcuffing them with plastic zip ties. Although Brandon is quick to point out that he does not see himself as a "violent revolutionary," he and Scott came back to New Orleans "heavily armed" with the supplies that Malik asked for, and ready to do whatever was necessary. Malik's home was established as a "base of operations." Along with others, they went out armed with semiautomatic weapons and high-powered rifles to confront the white militias. Brandon and Scott were able to communicate to the militias that their efforts in Malik's neighborhood were no longer wanted and wouldn't be tolerated. According to Brandon, adopting the language of war, there was a "stand down."

Brandon's next order of business was to help King, whom he had failed to reach a week earlier. He got as close to King's house as he could in his car and then took off on foot when he reached the high water from the levee breach. When the water got too high to walk in, he swam. Resting on top of a submerged car, he was approached by a boat full of National Guardsmen who were patrolling for survivors. Believing that he was waiting to be rescued, they tried to help him into the boat, but he refused, telling them that he was trying to reach his friend. They responded that if he got in, they would get his friend later. Brandon, whose thin trust for law enforcement had only diminished with what he had seen since the storm, refused, saying, "I am not leaving this spot until you go get my friend." They didn't call him on it or try to overpower him and instead went and found King, who was waiting on his porch. When the guardsmen returned with King to pick up Brandon, King told him, "I knew y'all would come."

Together, Malik, King, Scott, and Brandon decided to start Common Ground with the idea, reflected in the name, that they could bring together people from different backgrounds and orientations—from anarchists to Catholics—to address the issues that Hurricane Katrina created for poor communities in New Orleans. Though for Brandon this initially entailed buying an AK-47 and readying for "guerilla warfare" with the New Orleans Police Department as well as Blackwater (a private security firm), the Bureau of Alcohol, Tobacco, and Firearms, and other groups that had been brought into the city to restore order, fortunately it did not come even close to this—there was much more need for hazmat suits, respirators, and hammers than for guns in the organization's struggle to serve poor New Orleanians.

Among Common Ground's first actions were the establishment of a health clinic in the west bank neighborhood of Algiers and the creation of the Ninth Ward Project, an effort to thwart a perceived "land grab" that Common Ground believed lurked beneath the land use discussions that suggested the use of eminent domain in poor, flood-damaged neighborhoods.

With a small group of volunteers, Common Ground put a flyer on nearly every door in the Ninth Ward, eleven thousand homes in all. With a hammer in a black hand pictured in the upper left corner, the pamphlet announced, "Welcome Home Ninth Ward! Cooperation and Mutual Aid! Solidarity not Charity!!" The flyer introduced Common Ground and explained its intentions.

> The Common Ground Collective is based in Algiers. We are comprised of local and outside volunteers. Our lives are dedicated to working toward social justice for all peoples. We see that there was great inequality before the storm in the ninth ward. We believe this inequality continued during the storm, and we see that this inequality is continuing NOW, after the storm. . . .

This is a determining time for residents of the Ninth Ward. It is critical that the residents return home. Common Ground will aid local efforts in the creation of services and share a common vision of cleaning up and rebuilding the Ninth Ward. It will not be comfortable at first, but needs will be met. WE WILL SURVIVE this by WORKING TO-GETHER.

If we all work together to clean and rebuild, and work through the discomfort, we can keep the ninth ward community in the hands of those who live here. In order for this to happen, residents must return and be willing to help and communicate with each other. Only then can we work towards establishing a ninth ward free medical clinic, distribution center, and volunteer work crews to remove trash, and volunteers to help rebuild and repair damaged homes.

For thousands of people returning to devastated homes and empty neighborhoods, the flyers welcomed them home and offered a vision of their neighborhood's future that took issue with the dominant voices at the time, which called for a moratorium on rebuilding in much of the Ninth Ward. The day after the first flyers were posted, Brandon received his first call from a resident who had found his number on the bottom of the flyer. She wanted to know about having her house gutted. The next day there were another two calls. On the third day there were more than seventy calls, and after that Brandon stopped trying to keep track.

Given the community's response to Common Ground's offer of assistance, Brandon decided to locate volunteers directly in that community to establish both a distribution center where residents could get basic groceries and cleanup materials without having to drive a half hour across town to the open grocery stores in unflooded neighborhoods. He also created a dormitory for the volunteers who began flowing in to work. The volunteers were people who had been moved to help in New Orleans by what they had seen on television but who weren't interested in working with mainstream charities. They had heard about Common Ground, projected as a sort of alternative Red Cross, on left-wing radio, in the progressive independent press, and on the Internet. By Christmas, a small army of volunteers had gutted three hundred homes, had distributed tons of water and supplies, and had already established a presence in the Lower Ninth Ward, a neighborhood so badly damaged and so underserved that even a year after the storm, Common Ground volunteers were among the handful of people living in a neighborhood where more than ten thousand people had lived before Hurricane Katrina. In fact, Brandon was the first person to live in the most devastated portion of the Lower Ninth Ward when he rented and then gutted a small blue house not far from where the levee breached, a house that has since acted as the distribution center and base of operations for Common Ground in the Lower Ninth Ward. At this time there was still a curfew in the neighborhood that prevented residents from returning, but Brandon believed that because he was white and because he ran an organization that had lawyers and ready access to the local and national press, the curfew would not be enforced and the area would be opened to the neighborhood's real residents.

In talking to a number of people in Common Ground, it becomes clear that this mode of operation seemed to permeate the group's tactics and vision. Malik Rahim made this explicit in a video on Common Ground's Web site: "Brandon Darby used the fact that he was white, had white privilege, to make a difference in the black community. . . . If it was just residents, it would not have stopped the thing. But when they see that there were people there from all over the world, we can do this."[1]

In a manner that mirrors the internal struggles of past movements in which the groups with the most in common had the least capacity to work with one another, other progressive activist groups in New Orleans, especially those with black leadership, took umbrage at Common Ground's vision and its view of itself as being the boldest, most effective relief organization in New Orleans. In an "open letter" decrying the ineffectiveness of the People's Hurricane Relief Fund (PHRF), an organization founded by, among others, Curtis Mohammed, an old-school black activist who had been a Student Nonviolent Coordinating Committee organizer in the 1960s, Scott Crow wrote,

> PHRF in my humble opinion from the beginning has done little to NOTHING in the helping of NOLA [New Orleans, Louisiana] victims since the beginning of the disaster. They have raised a lot of money on the backs of work that many other groups really have done, and placed themselves in a position of visible, political power as the voice of the NOLA region when they have NOT done work in the region.

Scott went on to contrast the origins and efficacy of the two organizations:

> While we at (CGC) were fending off white armed militias, beginning our large scale food/water delivery, the first clinic, and cleaning dead dogs and debris out of the street, PHRF called ALL available activist organizers to Baton Rouge for a "power meeting". . . . This is when there were very few on the ground doing work. . . . After it was all said and done CLU/PHRF raised $150,000 without doing a single piece of work yet, while we at Common Ground with about 30

people on the ground doing real, dirty, work had collectively about $200. . . .

They have criticized CGC for mostly being a "white" organization and that we should not be doing this work. When we have repeatedly called for the "coalition" members to come and replace us they respectfully decline. Members have repeatedly told us to get out of here and work with our "own" people. When we ask: Who will do this? They never have an answer. . . .

In closing I want to say I do not want to see PHRF go away. I just want to see them actually do the work they are taking credit for and raising money about.

People at PHRF were not pleased. Shana griffin,[2] a thirty-one-year-old black mother who grew up in a New Orleans housing project and who worked with PHRF and other groups on women's issues, and Brice White, a white twelve-year New Orleans resident, DJ, and activist who had been working on environmental justice issues with PHRF, responded on the same e-mail listserv on which Scott's open letter had been sent:

We find it comically absurd as well as dangerous that you, a white male from Austin, Texas, would have such lessons and reprimands for a coalition group that is led wholly by Black people from Louisiana and Mississippi. . . .

What we find most disturbing about your open letter is the level of comfort you exhibit in challenging the leadership of a Black led multi-racial Coalition. You wouldn't go to Chiapas and critique the leadership of the Zapatistas, nor would you go to Palestine and critique the leadership of the Palestinians, yet you are very comfortable challenging the leadership of displaced Black residents of New Orleans and the Gulf Coast. Your remarks illustrate how out of touch with reality are the vast majority of activists, and in particular the loosely affiliated, overarchingly white, national anarchist scene. Nowhere is this clearer than . . . in the constant replaying of the heroic saga of rescue, guns, guts, and glory on pirate radio in New Orleans. In the months following Katrina, we have been forced to listen to this drivel replayed over and over again. Seemingly, the only purpose of this constant replay is to further support the myth of the great white liberators in the weeks after Katrina. . . .

These shady, divisive tactics, attempting to pit community members and comrades against each other remind us that with friends like these, we don't need COINTELPRO [the FBI's counterintelligence program from the 1960s and 1970s].

When I met with Brice, his anger at the failure of progressive groups to come together was still sharp. He attributed much of the trouble to the inability of new progressive organizations to break out of "the old molds of out of touch, white, left-wing organizations of the 1960s." He saw the Common Grounders as white, middle-class people coming down to New Orleans to "relive the dream" of the 1960s counterculture and antiwar movement, and perpetuating some of the same "outside/in, top/down" hierarchies that portrayed outside activists as heroes whose actions and images were projected while crowding out local community members who knew the issues best and who ended up getting stuck with the legacy of the outside activists' actions when they were long gone. Brice pointed to the Common Ground video and rejected with disgust comments like those that came from a volunteer from Maine who referred to Common Grounders as "freedom fighters" who are "making history" and "will be remembered for generations." Brice commented, "Damn that feels good to say doesn't it? It's even better to believe it."

Brice said that he believes that many of the people drawn to work with groups like Common Ground are running after that sense of wanting to be part of the new "radical movement." He heard these folks talking about the glory days of the Seattle World Trade Organization protest as the height of this movement. He rejected the idea that New Orleans should end up another Seattle, a city on a circuit for national groups and individuals to play out their "revolutionary experiments" when they couldn't "have cared less about New Orleans or the generations of revolutionary folks that lived here" before Hurricane Katrina. Although Brice was respectful of Malik, he felt that these outsiders were attempting to cloak themselves in his legitimacy but acting largely independently. His bitterness toward Common Ground centered on his perception that the organization was projecting a message in its fund-raising and informational materials that it was the only group doing anything in New Orleans—that its volunteers were the only ones gutting houses in the Lower Ninth Ward, doing distribution, or helping the poor—and that this diminished the sense that local people here can lead. He explained:

> The mantra that outsiders like to repeat and is constantly perpetuated by Common Ground is that nothing was going on before they got here. This is offensive and untrue. Things look different here and there is no liberal establishment that exists in a lot of other places like Austin, the Bay Area, and New England to gloss over the realities of racism and poverty in America. New Orleans is a raw place, before the storm and after, and despite the simple analysis of organizations like Common Ground, the roots of life and resistance to oppression run deep here. The residents of New Orleans need to guide their own self-determination and are doing so already,

just not always in the ways that outside folks may see or think is right. The most beneficial thing that could be done now is to clear out the space for residents to come home.

He sums up his feelings: "Common Ground? When are they leaving?"

When they are not attacking one another, these social justice groups have attempted to address significant discord stemming from the accusation of internal injustices. In its young life, Common Ground has already faced charges that the machismo of the organizational leadership created an environment that was hostile to women and that the organization failed to address significant complaints of both sexual harassment and sexual assaults among the volunteers. In spring 2006, Common Ground responded with formal policies condemning racism and gender discrimination and set out standards and practices for addressing these kinds of issues. The living and work environments for volunteers were also brought into question, with some volunteers complaining of toxic and unsafe work environments, as well as a dormitory for volunteers that has periodically had outbreaks of lice, staph infections, and giardia due to unsanitary conditions. Michelle Shin, a woman from Oakland who began directing the Lower Ninth Ward Project in 2006 after months as a volunteer, explained that many of the problems with sexual discrimination and violence as well as issues with the living environment stemmed largely from the unexpected success of the organization in bringing large numbers of unscreened volunteers from around the country into cramped living quarters, and that these issues had been addressed as the organization became more experienced in managing the volume of volunteers who staff its projects. She insisted that, as a woman in a leadership position, she felt respected within Common Ground and that the organization was an example of how a community-based organization should work. Regarding concerns that New Orleans would be better off without the organization, she agreed to an extent. She believed that poor people in New Orleans are better off because of the existence of Common Ground, but she also believed that the city and the organization will be even better off once community members take over jobs like hers. Despite the fact that it is still an all-volunteer organization, with no paid staff, that process seemed already to be underway down at the Common Ground House in the Lower Ninth Ward.

BY THE TIME you reached the high, rusty metal bridge on Claiborne Avenue that connects New Orleans to the Lower Ninth Ward, you had already seen your fair share of urban destruction rendered by Hurricane Katrina and decades of neglect. But as you reached the bridge's zenith and gazed out to your left, the landscape was like nothing you had ever seen in the United States. Blocks with homes strewn randomly where they used to sit neatly and orderly stretched for miles. Once you reached the Lower Ninth Ward, heading north into the neighborhood closest to the levee breach, it was even worse; the disarray was the same, but with the intimate details of peoples' lives more in evidence—destroyed record collections, molding dolls, and, saddest of all, rotting memorial flowers for the individuals who died there. As blocks were cleared of the remains of these lives, the concrete pilings that had held the houses remained, evenly spaced and a couple of feet high, like headstones.

The Common Ground House, painted bright blue, sat in the midst of all of this at the corner of Deslonde and Derbigny

Streets, only a few blocks from the levee breach. People bustled in and out, mostly white volunteers and mostly black residents seeking supplies or assistance, in the otherwise lifeless neighborhood. Under a blue tarp stretched out as a shade in front of an adjacent house that functioned as a distribution center, several black men and women sitting on rickety old metal chairs directed traffic and helped people find what they needed. A woman who appeared to be in her midfifties introduced herself to me as Miss Carol and told me that she was the "mother" of the volunteers down here. As proof, she pointed to a sign, made by some of the volunteers, reading "Ms. Carol is the mother here." She explained that she liked to spend time helping out at the distribution center because it made her feel good to be back in her neighborhood. Her house has been gutted but not yet rebuilt. She introduced me to Albert Bass, who, she said, was living around the corner.

Albert was a thin black man with a look of experience and a life of hard work, who was, nonetheless, probably younger than fifty. He had a short salt-and-pepper beard and close-cropped hair. The white of one of his eyes was filled with blood. He explained that, while driving a Common Ground truck the week before, he had been in an accident that left him with a broken jaw that needed surgery, but he was putting it off. He only smiled when I asked him if it hurt , but his smile was without derision or condescension. He told me that he had been with Common Ground for the past few months since his wife brought him down there to get something to eat. He had been living in his house, gutted by a church group a few months earlier, without water or electricity, and with no sheetrock on the walls. When he saw the energy of the people at Common Ground, he was inspired and "jumped in full force." Unable to find work in town as a dental technician, work he had done for two decades, Albert had been volunteering with Common Ground since his first visit and was about to be given a supervisory role, "running distro" for the Lower Ninth Ward Project. He talked about Common Ground as though it had saved his life, the way people newly off booze talk about Alcoholics Anonymous.

He invited me to see where he lived. We drove a few blocks to his house, but even in the minute or two it took, he pointed out several homes where people had died: "An old lady lived there. Didn't make it. A man and his wife lived in that house twenty-five years, drowned there. You see that house, it used to be a few blocks away. It's hard to see, but it is actually sitting on another house. My friend died in the crushed house." It was all expressed evenly, mentioned in passing as if it were normal. He had explained all this before.

His block, Andry Street between Roman and Prieur Streets, was dusty and still. All the houses were vacant. Almost none had been gutted, or even touched since the storm. "This used to be a normal, everyday neighborhood," he explained, breaking through the current picture to a time when people lived here. "My grandfather built this house in the 1930s. This is where my roots are."

He took us into the house. In the back corner, past wall framing and a length of buckled hardwood floor, was a mosquito netting tent where he had set up his bed. He had some canned food and a propane stove in what used to be a separate room but which, without the sheetrock, was just another area of the house a few feet from his bed. He walked us through and told us that on the day of the storm, he and his wife decided not to evacuate because they had waited until it was too late and had heard about the terrible traffic. Everything seemed fine at first, but on the Monday after the storm hit, he noticed that his toilet was overflowing in the bathroom. The next thing he knew, the water was rising in the house and his fridge began floating. He and his wife ran upstairs into the attic, and in little more than ten minutes from when he first noticed the toilet, water was up to his ankles in the attic. His wife started panicking, and as he looked around for a tool to cut through the roof, he noticed a knife and a crowbar sitting beside him on a table, things he swore he had never seen before in years of living there. I suggested that maybe his grandfather had put them up there for fear of flooding, and said it was good luck. He cut me off. "No. Not luck. God."

He worked his way through the roof with the knife and then widened the hole with the crowbar. He lifted his wife, and then himself, through the hole. When he got out, he saw his neighbors on their roofs and was happy to see that they had made it out alive. Later, a man from around the corner rescued them in a boat and brought them to a church. Albert and other men went through the water, found stores that had been broken into, and brought back food. The Coast Guard came to the church and began bringing people across the St. Claude Bridge, another bridge out of the Lower Ninth Ward into New Orleans. People gathered there for three days, unwilling to walk for miles to the Superdome or the Convention Center and repelled with guns when they attempted to cross back over the bridge. The group, including many elderly people from the Villa St. Maurice old folks' home, was there for three days, "looting" stores to survive, before they were picked up on buses and taken to Baton Rouge.

Albert told me that after all he had been through, he was desperate to see his neighborhood rebuilt and he believed that "these kids from Common Ground came here and saved this neighborhood." When I asked him about whether it mattered to him that so many of the volunteers and people associated with Common Ground were white, he answered pragmatically, "It's not about me. It's not about that white boy. It's about the Ninth Ward, and if Common Ground hadn't come, they could have taken a bulldozer and gone through the whole damn place."

Back at Common Ground, Albert took me into a back room and pulled out a long, slender object covered with plastic bags. He pulled the bags aside and exposed a piece of wood, shaped like a large painting, with a carving of a Spanish knight on a horse carrying a flag. "It's Don Quixote," Albert explained. "Someone gave it to me nine years ago in exchange for some dental work. Me and Don survived the storm, and now we're trying to make it home." Albert, a brave and dignified man who suffered greatly in the very real world, posed for a photo holding Don, the errant knight, his salvaged prized possession.

WEEKS LATER, I passed the Blue House and was greeted by Albert as I walked to the memorial at the point where the Lower Ninth Ward levee breached. An event was being held there, organized by a number of groups working together, including both People's Hurricane Relief Fund and Common Ground, to commemorate the one year anniversary of Hurricane Katrina. Albert smiled and said he would catch up with me later because he was busy making sure that there would be enough water for the hundreds, maybe thousands, of people who were expected to attend the memorial and the subsequent march to historic Congo Square.

As I got closer to the levee, groups of people, mostly black, were gathering. A man wearing a t-shirt with pictures, looking like mug shots, of George Bush, Dick Cheney, and Homeland Security Secretary Michael Chertoff, with the caption "Wanted for Murder" written below, looked out over the neighborhood, now almost completely cleared but for a few houses and some debris, and said to his friend, in a hushed tone, "It looks like a graveyard down here."

Mama Olayeela, a black storyteller and cultural activist in her sixties, dressed in flowing white robes, called out, "Ashé," the West African word for the power that permeates the universe and everything in it, quietly demanding the attention of the large group that had gathered around her. She said in a clear voice, loud enough so that everyone could hear her—the reporters and television cameras in close, the families clustered around her and those at the foot of the levee, and the onlookers: "So many of our brothers and sisters lost their lives, and we did not give them a proper burial. It is the duty of the living to take care of those who died." People began calling out names of people who died, some through tears, some with defiance, some in a whisper. "Leslie L. Robinson." "Caryann Brown." "Dawn Thomas." "Austin Leslie." "Estelle James."[3] With each name called, Mama Olayeela poured water on the ground from a Anheuser-Busch can of purified water, one of the nearly one million cans, resembling Budweiser and made by the beer company, that had been brought in by FEMA when food and water were still scarce in the weeks after the storm. When the string of calls ceased, Mama Olayeela said, "And those who are unnamed. Let them all feel the light in the other village they have gone to."

A few other speakers addressed the crowd gathered under the hot morning sun and were greeted with cheers after comments like, "The devils are trying to wash us away," "We need to help each other come home," and "It is our neighborhood, it is our land!"

After the speakers, the march began to gather at the foot of the levee, the ground zero of the destruction of the Lower Ninth Ward, at the corner of Jourdan and Galvez. The telephone pole on which homemade street signs hung was still tilted at a seventy-degree angle from the force of the water. The parade began as an old black hearse, which led the procession, started creeping down Galvez Street. Behind the hearse, two men marched with a wide NAACP banner, then two others with a Malcolm X banner, then people with all variations of signs insisting on "The Right of Return" and justice for the Ninth Ward expressed in innumerable other ways. Two black teenage boys walking near me, dressed in baggy pants, enormous black t-shirts, and baseball caps, spoke to one another sadly and earnestly. "It's hard to even figure out what block you lived on," one said, as he scanned the devastated landscape where he had lived his entire life until a year earlier.

Down the block I saw a black man in his thirties or forties, holding a sign with pictures of a neatly dressed elderly couple. Beneath the picture was written, "World's Greatest Grandparents." I asked him about the sign, and he told me that the storm had taken his grandparents, both one year short of eighty years old. He then pointed to the colorful writing on his t-shirt, "The Chain Has Been Broken, Only God Know Why, Gone But Not Forgotten," around three other photos of an elderly man, a middle-aged woman, and a young girl. "All these people died in Katrina," he explained, "four generations of my family." He looked as though he was about to cry, but he marched on in the ninety-degree heat.

Seeing me, a white man in the midst of a largely black memorial, writing in my little notebook, a black man with a video camera approached. With the camera close to my face, he asked, "Do you believe that what happened here was justice?"

"No," I responded, "I don't. Do you?"

"I believe it was injustice. But what are we going to do about it?"

Nervously, I considered his question and responded that all that had happened here was part of a bigger and longer struggle and that those who were touched by it would have to insist on change, just as in the past people had insisted on change.

He looked back at me incredulously. "With all this history, with all that has happened, you think *they* are ever going to change things? What you think that their word even means to us even if they promised change?" He walked away and pointed the camera at a little black girl a few feet away from me, and asked, gently, "Do you believe that what happened here was justice?" She was too nervous to answer.

A few blocks down I met a little boy who would have answered quickly in the negative. He looked seven or eight years old and stood a little more than four feet tall. He was holding a sign that read, "One Year Later, Where's the Help?" Next to him, his even younger, smaller little brother held a sign that read, "End Racism." When I walked up to the older brother and asked him his name and about his sign, he looked up at his grandmother for permission to talk to a stranger, and she nodded to him. "Anthony Lewis," he said quietly. "My sign means 'let us come home.'" He was born and raised in the Lower Ninth, like his grandmother, but had been living in Atlanta since Katrina. As young as he was, he looked weary.

At this point in the four-mile march, after we had crossed the

Industrial Canal and passed into the more functional but still decayed stretch of the city that runs into the French Quarter, everyone was tired, and the heat and distance had slowed the procession. Just then, I began to hear the loud sound of music. Looking around, I saw the Hot 8 Brass Band gathering at the front of the procession, taking the reins of the march from the hearse. As they started playing "Shoo Fly, Don't Bother Me," people began to dance and second-line behind them. Then, as if from nowhere, the Comanche Hunters, a tribe of Mardi Gras Indians, appeared dressed from head to toe in their full garb of feathers and beads, the chief holding a standard shaped like a big red nine. Suddenly, and not surprisingly in this city, the tragic, when it was at its worst, when it was almost unbearable, had turned joyous. The solemn march had become a parade and wilting marchers now looked full of life. The music, the feathers, and the beads helped us remember what was special and exceptional about our city and allowed us to forget the problems we faced, the old ones that existed before the storm and the new ones that had floated in since, and how these problems existed across our country in small towns and big cities, and most every other place in between. Before long the music would stop, and then the work, the grief, and the struggle would continue.

CHAPTER 23

In the Parish

For Rent, St. Bernard Parish, Mardi Gras Day

St. Bernard Parish is trying to recreate the isolated, backward community it maintained so carefully prior to Katrina. In passing an ordinance that restricts rentals to blood relatives, this formerly almost entirely white parish would be freed of most of its Hispanic and African-American residents and pushed back to its status prior to the storm, the 1950s. . . . St. Bernard needs outside assistance if it is ever to enter the second half of the 20th century, much less the 21st. This racist ordinance needs to be declared unconstitutional and the leaders closely monitored until they repent or resign.

Letter to the Editor, Times-Picayune, October 1, 2006

I am proud of St. Bernard for wanting to maintain its affordable, but also stable, family-oriented atmosphere. I am tired of people . . . who attribute our desire for stable, family-oriented neighborhoods to racism!

Response from a St. Bernard Parish resident,
Times-Picayune, October 4, 2006

AS YOU DRIVE EAST on Claiborne Avenue through New Orleans's famously devastated Lower Ninth Ward, you pass the destroyed remains of the Jackson Barracks, a nineteenth-century military base, and then, suddenly, the print on the street signs and the race of the people on the streets change, and you find yourself on Judge Perez Drive in St. Bernard Parish. Both sides of the parish line were so devastated by Hurricane Katrina that the view here would bring to tears both William C. C. Claiborne, the first elected governor of the state of Louisiana, and Leander Perez, the political boss of St. Bernard and Plaquemines parishes throughout much of the early and mid-twentieth century, for whom these streets were named. Most Americans have seen the consequences of the storm on television and heard about people, mostly black and poor, dying in their attics in the Lower Ninth Ward and about the utter devastation left behind after the storm. Far fewer have heard of the struggle on the St. Bernard side of the parish line, where people, overwhelmingly white, toil in obscurity and against monumental obstacles in creating a future in a parish that extends with little fingers of land through the bayous out to the Gulf of Mexico, and where nearly all homes were rendered uninhabitable by the storm.[1] People here feel overlooked but unsurprised. Being ignored, kicked around, set aside, these are facts that are etched into their collective history from a century of environmental exploitation, an intentional levee breach during the

1927 flood to save New Orleans's Garden District, devastation from Hurricane Betsy in 1965, a "trappers' war" with outsiders down in the marsh, and now Katrina.

In the early 1960s, Bill Schmidt took this drive across the parish line and moved his family here for good. Schmidt had grown up in the proud but castigated white working-class Lower Ninth Ward, where New Orleans "y'at" (quintessential neighborhood New Orleanian) culture was in full bloom, with ethnic whites speaking in a manner that sounded more Brooklyn than Montgomery. He was in the last wave of an exodus of his white friends and neighbors from the Lower Ninth, where the Orleans Parish School Board had recently begun integrating the city's schools by ordering William Frantz Elementary School to accept one brave young black girl, Ruby Bridges.

According to Liva Baker's *Second Battle of New Orleans*, this was the "worst possible choice of schools from which to launch racial desegregation." As she described,

> Ninth Ward whites were not much better off [than their black neighbors]. Originally settled by German, Italian, and French immigrants, the area began life as a truck-gardening section in the nineteenth century and remained a predominantly white working-class section in the twentieth. Over the fifteen years since the end of World War II, white New Orleanians had been moving to the northeastern outskirts of the city, out toward Lake Pontchartrain, as fast as swampland could be reclaimed, leaving the Ninth Ward to those who couldn't afford to move. Many of them had been defeated in the competition for material success and were least equipped psychologically to handle the added humiliation they believed racial desegregation of their children's schools would impose. That they lived in a housing project already had de-

moted them to the level of the black families who lived in the nearby all-black neighborhood. "At least I'm not a nigger" counted for less now than it once had. The prospect of black children transferring from the neighborhood black schools to the neighborhood white schools promised the final injustice.[2]

Rather than integrate, white Ninth Ward residents moved, mostly to what locals call, simply, "the Parish," where the population grew by nearly 500 percent between 1950 and 1970, to more than fifty thousand residents.[3] The new residents of St. Bernard could be sure that the local leadership wouldn't cave in to the ACLU, the NAACP, and all of the other pressures of laws and judges that had undone their previous community. Perez, the political boss, had made his views on such groups clear, once exclaiming that the membership of the NAACP and the desegregation movement were "all those Jews who were supposed to have been cremated at Buchenwald and Dachau but weren't," and taking a bold stance against the national effort to integrate the South.[4] Perez was actually one of the principals in the schism of the Democratic Party in 1948, following the decision of the U.S. Supreme Court in *Shelley v. Kramer* that outlawed racial prohibitions in property titles, and he led the Louisiana delegation at the Democratic convention to cast its electoral votes for Strom Thurmond that year.[5] It was this sort of principled stability that families like Schmidt's sought out in the parish. And for the next forty years, up until Hurricane Katrina, they found it here in this hardworking, low-crime community of sixty-five thousand, nearly 90 percent of which was white.[6]

The long-sought stability and security were no longer apparent on Bill Schmidt's Pecan Drive, which, like almost every other street in the parish, took many feet of water during Hurricane Katrina. Of the forty brick ranch houses on the block, most were still lifeless shells, five had been cleared entirely down to the concrete slab, a few had white FEMA trailers parked out front, and only two had been renovated and housed their owners, a consequence of the fact that not a single resident of St. Bernard Parish had yet received a cent of the billions that Congress allotted for redeveloping the Gulf Coast. One of those houses, neat and tidy amidst the boarded-up homes and overgrown yards, belonged to Bill Schmidt. In that house, in Schmidt's desire for things simply to return to the way they were, a second flood began, this time one of controversy, recriminations, and accusations of racism.

Schmidt, afraid that his neighborhood would reemerge transformed after Hurricane Katrina, proposed an ordinance to the parish council that would prevent people from renting their homes to people unrelated by blood. In late September 2006, the parish council took this up and the proposal became law—and Schmidt's block along with a thousand others in St. Bernard Parish were protected from change even while they were suspended in devastation.

Anger at the ordinance was immediate in this region where race and its complexities provide the subtext and backdrop for nearly every nuance of public life. The Greater New Orleans Fair Housing Center sued, pointing out that 93 percent of St. Bernard Parish property owners were white and that the ordinance effectively discriminated in the same manner that was found unconstitutional in *Shelley v. Kramer* five decades earlier, even if the reality of race was hidden in the language of blood. Its brief argued, "St. Bernard Parish seeks to perpetuate segregation by preserving the parish as an overwhelmingly all-white enclave."

The council presented a world-weary and defiant face in light

of the lawsuit and attacks in the local press. The parish council-
man Craig Taffaro, who represents Chalmette, the St. Bernard
Parish seat, much of which is now a brownfield site because of an
oil leak from an international oil company's refinery during Katrina, denied any racial motivation and mocked those who im-
puted one: "What a tremendous burden it must be to believe that
everything is motivated by race. Our motivation is simply to do
what's best for our recovery and to restore and maintain our pre-
Katrina quality of life."[7]

Another council member cited the uniform gratitude of his
constituents for the council's passing the ordinance, and explained
that the council would not revoke it. At the next council meeting,
they lawyered up and hunkered down for a fight, over the objec-
tion of the eccentric, outspoken, and white—like the rest of the
members—council president, Lynn Dean, who had voted against
the ordinance and who wrote in his column in the *St. Bernard
Parish Voice* that it was intended to keep blacks from moving to the
parish. Dean tried to simplify the issue at the meeting: "Our
parish is broke. We don't have the money to fix roads. We are
going to hire an attorney, and when it's all over with, we are going
to lose."[8] The meeting ended in closed session, with the council
moving to censure Dean for his outrageous invocation of race in
criticizing the ordinance.

But things had changed by the council meeting the following
month. In the late-morning December sun, in a double-wide
trailer behind the destroyed parish government building on Judge
Perez Drive, the council said the Pledge of Allegiance, prayed to
Jesus Christ, and worked its way through its regular business—
naming the parish's "Teacher of the Year" and castigating the director of the company with the contract to disburse billions in

federal rebuilding funds for failing to disburse a single dollar to its residents or to any of the council members, all of whom lost their homes to the storm—before reaching the business of the rental ordinance, which had brought me and a few other print and television journalists to their down-to-earth and informal meeting. On the docket was a new ordinance, to revoke the "blood ordinance," maybe at the urging of their two-hundred-dollar-an-hour lawyer, maybe because they just realized that they had better things to do than fight the rest of the world on this.

Bill Schmidt, reading from prepared notes, spoke against revoking the ordinance, arguing against the tide: "They say it's a racial thing. . . . I don't want to hear this baloney about this being about race. . . . We just wanna live as we lived before." And then defiantly, but sadly, "I'm from the Ninth Ward. I've always lived with this negative image. I'm looked down at by the rich people. I don't care what other people think about the parish." And even though most of the council seemed to relate to him, to feel the same way, they voted unanimously to back down from this fight and to revoke the ordinance, and then moved on to the business of rebuilding.

The television cameras and journalists left quickly after the ordinance was revoked, eager to file the story in time for the evening news. I sat for a while and listened to the council address the true and seemingly insurmountable obstacles the parish faces. Levee maintenance. Oil contamination. Sewer funds. Closing the industrial canal built through the parish, which had worsened Katrina's destruction. With each issue, the council members seemed almost powerless in the face of the human, natural, business, and financial forces against them. And it became clear how the rental ordinance had risen to the top of the stack of parish business. It was easy. It brought the people of the parish together, at least most of them. It was about making an "us" and saying "the hell with you" to all those "thems."

As I walked out of the meeting, probably by then the only face that everyone didn't recognize, a man walked up to me and spoke bitterly, "Now you can go tell the people up in *New York* and *Washington* all about it." I tried to explain that I lived in New Orleans. That we weren't all against them. That we hoped for the best in their recovery. But he seemed unconvinced. I got in my car and drove back down Judge Perez Drive across the parish line.

CHAPTER 24

Not Resigned

Thou Shalt Not Kill, Central City

IN ONE TWENTY-FOUR-HOUR PERIOD in January 2007 in New Orleans, a small city of two hundred thousand residents, six people were murdered. The previous year's total of 161 murders had made New Orleans the deadliest city in the United States by a significant margin. I suppose it was only a matter of time before the violence touched my life directly.

As I worked at my computer in the late morning one day that month, I received a call from my friend Kittee. She asked sharply, "Where are you?"

"I'm at home," I responded.

"I have awful news," she said, and then very quickly: "Someone broke into Paul and Helen's house. Helen was shot and killed. Paul was holding baby Francis and was shot three times. He's still alive. Francis is okay."

Paul Gailiunas—Dr. Paul, I call him—had been my physician for several years at the Little Doctors Clinic, a health center for poor people that he founded in Treme, one of America's oldest black neighborhoods.

I had started to see Paul after my previous doctor mocked one of my colleagues about our work representing people on Louisiana's death row. When I met Paul through a friend, I asked him directly, "Are you in favor of the death penalty?" He responded, with a smile, "Eh, I'm Canadian," clearly feeling that was answer enough.

And it was, coming from the founder of our local chapter of

Food Not Bombs and the front man for the Troublemakers, a band whose songs celebrate Emma Goldman and the idea of universal health care in such a lighthearted tone that it would scarcely have alienated the most ardent conservative.

Helen Hill was Paul's perfect match. She was ceaselessly kind and generous, she had long ago forsaken even dairy products because producing them involved potential cruelty to animals, and she made award-winning experimental animated films while teaching art and filmmaking to kids, adults, anyone who was interested. She'd spent much of the previous year restoring reels of 16-millimeter film on which she had drawn by hand, which had been damaged when their house took four feet of water during Hurricane Katrina.

She had a new film under way, inspired by discarded hand-sewn dresses, made by an elderly New Orleanian, which Helen had found in the trash after the woman's death. The film interwove the story of the old woman and her dresses with Helen's own flood-torn life, which took her, Paul, and Francis to Columbia, South Carolina—Helen's hometown, where she later was buried—for almost a year.

Helen had longed to return to New Orleans, despite Paul's concern that crime and potential hurricanes made it too dangerous for their family. So Helen campaigned, sending Paul's friends in New Orleans blank postcards, addressed to Paul, for us to write and mail to him. In mine, I pleaded with Paul—"We need you"—the way I do with anyone who is thinking about leaving, coming to, or even just visiting New Orleans. In my card I reminded him about my client Ryan, whom he had treated at no charge for a terrible seizure disorder that had gone unattended during Ryan's years of wrongful imprisonment. "Ryan needs you." After what I am sure was a flood of similar cards, Paul relented.

I saw Paul and the baby the day after their return to the city, at the parade on the anniversary of Hurricane Katrina. Francis had on a little railroad conductor's hat, a t-shirt depicting a cartoon love affair between red beans and rice, and a little sign pinned to his back, in Helen's pretty script: "New Orleans Native. I Got Back Yesterday!"

The day of the anniversary was solemn but optimistic. People still clung to a can-do attitude. Paul, for one, could help make the city's people well and improve health care for the poor. Helen could make art depicting the city's life. Others could rebuild schools, demand better levees, reconstruct their homes. It still felt as if our grassroots efforts, along with some real help from a government finally forced to make good on its obligations, could create a more just, fair, and safe city. It might have been naive, but it really seemed possible.

After wandering this beautiful, falling-over city the afternoon after Helen's murder, forcing myself to remember why I love it here so much, I came back to my garden and picked flowers, those hardy few that had weathered the recent cold. I put them in a vase, wrote out the verses to Edna St. Vincent Millay's "Dirge without Music"—"I am not resigned to the shutting away of loving hearts in the hard ground / So it is, and so it will be, for so it has been, time out of mind"—and drove to the couple's home, which my wife and I had recently visited for Helen's open studio. On the steps leading up to their old shotgun house I set down the poem and the vase, just feet from where Paul had been found by the police, shot, bleeding, holding his baby.

On the way home, I stopped by a neighborhood bar to drink a beer and to try to eat something. As I forced a bite of food down, a picture of Paul and Helen, followed by one of Francis, appeared on the television in the corner. "Oh, my God," I groaned. The bartender was kind. She asked me whether I knew them, and talked to me about her fears living with her new baby in a city with no functional schools, no real plan for redevelopment, and spotty or nonexistent basic services. The TV news switched to a weather report: torrential downpours were expected to dump a half-foot of rain overnight.

I drove home in the twilight and arrived uneasy and restless. Remembering the coming rain, I resolved to make myself useful to my block by digging out a sewer so backed up that the street— on high ground by New Orleans standards—floods at even the hint of rain. I had done this many times before, having realized that my innumerable calls to the city were in vain.

I pried up the hundred-pound cast iron cover with a shovel and then shimmied it from side to side until I had the two-by-four-foot sewer open. It was full to the top with debris. I shoveled out the leaves, dirt, Popeye's cups, and other garbage until the small brick rectangle was as clean as it was a century ago, when New Orleans first created this drainage system.

Then I set to work on clearing the cylindrical drain—about as wide as a hubcap, at the bottom corner of the cleaned-out basin— so that the rain could find its way into the city's sewers, away from our houses, cars, and belongings. I got down with a small shovel and burrowed through the muck until it seemed to open at the other side. Reaching in, though, I could feel that beyond the drain lay more dirt and leaves, packed hard.

Indeed, it became clear to me that the whole sewer line running beneath the street was solid with waste, impenetrable to arms and shovels—that my street would flood again that night. The problem, I realized, is bigger than me.

I know. But I do not approve. And I am not resigned.

CHAPTER 25

Epitaph

Piano. Inside Out. Central City.

And some there be which have no memorial; who perished, as though they had never been; and are become as though they had never been born; and their children after them.

But these were merciful men, whose righteousness hath not been forgotten.

Ecclesiasticus 44:9–10.

MORE THAN A YEAR after the storm destroyed New Orleans, it has become hard to be optimistic about the city's future. Much of what was wrong with the country, "the whole country's garbage," had long been flowing down the Mississippi to us. Hurricane Katrina seems to have blown in the rest. The weeks and months following the storm made us rally, made us believe, in some mad delirium, that we could return to our homes and to a city so decimated that we could begin again, remaking it in a manner that reflected the common good. I believed we could make a city where rich and poor children alike could learn in schools, where hospitals could be rebuilt to provide decent health care to people regardless of their income, and where people could live in homes where they would be safe from the ravages of both the environment and crime. This was the phoenix that I hoped would rise from the ashes of all of this misery. And misery did abound.

The most recent count put Louisiana's death toll at 1,580 people. Most of these people came from the weakest segments of the population; more than 70 percent of the dead were over sixty years old. Following Hurricane Katrina, the *Times-Picayune* profiled each of the city's dead in brief obituaries. The faces in the *Times-Picayune* were almost uniformly the faces of the old, the infirm, or children, the people who needed the most help from their government in this predictable disaster but who instead met with horrifying watery deaths. They deserved better.

No one should be surprised at the extent to which these people were abandoned by their government. The diminution of the role of government as an agent of help and assistance is part of the Republican revolution that the rest of us, barely, lived through. The dominant voices in the political discourse of the 1980s, 1990s, and hopefully only the first half of this decade, those who had the ears of the people in power, are people who don't believe that government should play a role in people's lives, people like Grover Norquist, the conservative activist president of Americans for Tax Reform, who famously explained his notion of effective governance: "I don't want to abolish government. I simply want to reduce it to the size where I can drag it into the bathroom and drown it in the bathtub."[1] Except for our remarkable spending on the military and, to a lesser extent, prisons and attempts at crime prevention, Norquist and his allies in the Republican Party have made remarkable progress in their efforts. Indeed, government has been so diminished in the lives of American citizens that the most vulnerable citizens of the richest country in the world drowned—the old and the infirm in nursing homes, and children in their front yards before their parents' eyes—as the federally built and maintained levees crumbled under the pressure of a strong but not exceptional storm. Along with these unfortunates, our values and our belief in the common good were nearly drowned in the flood, with the hands of Norquist, Bush, and all the other "that government which governs least, governs best" types around our necks, holding our heads beneath the water until they believed we had succumbed at last.

Believing these values to have drowned, these folks could then get on with the important business of repealing the estate tax, a measure of supposed great concern to the yeomen farmers of the State of Louisiana, where one twenty-fifth of 1 percent of the population of the state, the extraordinarily rich, would be the only people to receive any benefit, while the repeal would cost the federal government twenty-four billion dollars every year, many times the amount required to maintain proper levees, and enough to provide health care for ten million uninsured Americans.

In the many moments when I became disillusioned, too focused on the fact that our government stood by as the dead carcasses of New Orleanians were left on the street and eaten by dogs, I looked back and tried to see how far we had come.[2] Liberal politics has won the big philosophical debate of our times. However limited our rights and expectations have become, at least government is now understood as having obligations to its citizens. However inadequate the sum, people unable to work receive Social Security. Children receive Medicaid and the elderly receive Medicare. The poor are provided with subsidized housing. The government protects workers' rights and regulates corporate malfeasance and the impact of industry on the environment. Even though we have lived through years of backlash, conservatives have managed only to nibble away at the margins of these entitlements; no one seriously entertains arguments that Social Security, welfare, or housing aid for poor families should be abolished altogether. Obviously, reality has fallen short of the vision of a government earnestly invested in the common good, but there seems to be little need to argue the principle that the common good of the people is the necessary province of government.

As everyone has in New Orleans, I have had my own struggles during this time. Under the weight of the storm, my marriage began to collapse after my wife and I returned to our destroyed home. My truck died by the side of a Mississippi highway when I was moving out of my home to a shack in the Mississippi coun-

316 / *Against the Ropes*

tryside. My dog was diagnosed with terminal cancer. But life has a way of sorting itself out sometimes, however tenuously, and my life became like the old joke about the country song played backward: you get your wife back, you get your truck back, you get your dog back. I know too well that not everyone's luck is so good and that many people have troubles graver than mine. But I do believe that the tide will turn similarly for my city, and for the poor and disenfranchised in this country. That the important values that animate our democracy were not drowned in the flood. That the losses we suffered haven't been in vain.

The citizens of this country never intended to vote into office leaders who would allow what happened in New Orleans to occur. Ultimately, voters will hold politicians accountable for clinging to a self-interested political ideology that betrayed the government's obligations to its people. Indeed, they have already started.

How the Other Half Lives, Jacob Riis's work that exposed the reality of the lives of immigrants in New York City's slums, ended with a quotation from James Russell Lowell's poem "The Vision of Sir Launfal," sounding very much like scripture: "Think ye that building shall endure which shelters the noble and crushes the poor?"[3] Throughout our history we have seen such buildings, but in these moments the people have led, in our noble tradition, and worked to lessen the burden of those who struggle. This is why thousands of people have come to New Orleans and the Gulf coast to help. This is how the tragic deaths of more than a hundred women in the fire at the Triangle Shirtwaist Factory ultimately led to the New Deal more than twenty years later. This is what the dedicated citizens of New Orleans and this country will make real for themselves. This is the best that anyone can ever hope will arise from tragedy.

NOTES

PROLOGUE

1. Susan Saulny, "A Legacy of the Storm: Depression and Suicide," *New York Times*, June 21, 2006; Matthew Penix, "Post-Katrina Depression Triples Suicide Rate in New Orleans," *New Orleans CityBusiness*, July 3, 2006.

2. A STRANGER COMES TO TOWN

1. National Public Radio, *All Things Considered*, "Bush Tours New Orleans Damage," September 12, 2005.

3. "THIS BLUES IS JUST TOO BIG"

1. Staff Reports, "Hurricane Katrina—the Aftermath. Weblog for Day 5," *Times-Picayune*, August 31, 2005.

2. Robert D. McFadden and Ralph Blumenthal, "Bush Sees Long Recovery for New Orleans; 30,000 Troops in Largest U.S. Relief Effort," *New York Times*, September 1, 2005.

3. Staff Reports, "Hurricane Katrina—the Aftermath. Weblog for Day 5."

4. Ibid.

5. *Merriam-Webster's Dictionary of English Usage* (Springfield, MA: Merriam-Webster, 1994) labels the correction as antiquated: "Any handbook that tells you that 'nauseous' cannot mean 'nauseated' is out of touch with the contemporary language. In current usage it seldom means anything else."

6. National Public Radio, *All Things Considered*, "Mourning for a Flooded Crescent City," August 31, 2005.

4. A DOLLAR SHORT

1. According to the 2003 data from the U.S. Census Bureau, 25.8 percent of the city's population lives below the poverty line. See http://quickfacts.census.gov/qfd/states/22/22071.html. This is more than twice the national average, but is close to the percentages in other American cities such as Miami (28.5), Los Angeles (22.1), Atlanta (24.4), and New York City (21.2). Notwithstanding the fact that poverty seems to be entrenched in cities across America, the census makes clear that these problems remain greatest in the South, which suffers disproportionately from poverty when compared to the rest of the nation. See Bureau of the Census, *Statistical Brief*, "Poverty Areas," 1995. Posted online at www.census.gov/apsd/www/statbrief/sb95_13.pdf.

2. Helen Prejean, *Dead Man Walking: An Eyewitness Account of the Death Penalty in the United States* (New York: Vintage, 1994), p. 3.

3. For the history of the development and decline of the St. Thomas Housing Project, see Greater New Orleans Community Data Center, "St. Thomas Neighborhood Development Snapshot," posted at www.gnocdc.org/orleans/2/59/snapshot.html.

4. A chilling account of the intersection of crime and poverty in the St. Thomas Project was offered in Rick Bragg's article, "Children Strike Fear into Grown-Up Hearts," *New York Times*, December 2, 1994.

5. Greg Thomas, "Neighborhoods Rejoice; Lower Garden District,

Irish Channel Renovators Thrilled about Plans for New St. Thomas,"
Times-Picayune, October 26, 1996.

6. See, e.g., Michelle Krupa, "Smack's Back; As Heroin Makes a
Comeback, a Different, Easier-to-Use Form of the Drug and a Younger
Breed of User May Be Fueling Violent Crime in the Area: Violent
Crimes on N.O. Streets Driven by Heroin," *Times-Picayune*, July 11,
2002.

7. Stewart Yerton, "$6.15—Raising Minimum Wage: Yes or No,"
Times-Picayune, January 6, 2002.

8. Stephanie Grace, "Election Set on Raising Wages in N.O.; Judicial Order Prompts Action," *Times-Picayune*, September 21, 2001.

9. Stewart Yerton, "N.O. Voters Approve Minimum Wage Increase,"
Times-Picayune, February 3, 2002.

10. Ibid.

11. New Orleans had approximately 225,000 workers, according to
the 2000 census.

12. Susan Finch, "Minimum Wage Increase in N.O. Upheld; Opponents to Appeal to La. Supreme Court," *Times-Picayune*, March 26,
2002.

13. *New Orleans Campaign for a Living Wage v. City of New Orleans*,
02–0991 (La. 09/04/02); 825 So. 2d 1098.

14. In addition to *Sun Tzu: The Art of War for Managers; 50 Strategic
Rules* and *Sun Tzu for Success: How to Use the Art of War to Master Challenges and Accomplish the Important Goals in Your Life*, the modern businessman can also arm himself for battle with the successful Art of War
Plus . . . series, including volumes on *The Art of Management, The Art of
Marketing*, and *The Art of Career Building*. For a Western perspective, the
war of business can be learned from *Machiavelli on Modern Leadership:
Why Machiavelli's Iron Rules Are as Timely and Important Today as Five Centuries Ago, The Mafia Manager: A Guide to the Corporate Machiavelli*, or,
more humorously, *What Would Machiavelli Do? The Ends Justify the
Meanness*.

5. POOR, NASTY, BRUTISH, AND SHORT

1. The *Oprah Winfrey Show*, September 6, 2006.

2. Ibid.

3. Gwen Filosa, "At Least 10,000 Find Refuge at the Superdome," *Times-Picayune*, August 29, 2005; Staff Reports, "National Guard Pours into New Orleans, Mississippi," *USA Today*, August 31, 2005; Mary Foster, "Superdome Evacuations Enter Second Day," Associated Press, September 1, 2005.

4. See, e.g., National Public Radio, *Weekend All Things Considered*, "Humanity Prevails in New Orleans," September 3, 2005; CNN, "Sniper Fire Halts Hospital Evacuation," September 1, 2005.

5. See, e.g., Jeff Jacoby, "The Looting Instinct," *Boston Globe*, September 4, 2005; Emily Smith, "USA 2005 . . . and Rats Are Eating Corpses in the Street," *The Sun* (London), September 3, 2005.

6. "Breaking News from the *Times-Picayune* and NOLA.com; Hurricane Katrina: The Aftermath; Weblog for Day 4," *Times-Picayune* (Web edition), August 30, 2005.

7. Howard Witt, "New Orleans Ravaged," *Chicago Tribune*, August 31, 2005; "Looting," *The Advocate* (Baton Rouge), August 31, 2005.

8. Chris Graythen/Agence France-Presse, posted on Yahoo! News on August 30, 2005. See also James T. Campbell, " 'Looting' vs. 'Surviving,' Media Missed the Nuance," *Houston Chronicle*, September 18, 2005.

9. Dave Martin/Associated Press, posted on Yahoo! News on August 29, 2005.

10. Dave Martin/Associated Press, posted on Yahoo! News on August 30, 2005.

11. Aaron Kinney suggested in "Looting or Finding," *Salon*, September 1, 2005, that the differences among the captions of the wire service photographs were the result of specific determinations made by the individual reporters based on what they had observed. This overlooks, however, the broader contours of the media's role in stirring up racialized—and false—depictions of crime and violence in the poor, mostly black city of New Orleans following Hurricane Katrina or the fact that

there were other sad linguistic correlations following the storm, such as use of the term *groups* for groups of whites and *gangs* for groups of blacks. See Rod Watson, "Race Relations Sublime and Ridiculous," *Buffalo News*, January 5, 2006. Furthermore, the use of the terms *loot* and *looter* was both unfair and misleading, given that the vast majority of people who were taking food were not using force and were acting out of necessity. The potency of these terms was all too evident after Katrina when "looters will be shot" remained painted throughout Uptown New Orleans. Yahoo! News, which originally posted the photographs, at least took the matter sufficiently seriously to apologize to its readers: "Yahoo! News regrets that these photos and captions, viewed together, may have suggested a racial bias on our part" (September 1, 2005, http://news .yahoo.com/page/photostatement).

12. Davidduke.com, "Heineken, the Beer of Choice for New Orleans Looters," September 20, 2005, www.davidduke.com/?p = 410 (last checked October 10, 2006).

13. This song was written by Chuck Redden, the owner of two Monroe, Louisiana, radio stations and was first heard on the *Walton and Johnson* syndicated morning radio show. A slightly toned-down version of the song was released by Ray Stevens, a country music comedian. More recently, Redden put out "Chocolateville," another, equally offensive song that parodies blacks in New Orleans.

14. Certainly, many in Louisiana agree with Duke. He won the majority of the "white vote" in Louisiana when he ran for governor in 1991. See, e.g., Jonathan Tilove, "Democrats Pursue South's White Men," *Times-Picayune*, August 28, 1996.

15. See, generally, Brian Thevenot and Gordon Russell, "Rape. Murder. Gunfights. For Three Anguished Days the World's Headlines Blared That the Superdome and Convention Center Had Descended into Anarchy. But the Truth Is That While Conditions Were Squalid for the Thousands Stuck There, Much of the Violence NEVER HAPPENED," *Times-Picayune*, September 26, 2005; Staff Reports, "Children's Hospital in New Orleans Reopens," *New Orleans CityBusiness*, October 7, 2005; John Laplante, "Storm Also Drowned Information," *The Advocate* (Baton

Rouge), March 26, 2006; Miriam Hill and Nicholas Spangler, "Shots at Helicopters Shrouded in a 'Fog': Reports of Gunshots Aimed at Rescue Helicopters in New Orleans on Sept. 1 Now Appear to Have Been Little More Than Rumors," *Miami Herald*, October 3, 2005.

6. NOT IN MY BACKYARD

1. CBS, *60 Minutes*, "The Bridge to Gretna," December 18, 2005.

2. Gardiner Harris, "Police in Suburbs Blocked Evacuees," *New York Times*, September 10, 2005.

3. Larry Bradshaw and Lorrie Beth Slonsky, "Hurricane Katrina: Our Experiences," *EMS Network News*, September 6, 2005.

4. CBS, *60 Minutes*, "The Bridge to Gretna," December 18, 2005.

5. Ibid.

6. CNN, *Anderson Cooper 360 Degrees*, "Brown Resigns," September 12, 2005.

7. National Public Radio, *Morning Edition*, "Evacuees Were Turned Away at Gretna," September 20, 2005.

8. Ibid.

9. Katy Reckdahl, "Ties That Bind," *New Orleans Gambit*, January 14, 2003.

10. Joel Divine, Richard Bourke, and Joseph Hingston, "Black Strikes," September 2003. Available at www.blackstrikes.com.

11. Ibid.

12. Rob Nelson, "Group: Jeff Juries Formed Unfairly; It Says Too Many Black People Omitted," *Times-Picayune*, September 24, 2003.

13. *State v. Harris*, 01–0408 (La. 06/21/02); 820 So. 2d 471.

14. *Miller-El v. Cockrell*, 537 U.S. 322 (2003); *Miller-El v. Dretke*, 545 U.S. 231 (2005).

15. Katy Reckdahl, "Target Practice," *New Orleans Gambit*, April 12, 2005.

16. Ibid.

17. Natalie Pompilio, "There's Something about Harry," *Times-Picayune*, April 2, 2000.

18. Ibid.

19. ABC, *World News Tonight*, November 18, 1991.

20. The returns recorded by the Louisiana Secretary of State make clear that Duke won a majority in Jefferson Parish. See www.sos.louisiana.gov:8090/cgibin/?rqstyp = elcmpct&rqsdta = 1116911 0012919.

21. Mike Williams, "Duke's Angry Message Packs Power in Economic Hard Times," *Atlanta Journal Constitution*, October 19, 1991.

22. "Leaders Call Truce in Barricade Battle," United Press International, February 24, 1987.

23. Douglas Martin, "Fence Is Not Neighborly in a Suburb of Cleveland," *New York Times*, June 27, 1987.

24. See, e.g., "White New Orleans Suburb Backpedals on Barriers," *Chicago Tribune*, February 24, 1987.

25. National Public Radio, *Morning Edition*, "Evacuees Were Turned Away at Gretna," September 20, 2005.

26. Matthew Brown, "Bridge Exposes Racial Divide; Gretna Police Stand by Decision to Block Evacuees," *Times-Picayune*, September 22, 2005.

7. LEFT TO DIE

1. Alfred Blumstein and Allen J. Beck, "Population Growth in U.S. Prisons, 1980–1996," *Crime and Justice: A Review of Research* 26 (1999): 17–61; Fox Butterfield, "Number in Prison Grows Despite Crime Reduction," *New York Times*, August 10, 2000.

2. Human Rights Watch, *New Orleans: Prisoners Abandoned to Floodwaters*, September 22, 2005.

3. According to the Death Penalty Information Center's "List of Those Exonerated from Death Row," Dan Bright was the 118th person exonerated since 1973.

4. *State v. Bright*, 98–0398 (La. 04/11/00); 776 So. 2d 1134.

5. *Bright v. Ashcroft*, 259 F. Supp. 2d 502 (E.D. La. 2003).

6. See, e.g., Fox Butterfield, "Hard Time: Profits at a Juvenile Prison Come with a Chilling Cost," *New York Times*, July 15, 1998; Katy Reck-

dahl, "Can This Prison Regain Its Stripes? Tallulah Timeline," *New Orleans Gambit*, November 6, 2001; Human Rights Watch, *Children in Confinement in Louisiana*, October 1995.

7. Juvenile Justice Project of Louisiana, "Treated Like Trash: Juvenile Detention in New Orleans before, during, and after Hurricane Katrina," May 2006.

8. Ibid.

9. Ibid.

10. Ibid.

11. U.S. Department of Justice, Bureau of Justice Statistics, "Prison and Jail Inmates at Midyear 2005," May 2006.

12. Sentencing Project, "State Rates of Incarceration by Race," 2004. Posted online at www.sentencingproject.org/pdfs/racialdisparity.pdf.

13. Roy Walmsley, "World Prison Population List (Sixth Edition)," King's College London, International Center for Prison Studies, February 2005.

14. Editorial, "Creating the Next Crime Wave," *New York Times*, March 13, 2004.

8. BRING THE WAR HOME

1. See, e.g., Alan Zarembo, "Katrina's Aftermath; New Orleans Gets a Makeshift Jail; Suspects Are Being Put in Holding Cells Set Up in the Bus Station. Their Cases Will Be Processed through a Court System That Is Far from Normal," *Los Angeles Times*, September 7, 2005; Alex Berenson, "With Jails Flooded, Bus Station Fills the Void," *New York Times*, September 7, 2005.

9. THE DRY RUN OF THE APOCALYPSE

1. CNN, *Anderson Cooper 360 Degrees*, "Hurricane Katrina: Mission Critical," September 6, 2005.

2. Human Rights Watch, "Shielded from Justice: Police Brutality

and Accountability in the United States," June 1998. Posted online at www.hrw.org/reports98/police.

3. Paul Keegan, "The Thinnest Blue Line," *New York Times Magazine*, March 31, 1996.

4. Staff Reports, "N.O. Police Are Taped Beating Man, 64; AP Producer Also Punched on Film," *Times-Picayune*, October 10, 2005.

5. Frank Donze, "NOFD Hires, Police Up for Raises; Fire Union, EMS Chief Question Nagin Plan," *Times-Picayune*, July 26, 2006. Though I agree with little that is written by the folks at *National Review*, I think that Jack Dunphy, "Rebuilding a Police Department: A Few Suggestions for New Orleans," *National Review Online*, October 11, 2005, provides interesting insights into what is necessary to rebuild the police department from a law enforcement perspective.

10. HISTORY REPEATS ITSELF

1. See, e.g., Deroy Murdock, "State of Damage," *National Review*, September 22, 2005.

2. See, e.g., ibid.; MSNBC, *The Situation with Tucker Carlson*, September 15, 2005; MSNBC, *Scarborough Country*, September 16, 2005; Joe R. Hicks, "Levees Let Loose an Ugly Flood of Black Paranoia; Some Leaders Are Spreading Myths—as Unfair as They Are Untrue—That Are Doing Damage to Us All," *Los Angeles Times*, October 2, 2005.

3. See, e.g., Fox News Network, *The O'Reilly Factor*, October 14, 2005; Fox News Network, *The O'Reilly Factor*, August 29, 2006; Fox News Network, *Fox Hannity & Colmes*, September 19, 2005; MSNBC, *The Situation with Tucker Carlson*, September 15, 2005.

4. Federal News Service Transcript, "Hearing of the Select Bipartisan Committee to Investigate the Preparation for and Response to Hurricane Katrina," December 6, 2005.

5. Ibid.

6. MSNBC, *The Situation with Tucker Carlson*, December 7, 2005.

7. The history of the 1927 levee breach recounted here relies mostly

on John Barry, *Rising Tide: The Great Mississippi Flood of 1927 and How It Changed America* (New York: Simon & Schuster, 1998).

8. Ibid., p. 229.

9. Ibid.

10. Ibid.

11. Ibid.

12. James Gill, "The Truth Is Grim Enough," *Times-Picayune*, September 28, 2005.

13. Sara Vilkomerson, "Spike's Pique," *New York Observer*, March 20, 2006 (quoting from Bill Maher's HBO show).

14. See, e.g., Christopher Cooper, "In Katrina's Wake—Old-Line Families Escape Worst of Floods and Plot the Future," *Wall Street Journal*, September 8, 2005.

11. GOING HOME

1. Adolph Reed Jr., "The Battle of Liberty Monument," *The Progressive*, June 1993; James Gill, "Goose-Stepping Home," *Times-Picayune*, May 9, 2004.

15. SECOND LINE

1. Katy Reckdahl, "Why? NOPD's Shooting Death of a Young Trombone Player Leaves Onlookers and Bandmates Shocked and in Search of Answers," *New Orleans Gambit*, August 17, 2004.

16. GIDEON'S BLUES

1. Southern Center for Human Rights, "A Report on Pre- and Post-Katrina Indigent Defense in New Orleans" (March 2006), provides an excellent overview and description of the shortcomings of New Orleans indigent defense system before and after Hurricane Katrina. Posted at www.schr.org/indigentdefense/press%20releases/press_new_%orleans_prepost_katrina.htm.

2. Barry Gerharz and Seung Hong, "Down by Law: Orleans Parish Prison before and after Hurricane Katrina," *Dollars and Sense*, March/April 2006; Laura Maggi, "Judge Takes Public Defense to Task; Six Lawyers Quit, Causing Case Delays," *Times-Picayune*, September 18, 2006.

3. Christopher Drew, "Courts' Slow Recovery Begins at Train Station," *New York Times*, October 14, 2005.

4. "Justice System Struggles in New Orleans: Exposed by Katrina, Long-Neglected System Needs Expensive Overhaul," Associated Press, June 24, 2006.

5. Sharon Cohen, "Troubled New Orleans Criminal Justice System Struggles to Rebound and Improve after Katrina," Associated Press, June 24, 2006; Laura Parker, "People Arrested before Katrina Still Await Trial; Legal System in Tangles, and Many Remain in Jail," *USA Today*, February 27, 2006.

17. LIVE FROM THE CIRCLE BAR

1. Mary Foster, "Business Owners Say Starting Over Will Be Difficult, Maybe Impossible," Associated Press, September 17, 2005; Stephen White, "Never the Twain; Entire Store Emptied by Looters . . . Apart from Shania CD's," *Daily Record*, September 19, 2005.

18. CORPORATE LIMITS

1. According to the Census Bureau, the population of New Orleans at the beginning of the twentieth century was 287,104. Campbell Gibson, "Population of the 100 Largest Cities and Other Urban Places: 1790 to 1900," Population Division, U.S. Bureau of the Census, June 1993. Posted at www.census.gov/population/www/documentation/twps0027.html.

2. Gordon Russell, "An 1878 Map Reveals That Maybe Our Ancestors Were Right to Build on Higher Ground. Almost Every Place That Was Uninhabited in 1878 Flooded in 2005 after Katrina," *Times-Picayune*, November 3, 2005.

3. Leonard Huber, *Lakeview Lore* (published "to commemorate the opening of the Harrison Avenue Office of the First National Bank of Commerce," 1971, according to the New Orleans Public Library), Louisiana Room of the New Orleans Public Library.

4. Villavaso and Associates, LLC, "New Orleans East Renaissance Plan," June 2004, for the New Orleans East Economic Development Foundation, Louisiana Room of the New Orleans Public Library; Gibson, "Population of the 100 Largest Cities and Other Urban Places," 1900 and 1960. According to the Census Bureau, the land areas of San Francisco and Boston are 47 and 48 square miles, respectively, or 30,080 acres and 30,720 acres.

5. See, e.g., "Eastern New Orleans: I-10 Opens Up New Land," *Times-Picayune*, January 12, 1975; Cornelia Carrier, "Drained Wetlands: How Infirm a Foundation," *Times-Picayune*, April 17, 1975.

6. Villavaso and Associates, LLC, "New Orleans East Renaissance Plan," p. 11.

7. Ibid., p. 17.

8. See, e.g., Frank Donze and Gordon Russell, "4 Months to Decide; Nagin Panel Says Hardest Hit Areas Must Prove Viability; City's Footprint May Shrink; Full Buyouts Proposed for Those Forced to Move; New Housing to Be Developed in Vast Swaths of New Orleans' Higher Ground," *Times-Picayune*, January 11, 2006.

9. See, e.g., Martha Carr and Jeffrey Meitrodt, "What Will New Orleans Look Like Five Years from Now? Experts Have a Lot of Big Ideas, but Their Grand Plans Can't Happen Unless a Fractured City Rises to the Challenge," *Times-Picayune*, December 25, 2005; Gary Rivlin, "Wealthy Blacks Oppose Plans for Their Property," *New York Times*, December 10, 2005.

10. See, e.g., NBC, *Nightly News*, March 21, 2006; Sam Quinones, "New Orleans Rebuilding Plan Stirs Anger; Speakers Have Just Three Minutes during the Public-Comment Session, but It Doesn't Take Long to Say Not Enough Is Being Done," *Los Angeles Times*, March 21, 2006.

11. New Orleans East, Inc., "A Profile of New Orleans East for Gulf

South Research Institute" [1965], Louisiana Room of the New Orleans Public Library.

12. The history of this tract is detailed with great precision in Ray Samuel, " ' . . . to a point called Chef Menteur . . . ': The Story of the Property Known Today as New Orleans East, Inc.," New Orleans East, Inc., September 1959, and is discussed in the many volumes of New Orleans East, Inc.'s corporate planning documents held at the Louisiana Room of the New Orleans Public Library. The Johnson family's connection to New Orleans East, Inc., is mentioned in Oliver Houck, "Can We Save New Orleans?" *Tulane Environmental Law Journal* 19 (Spring 2006): 1–68; and Todd Shallats, "In the Wake of Hurricane Betsy," in *Transforming New Orleans and Its Environs*, ed. Craig Colton (Pittsburgh: University of Pittsburgh Press, 2000), pp. 121–140.

13. City of New Orleans Office of Policy Planning, "Neighborhood Profiles Project, Edgelake/Little Woods," ed. Darlene Walk et al., December 1980, Louisiana Room of the New Orleans Public Library.

14. James Mahoney, "Radical, Reformist and Aborted Liberalism: Origins of National Regimes in Central America," *Journal of Latin American Studies* 33, no. 2 (May 1, 2001): 221–256.

15. City of New Orleans Office of Policy Planning, "Neighborhood Profiles Project, Edgelake/Little Woods."

16. Peirce Lewis, *New Orleans: The Making of an Urban Landscape*, 2nd edition (Charlottesville: University of Virginia Press, 2003), p. 80; Carrier, "Drained Wetlands."

17. City of New Orleans Office of Policy Planning, "Neighborhood Profiles Project, Read Boulevard West," ed. Darlene Walk et al., December 1980, Louisiana Room of the New Orleans Public Library, p. 3.09.

18. Lewis, *New Orleans*, p. 81.

19. Ibid., p. 83.

20. Adam Nossiter, "Untouchable in Election: New Orleans's Central Issue," *New York Times*, April 18, 2006.

21. Carrier, "Drained Wetlands."

22. Save Our Wetlands, "History of the Eden Isles, Oak Harbor &

North Shore Estate subdivisions in Slidell, Louisiana," posted at www.saveourwetlands.org/edenislehistory.htm.

23. Save Our Wetlands, "Lake Pontchartrain Hurricane Barrier Project," posted at www.saveourwetlands.org/edenislehistory.htm; *Foy v. Lemieux*, no. 76–3998 (E.D. La. 1976).

24. Todd Shallats, "Holding Louisiana," *Technology and Culture: The International Quarterly of the Society for the History of Technology* 46 (January 2006): 102–117; and Shallats, "In the Wake of Hurricane Betsy."

25. *Save Our Wetlands v. Rush*, Civil Actions nos. 75–3710 and 77–976 (E.D. La. 1977).

26. Mark Schleifstein, "Refuge Plan Offered to Public," *Times-Picayune*, August 4, 1993.

27. Ibid.; Craig E. Colten, *Unnatural Metropolis: Wresting New Orleans from Nature* (Baton Rouge: Louisiana State University Press, 2005), pp. 179–184; Frances Frank Marcus, "Mercury Found in Proposed Site of Nature Area," *New York Times*, September 9, 1988; Sheila Stroup, "A Wonderful Life in the Marsh," *Times-Picayune*, November 6, 1993; Jeffrey Meitrodt, "3,000 Acres Near Sauvage Refuge Sold," *Times-Picayune*, June 10, 1994.

28. Fox News Network, Hannity and Colmes, "Are Environmentalists to Blame for New Orleans Flood?" September 13, 2005; David Schoenbrod, "The Lawsuit That Sank New Orleans," *Wall Street Journal*, September 16, 2005; John Berlau, "Dam Environmentalists: Why There's No Hope for the Obvious Solution to New Orleans Flooding," *Weekly Standard*, January 16, 2006; Government Accountability Office, Army Corps of Engineers, "Lake Pontchartrain and Vicinity Hurricane Protection Project," September 28, 2005.

29. A "contour map of land elevations" in New Orleans East by the Office of Policy Planning in Neighborhood Profiles Project, Edgelake/Little Woods, corresponds directly with maps of the extent of flooding in New Orleans East. See, e.g., graphic, "How Much Water Did You Get?" *Times-Picayune*, September 22, 2005.

30. See graphic, "Days under Water," *Times-Picayune*, September 19, 2005.

31. See graphic, "Victims of Katrina: Where They Were Found," *Times-Picayune*, December 20, 2005.

32. Martha Carr, "Rebuilding Should Begin on High Ground, Group Says," *Times-Picayune*, November 19, 2005.

33. Ibid.

34. See, e.g., Mike Davis, "Who Is Killing New Orleans?" *The Nation*, April 10, 2006; Adolph Reed and Stephen Steinberg, "Liberal Bad Faith in the Wake of Hurricane Katrina," *Black Commentator*, May 4, 2006.

35. Craig E. Colton, *Unnatural Metropolis: Wresting New Orleans from Nature* (Baton Rouge: Louisiana State University Press, 2005), p. 161.

36. Miriam Hill, Kim Hone-McMahan, and Dwight Ott, "Residents of Ninth Ward Insist Neighborhood Be Rebuilt," Knight Ridder, October 9, 2005.

37. Ceci Connolly, "9th Ward: History, Yes, but a Future? Race and Class Frame Debate on Rebuilding New Orleans District," *Washington Post*, October 3, 2005.

38. Carr and Meitrodt, "What Will New Orleans Look Like Five Years from Now?"

39. Houck, "Can We Save New Orleans?" p. 21.

40. Ibid., pp. 67–68.

41. Nossiter, "Untouchable in Election."

42. Coleman Warner, "Candidates Playing It Safe on Land Use: Nagin and Landrieu Are Equally Vague," *Times-Picayune*, May 13, 2006.

19. FAT TUESDAY

1. Billy Grady, "Couple Ties Can to Art World's Tail; Alliance Thrives on Weirdness," *Times-Picayune*, February 4, 1996.

2. Adam Nossiter, "Amid Revelry, Evidence of City's Cruel Transformation," *New York Times*, February 25, 2006.

3. James Gill, *Lords of Misrule: Mardi Gras and the Politics of Race in*

New Orleans (Oxford: University Press of Mississippi, 1997), pp. 7, 50.

4. According to the Census Bureau, New Orleans was the ninth largest city in America in 1870. Campbell Gibson, "Population of the 100 Largest Cities and Other Urban Places: 1790 to 1900," Population Division, U.S. Bureau of the Census, June 1993. Posted at www .census.gov/population/www/documentation/twps0027.html.

5. Gill, *Lords of Misrule*, p. 7.

6. National Public Radio, *Day to Day*, February 27, 2006.

7. Gill, *Lords of Misrule*, p. 223.

8. Ibid., p. 224.

20. HARD LOT

1. Wade McIntyre, "Megan Bell Going to Court over Oak Place Mobile Home Park," *Gonzales Weekly*, February 10, 2006.

2. David Mitchell, "Trailer Park Opponents Boo Officials, Advocates Point to Evacuees' Need, Appeal to Charity," *The Advocate* (Baton Rouge), February 2, 2006.

3. Ibid.; McIntyre, "Megan Bell Going to Court over Oak Place Mobile Home Park."

4. David Mitchell, "Hughes Opposes FEMA Trailers, Ascension Welcome Withdrawn," *The Advocate* (Baton Rouge), February 11, 2006.

5. David Mitchell, "November Trial Date Scheduled in Suit over FEMA Trailer Park," *The Advocate* (Baton Rouge), February 23, 2006.

6. See James Varney, "Trailer Cash; If FEMA Could Distribute the Fortune Spent on Trailers Directly to Those in Need of Housing, the Recipients Might Find a Much Nicer Place to Live, and Even Have Money Left Over for Home Repairs. But There's a Catch: That's Illegal," *Times-Picayune*, January 21, 2006.

7. Douglas Mitchell, "Resident Says Trailer Park Fears Unrealized," *The Advocate* (Baton Rouge), April 11, 2006

21. LA NUEVA ORLEANS

1. Ana Ester Gershanik, "Mexico May Re-establish N.O. Consulate," *Times-Picayune*, August 13, 2006.

2. Samantha Euraque, "Honduran Memories: Identity, Race, Place and Memory in New Orleans, Louisiana" (M.A. thesis, Louisiana State University, 2004).

3. Ibid.

4. Advancement Project, "And Injustice for All: Worker's Lives in the Reconstruction of New Orleans," July 2006. Posted at www.advance mentproject.org/reports/workersreport.pdf.

5. James Varney, "Nuevo Orleans? An Influx of Hispanic Workers in the Wake of Hurricane Katrina Has Some Officials Wondering Why Locals Aren't on the Front Lines of Recovery," *Times-Picayune*, October 18, 2005.

6. See H.R. 4437, The Border Protection, Anti-terrorism, and Illegal Immigration Control Act of 2005, passed December 16, 2005; John Pomfret, "Cardinal Puts Church in Fight for Immigration Rights," *Washington Post*, April 2, 2006.

7. Tyler Cowen, "An Economist Visits New Orleans: Bienvenido, Nuevo Orleans," *Salon*, April 19, 2006.

22. YOURS IN STRUGGLE

1. Common Ground Collective, *Solidarity, Not Charity*. Video posted at www.commongroundrelief.org/node/70.

2. Ms. griffin spells her name with a lowercase "g" as a commentary on her surname, which she refers to as a "slave name."

3. I was unable to find the names of these individuals among the official dead, a list that many say is incomplete, failing to include those who died after evacuating or from causes not immediately related to the rising water.

23. IN THE PARISH

1. See, e.g., Karen Turni Bazile, "Iraq Prepared Him for St. Bernard; Parish Hires Expert in Rebuilding Cities," *Times-Picayune*, October 15, 2005.

2. Liva Baker, *The Second Battle of New Orleans: The Hundred Year Struggle to Integrate the Schools* (New York: HarperCollins, 1996), p. 379.

3. See St. Bernard Parish.net, "An Online Guide for Living in or Visiting St. Bernard Parish," posted at www.stbernardparish.net/history.htm (last checked February 12, 2007).

4. Glen Jeansonne, *Leander Perez: Boss of the Delta* (Baton Rouge: Louisiana State University Press, 1977), pp. xv, 170–171.

5. Baker, *The Second Battle of New Orleans*, pp. 78–82.

6. U.S. Census Bureau, "St. Bernard Parish Quickfacts," posted online at http://quickfacts.census.gov/qfd/states/22/22087.html (last checked February 13, 2007).

7. Paul Rioux, "St. Bernard Sued over Rent Limit; Group Says New Law Upholds Segregation," *Times-Picayune*, October 4, 2006.

8. Karen Turni Bazile, "Bias Lawsuit Puts Council on Defensive; Lawyer Hired to Fight Allegation of Discrimination in St. Bernard," *Times-Picayune*, November 8, 2006.

25. EPITAPH

1. National Public Radio, *Morning Edition*, May 25, 2001.

2. A shocking sequence of photos by Allen Fredrickson, a photographer with Reuters/Corbis, shows a dog eating the leg of a corpse near the Lake Pontchartrain levee breach on September 6, 2005. One photo was posted on the National Geographic Web site and the Daily Kos blog; the sequence, including a later photo in which the corpse's leg appears to be missing, appears on Robert Lindsay's blog at robertlindsay.blogspot .com/2006/01/worst-katrina-photo-sequence-of-all.html.

3. Jacob A. Riis, *How the Other Half Lives: Studies among the Tenements of New York* (New York: Penguin, 1997).

INDEX

Page numbers in italics refer to illustrations.

Designer: Nicole Hayward
Text: 10/15 Janson
Compositor: Binghamton Valley Composition
Indexer: J. Naomi Linzer Indexing Services
Printer and Binder: Maple-Vail Manufacturing Group